STANLEY **COMPLETE**

PLUMBING DISCARD

Meredith® Books
Des Moines, Iowa

Stanley® Books
An imprint of Meredith® Books

Stanley Complete Plumbing
Editor: Ken Sidey
Senior Associate Design Director: Tom Wegner
Assistant Editor: Harijs Priekulis
Copy Chief: Terri Fredrickson
Copy and Production Editor: Victoria Forlini
Editorial Operations Manager: Karen Schirm
Managers, Book Production: Pam Kvitne,
    Marjorie J. Schenkelberg, Rick Von Holdt
Technical Editor, The Stanley Works: Mike Maznio
Contributing Copy Editor: Steve Hallam
Technical Proofreader: George Granseth
Contributing Proofreaders: Kathy Roth Eastman,
    Sara Henderson, James Stepp
Indexer: Donald Glassman
Electronic Production Coordinator: Paula Forest
Editorial and Design Assistants: Renee E. McAtee,
    Karen McFadden

Additional Editorial Contributions from
Greenleaf Publishing
Publishing Director: Dave Toht
Writer: Steve Cory
Production Designer: Rebecca Anderson
Associate Designer: Jean DeVaty
Editorial Assistant: Betony Toht
Photography: Dan Stultz, Stultz Photography
Illustrator: Dave Brandon, Art Rep Services; Tony Davis
Studio Assistant: Tom Maloney
Technical Consultants: Joe Hansa, Larry Schrader, Daniel Vejr

Meredith® Books
Editor in Chief: Linda Raglan Cunningham
Design Director: Matt Strelecki
Executive Editor, Gardening and Home Improvement:
    Benjamin W. Allen
Executive Editor, Home Improvement: Larry Erickson

Publisher: James D. Blume
Executive Director, Marketing: Jeffrey Myers
Executive Director, New Business Development: Todd M. Davis
Executive Director, Sales: Ken Zagor
Director, Operations: George A. Susral
Director, Production: Douglas M. Johnston
Business Director: Jim Leonard

Vice President and General Manager: Douglas J. Guendel

Meredith Publishing Group
President, Publishing Group: Stephen M. Lacy
Vice President-Publishing Director: Bob Mate

Meredith Corporation
Chairman and Chief Executive Officer: William T. Kerr

Chairman of the Executive Committee: E.T. Meredith III

Additional Photography:
John Holtorf/ Holtorf Photography: cover, page 1
Kohler Co.: pages 36, 37

With thanks to:
B. T. Premier Plumbing, Inc.
Builder's Plumbing & Heating Supply Company
Controlled Energy Corporation
Hamilton Concrete Products Co.
IPEX, Inc.
Kohler Co.
Star Water Systems
W/C Technology Corporation

All of us at Stanley® Books are dedicated to providing you with
the information and ideas you need to enhance your home and
garden. We welcome your comments and suggestions about
this book. Write to us at:
    Meredith Corporation
    Stanley Books
    1716 Locust St.
    Des Moines, IA 50309–3023

If you would like more information on other Stanley products,
call 1-800-STANLEY or visit us at: www.stanleyworks.com
Stanley® and the notched rectangle around the Stanley name
are registered trademarks of The Stanley Works and
subsidiaries.

If you would like to purchase any of our home improvement,
cooking, crafts, gardening, or home decorating and design
books, check wherever quality books are sold. Or visit us at:
meredithbooks.com

Note to the Readers: Due to differing conditions, tools,
and individual skills, Meredith Corporation assumes no
responsibility for any damages, injuries suffered, or losses
incurred as a result of following the information published
in this book. Before beginning any project, review the
instructions carefully, and if any doubts or questions remain,
consult local experts or authorities. Because codes and
regulations vary greatly, you always should check with
authorities to ensure that your project complies with all
applicable local codes and regulations. Always read and
observe all of the safety precautions provided by
manufacturers of any tools, equipment, or supplies,
and follow all accepted safety procedures.

Contents

CONTENTS (continued)

KNOWING YOUR LIMITS

If you are handy and able to work methodically, most of the projects in this book are within your reach. However, some are time-consuming and involve skills beyond plumbing. Understanding your limits and the constraints of time can assure an enjoyable, safe project.

Plan your time carefully; your family will not be able to use a plumbing fixture until you have finished the repair or installation. The "Prestart Checklist" at the beginning of each project will help you gather the needed tools and estimate the time needed to complete the project.

Even a well planned project can run into unforeseen problems. You may find yourself in need of tools or parts, so do your work while the stores are open.

Working safely and comfortably
Before attempting any project, turn off the water. Then turn on a faucet to make sure the water supply is off.

Take care not to touch nearby electrical outlets, especially if you are wet.

Plumbing can be physically demanding, not because of heavy lifting but because you often have to work in cramped areas. Make the work site comfortable. Spread towels as cushions, use a drop cloth to catch water and grime, and illuminate the area with a stand-up flashlight (page 41).

Hiring a pro
Even if you believe you are competent to do the work, you may not have the time. Rather than forcing your family to live in a work site for months, it may be worth the extra money to hire someone who can get the job done quickly. More importantly, local codes may require that only licensed contractors perform certain types of work. Some types of work call for the expertise of a qualified plumbing contractor.

Choosing a plumber
For a major job, obtain quotes from two or three plumbers. Ask for references and talk to former customers to see if they were satisfied. Make sure the plumbing contractor is licensed and bonded to work in your area and has liability and worker's compensation insurance so you will be protected in case of a mishap.

Levels of plumber involvement
Most professional plumbers would rather do all the work themselves. However, if you feel confident that you can work on a project and need only a bit of reassurance that you're installing things correctly, a plumber may agree to work as a consultant. Often an hour spent with a pro can save you plenty in materials and labor.

You might hire a plumber to do only the "rough-in" work of running supply and DWV (drain-waste-vent) pipes. Once the rough plumbing is installed, have a local inspector approve it before you finish paying the plumber. Then you can close up the walls and install the fixtures.

Working with a plumber
Once the work has begun, use this book to see how the job ought to be done. If you are dissatisfied, or if you do not understand what the plumber is doing, don't hesitate to ask questions.

Be firm but polite. Whenever possible, save all your questions for the end of the day, so you won't be a nuisance. However, if you feel the work is shoddy or the plumber is shrugging off your concerns, make it clear that you will not pay until you are satisfied. Have all work inspected.

Calling in a pro

Finding a quality plumbing contractor begins with a phone call, but requires follow-up with references, assurance of proper licensing and insurance, and a clear understanding of what, how, and when the work will be performed.

SAFETY FIRST

Most plumbing projects do not put you in harm's way. However, use common sense and take precautions to protect yourself and your home.

■ For most jobs, rule No. 1 is: **Shut off the water,** then run water until it stops to make sure it has been shut off.

■ If a job will cause you to get wet, **keep away from any live electrical receptacles or fixtures.** To be sure, first shut off the power at the service panel.

■ Be sure you know which pipes are which. In addition to plumbing pipes, your home may have gas pipes and pipes that carry hot water for the heating system.

■ When working with or near gas pipes, **shut off the gas** at a point prior to where you are working and open doors or windows to provide ventilation. Do not ignite any sparks or flames and avoid touching electrical devices.

■ Drain lines may contain gases, smelly or odorless, that are hazardous. Temporarily seal pipes with a rag and keep the area ventilated.

■ If at any point you are unsure of what you are doing, stop work. Consult this book and other resources until you gain confidence. Or call in a professional for advice.

■ When soldering copper pipe, protect all flammable surfaces that may be touched by the flame. Keep a fire extinguisher on hand.

■ Use the tool that's designed for the job.

■ Guard your eyes from metal fragments and debris by wearing eye protection. Wear long sleeves and use gloves when necessary. Use GFCI-protected extension cords (page 20).

GETTING READY

Some homeowners avoid plumbing chores because they see them as difficult and messy, if not downright dangerous. As a result, they call in a plumber for minor problems they could easily handle themselves. Others tackle the most complex plumbing operations, often with disastrous results.

Armed with this book, you can determine which projects are within your reach, and which are best left to pros. Better yet, you'll discover that plumbing need not always be knuckle-scraping and filthy, but actually can be satisfying.

Scoping out the job
Typically any plumbing that is exposed, not hidden in walls, can be easily approached by a handy person with no special knowledge or skills. Faucets and traps can be dismantled, unclogged, and repaired or replaced using inexpensive tools. Trips to the hardware store for replacements parts are usually more time-consuming than the chore itself.

The work becomes more challenging when the fixtures get heftier and more complex. You can replace a bathroom sink in short order, but a kitchen sink, with its mass of plumbing underneath, is a bigger job. Plumbing and fittings that are partially hidden, such as a shower faucet and its supply lines, may require carpentry, tiling, and other skills.

Anytime you install a plumbing fixture where there was none before—in other words, whenever you need to run new pipes—you've entered a whole new arena. New plumbing must conform to strict codes and must be inspected by a local building department.

Getting the work done
Often the most difficult part of a job is not the actual plumbing but dealing with obstacles. You may have to squeeze into cramped quarters. Use a kneeling pad, a drop cloth, or even an old pillow to make the work site as comfortable as possible. Position a flashlight or work light so you can see clearly.

There is one basic rule for most plumbing projects: **Shut off the water and test to make sure the water is off.** Keep a bucket and some old towels handy to catch the small amounts of water that may dribble out of pipes.

Before tackling a project, understand plumbing in general and your system in particular.

CHAPTER PREVIEW

Shutting off the water
page 8

Drain, waste, vent system
page 10

Supply system
page 12

Principles of venting
page 14

Septic systems and wells
page 16

Consider using separate buckets for different categories of tools. One bucket can hold general carpentry tools, while another holds tools for cutting and joining pipe.

Because most of a plumbing system is behind walls and ceilings, demolition is one of several carpentry skills needed in a plumbing project. Allow plenty of working space when opening up a wall—making a large patch takes slightly more time than a small patch.

Plumbing tools
page 18

Carpentry tools
page 21

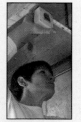

Pipes
page 24

Supply pipe fittings
page 26

Drain and vent fittings
page 28

Mapping a home system
page 30

Plumbing codes
page 32

Accessible installations
page 36

Making drawings
page 38

SHUTTING OFF THE WATER

It's the basic prerequisite for most plumbing projects: Shut off the water to the work area, then test to make sure the water supply is shut off. Failing to shut off the water leads to the sort of disaster you see in the comics: water spraying uncontrollably all over the place.

Every adult family member should know how to shut water off, both at the fixtures and to the entire house.

Fixture shutoffs

Most homes built in the past 40 years have a separate stop valve (also called a fixture shutoff valve) for each faucet, toilet, and fixture. A supply tube (sometimes called a riser) runs from the stop valve to the fixture. (A faucet has two stop valves, one for hot water and one for cold; a toilet needs only a cold-water shutoff.) If a fixture does not have a stop valve, you will have to shut off water to part or all of the house before working. It's a good idea to install a stop valve so you can stop the flow quickly in case of emergency *(pages 124–125).*

A stop valve typically has a chrome finish and an oval handle. In an older home, it may be shaped like a house valve with a circular handle, or it may have a decorative ceramic handle.

Most stop valves are inexpensive and made for light duty because they will be used only for emergencies or repairs. That means they might not shut off the water completely. Do not crank down on its handle with pliers; you may break the valve. See *pages 122–123* to repair a faulty stop valve or supply tube.

Main shutoffs

Every home has at least one main shutoff, which controls water flowing to the entire house. Often there is one main shutoff inside the house and another outside.

An inside main shutoff is usually located near the point where water enters the house. Often it is near the water meter. There may be two valves, one on each side of the meter. If your home has no meter (some homes don't), look for a large pipe that enters the house, often through a basement floor or at the bottom of a crawlspace. The shutoff should be somewhere along the run of that pipe.

In regions that experience mild winters, the main shutoff valve may be located outside of the house.

Stop valves

Kitchen sink stop valves often are hidden amid the jumble of pipes and tubes under the sink. Stop valves allow you to shut off water to the kitchen faucet. There may be a separate stop valve for the dishwasher.

A saddle tee-valve tied into a supply pipe runs cold water to a refrigerator's icemaker. Although a saddle tee is a handy way to tap into a line, some municipalities forbid its use. Check local building codes.

In-faucet stop valves can be found on some tub/shower faucets. Use a large slot screwdriver to turn water on and off.

An outside shutoff valve is located near the point where a pipe branches off from the utility's main line to bring water to your home. If you have a parkway—a narrow strip of land between the sidewalk and the street—the outside shutoff will likely be found there. If you cannot find yours, ask your municipality where to find it.

In temperate regions, an outside shutoff is usually housed in a plastic or concrete underground container, sometimes called a Buffalo box (below). Usually the box lid can be pried up, but you may need to dig away vegetation to free it.

In colder regions, the shutoff will be below the frost line, typically at the bottom of a tube covered with a cast-iron cover. It may be necessary to buy a "key" to be able to reach down to the valve and turn the water on and off. Keys are usually the same size and type throughout a neighborhood. Often your municipality will let you borrow a key for your shutoff.

Intermediate shutoffs

You may find other shutoff valves located on exposed supply pipes in a basement, crawlspace, utility room, or access panel behind a bathtub *(page 12)*. These will probably be in pairs, one for hot and one for cold water. (If the water has been running recently, you can tell which pipe is hot by feeling them with your hand.) These are probably intermediate shutoffs, meaning they control water supply to a portion of a house.

To find out what a shutoff valve controls, close it and go through the house turning on faucets and flushing toilets. Remember that a toilet with a tank will flush once after the water is off; listen or look for water refilling the tank after the flush.

If you have hot-water heat in your home, there will be shutoff valves near the boiler. These have nothing to do with the supply pipes for your plumbing fixtures.

Water meters

To keep track of water usage or to check that the utility is charging correctly, read your water meter. If your meter has a series of dials, each is labeled for the number of cubic feet it measures. It may be that some dials turn counterclockwise while others turn clockwise. A meter with a digital readout simply displays the amount of cubic feet of water used. Note the number at the start of the month or billing period, then read it again at the end and subtract the first number to calculate your use.

Shutoff valves

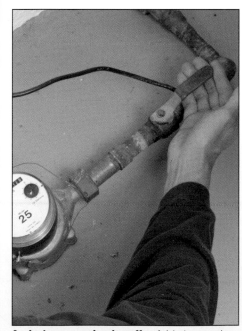

An in-house main shutoff, a fairly large valve located near the point where water enters the house, shuts water off for the entire house. As shown above, the shutoff valve is located next to the water meter.

A Buffalo box is another type of whole-house shutoff. Common in the South and Southwest, this buried box can be found outdoors. Pry off the lid. Inside you'll find either a standard valve that you can turn with your hands or one that requires a special key.

Intermediate shutoff valves control water flow to part of the house. There will be two or more pairs of these.

DRAIN, WASTE, VENT SYSTEM

Drain-waste-vent (DWV) pipes carry waste and water out of the house without gurgles or fumes. Never install or replace a DWV pipe without consulting a building inspector. These pipes must be installed according to precise specifications.

Drainpipes

The centerpiece of a DWV system is the **main stack,** usually a pipe 3 or 4 inches in diameter, which runs straight up through the roof. A **secondary stack**, perhaps 2 or 3 inches in diameter, serves a branch of the system.

Branch drainpipes of smaller diameter—typically 1½ or 2 inches—carry water from specific fixtures to a stack.

Drain stacks in older homes are often made of cast iron, which rusts through after 80 years or so. In older homes, the branch drains typically are made of galvanized steel, which is much more likely to rust and corrode shut. In newer homes, plastic pipe is used for stacks and branch drains. The first plastic pipe to be used was ABS, which is black. Since the 1970s, ABS has generally been replaced by white- or cream-colored PVC pipe. In rare cases, drainpipes are made of copper.

Drainpipes must be sloped so water runs freely through them, usually about ¼ inch per foot. Codes require special fittings make sweeping turns rather than abrupt turns, so waste does not get trapped in the pipes.

Drainpipes often have **cleanouts**—places where a plug can be temporarily removed—so the pipes can be augered to clear a clog.

The main drain line

Water travels downward through the stacks to the main drain line, which leads to the municipal sewage system or to a septic system. In older homes, the main drain may be made of clay pipe or other porous material. Tree roots sometimes work their way into the main line, causing wastewater to back up into the house. The solution is to call a company that specializes in augering main lines.

Vent pipes

For water to flow smoothly, without gurgling, there must be an air passageway behind the water (below). Vent pipes extend from the drainpipes up through the roof to provide that passage. Vent pipes also carry odors out of the house.

The drainpipe for each plumbing fixture must be connected to a vent that supplies the pipe with air from the outside. In some cases, the drainpipe is connected directly to a main or secondary stack pipe, which travels straight up through the roof. More often, a drainpipe is connected to a **revent** pipe that reaches up and over to tie into the main vent stack.

Plumbing codes strictly prescribe where vent pipes can connect to the stack and how far they should travel. In most cases, a "wet" section of pipe—the part that carries wastewater—cannot be used as a vent, even if it is usually dry. Examine the illustration on the opposite page, and you'll see that all the vent pipes lead to sections of a stack that never carry running water.

If your drainpipes gurgle when you run water in a sink or flush a toilet, call a professional plumber for an inspection. A vent may be stopped up and need clearing. Or the plumbing may be incorrect, and you may need a new vent line.

In some cases, local codes allow for other venting strategies. For instance, a basement sink might be vented with a special wall vent, which simply runs out the wall. Or a cheater vent, a small device that draws air from the room rather than outside, may be allowed.

Why venting is necessary

Try to quickly empty a bottle with a narrow mouth, and it will gurgle and glug as it slowly empties. Open the vent cap on a plastic gas container and it flows smoothly. That's because the vent hole allows air to enter behind the flowing liquid, producing a quick, glug-free flow. Vent stacks in a household plumbing system work the same way.

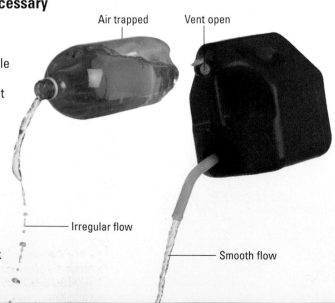

Air trapped

Vent open

Irregular flow

Smooth flow

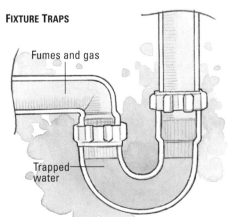

FIXTURE TRAPS

Fumes and gas

Trapped water

The drain water for every fixture must run through a trap—a section of pipe shaped like a sideways P or an S. Because of its shape, it holds water, creating a seal that keeps fumes and gases from entering the house. A toilet has a built-in trap. Sink traps are made of chrome-plated brass or plastic with joints that can easily be taken apart.

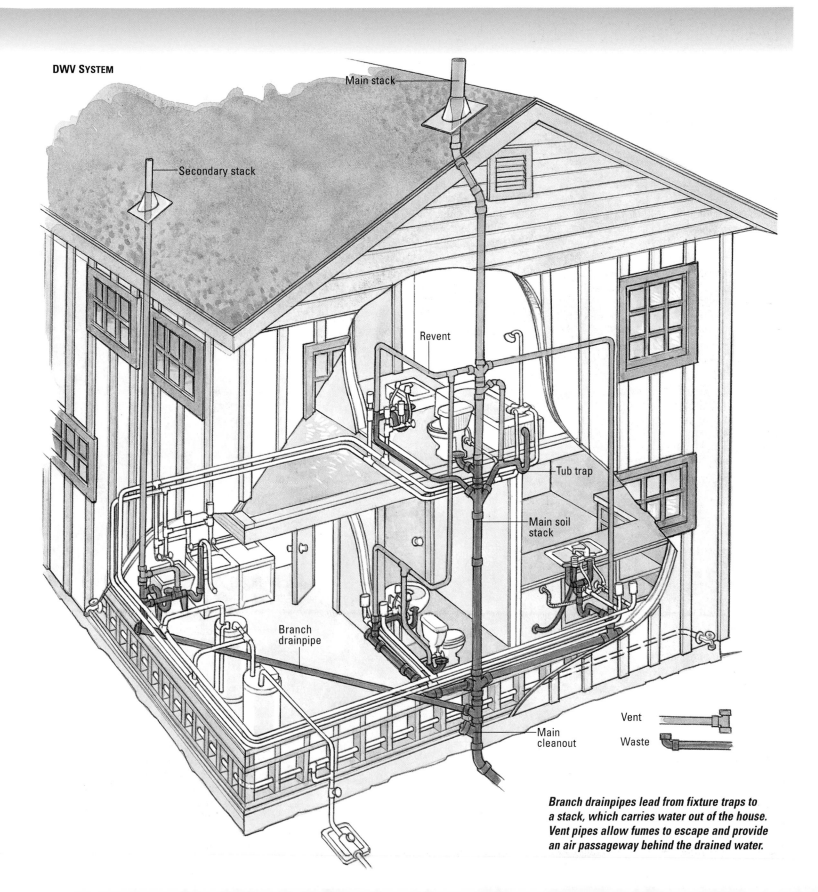

DWV SYSTEM

Main stack

Secondary stack

Revent

Tub trap

Main soil stack

Branch drainpipe

Main cleanout

Vent

Waste

Branch drainpipes lead from fixture traps to a stack, which carries water out of the house. Vent pipes allow fumes to escape and provide an air passageway behind the drained water.

SUPPLY SYSTEM

Pipes that carry water into the house are less complicated than the drain-waste-vent (DWV) pipes. Typically a single pipe runs to the water heater, where it divides into cold and hot pipes that supply faucets, fixtures, and toilets. Shutoff and stop valves make it possible to turn off the water along the supply system *(pages 8–9)*.

Water purity

If the water comes from a utility company, it is tested regularly to ensure it is safe to drink. If you have a private well, testing for purity is your responsibility. If your water tastes bad or produces stains, running the main supply line through a water softener and/or a water filter may help.

Water meter

If your water bill is the same from month to month, you probably have unmetered water. If you have a water meter, the bill reflects how much water enters your house. A water meter may be found inside the house, or it may be in the Buffalo box outside.

Water heater

Near the water heater, one pipe branches off to supply cold water throughout the house, and another enters a gas or electric water heater, which typically holds and heats 30 to 50 gallons of water. A supply pipe exits the heater to deliver hot water throughout the house. If you often run out of hot water while bathing, consider buying a water heater with a larger capacity.

Supply pipes

Supply pipes run in pairs throughout the house. Vertical pipes are called risers.

Supply pipes may be copper, galvanized steel, or plastic. Galvanized steel pipes rust and corrode in time, causing leaks that lower water pressure. Plastic PVC supply pipes have been banned by most communities for interior use because the joints may come loose in time. Newer plastic pipes, made of rigid CPVC or flexible polyethylene (PE), are more reliable and are permitted in many areas. Copper is the material of choice in most areas. It is long-lasting and its smooth surface does not collect deposits that slow the flow of water. A properly soldered joint, using lead-free solder, is as strong as the pipe itself.

A nail or screw can easily pierce a copper or plastic supply pipe, so plumbing codes prescribe measures to keep supply pipes out of harm's way. Pipes within walls should be placed in the center of studs so that nails cannot reach them. Protective metal plates may also be required.

Pipe sizes and water pressure

The larger a pipe's inside diameter, the greater the water pressure. If water pressure is too low, the problem may be the supply pipes.

The pipe bringing water into a house is typically 1 inch or 1¼ inches inside diameter. Soon after entering the house, the size narrows to ¾ inch. Pipes that carry water from room to room may be either ¾ or ½ inch; the larger size is preferable. Pipes that supply water to specific fixtures are usually ½ inch to the stop, then ¼ inch.

A bathtub access panel

Bathtub plumbing is complicated, so many homes have an access panel to allow you to reach it. To find an access panel, look in the adjacent room or closet, on the wall directly behind the tub faucet.

Locating supply lines

Hot supply · Cold supply · 2-21-94

Near the water heater, supply lines branch into cold and hot pipes— an excellent place to start tracing your supply system. Most water heaters stamp "hot" and "cold" on the top of the metal housing.

Reducer · Reducing Tee

Some lines reduce in dimension along their run. Here a pipe steps down in size from ¾ inch to ½ inch.

HOUSEHOLD SUPPLY SYSTEM

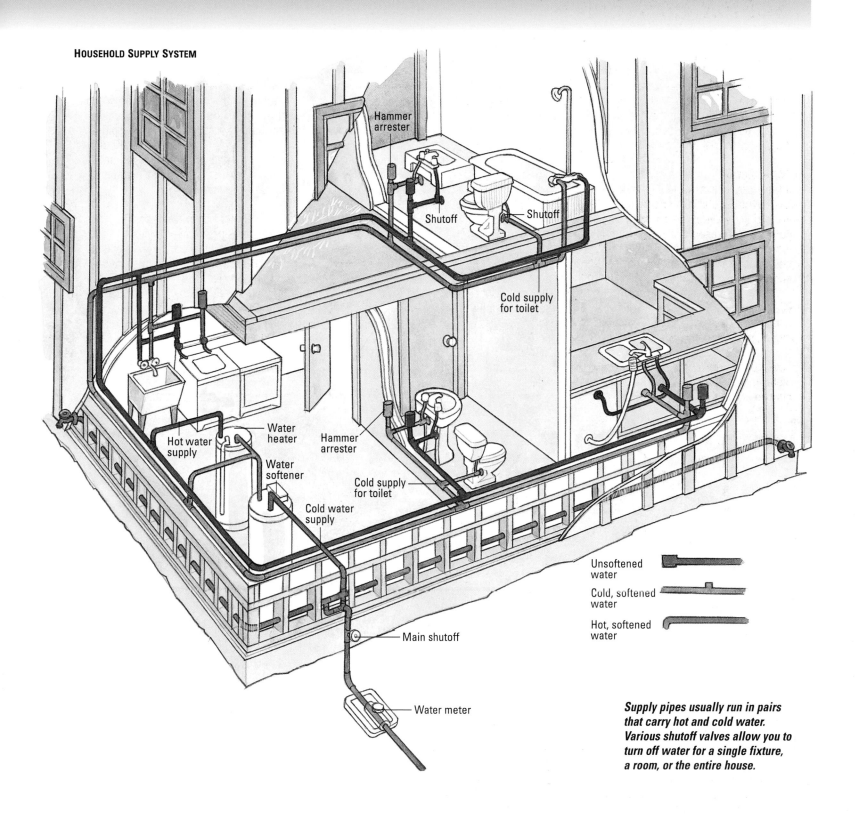

Hammer arrester

Shutoff

Shutoff

Cold supply for toilet

Hot water supply

Water heater

Water softener

Hammer arrester

Cold supply for toilet

Cold water supply

Main shutoff

Water meter

Unsoftened water

Cold, softened water

Hot, softened water

Supply pipes usually run in pairs that carry hot and cold water. Various shutoff valves allow you to turn off water for a single fixture, a room, or the entire house.

PRINCIPLES OF VENTING

How will the drain be vented? That's the first question that must be answered as you plan for plumbing a new appliance or an addition to your system. When developing a plumbing system plan, you may have the option to choose from several venting types; keep in mind that each option may present its own problem or complication. Before finalizing a plan, have the venting scheme approved by the local plumbing inspector.

Vent types

A **true vent** is a vertical pipe attached to a drain line that runs up through the roof with no water running through it. If a fixture is close to the stack and is on the top floor,

the upper part of the stack serves nicely as a vent (as is the case for the toilet shown below). However, many fixtures are not so conveniently located and other solutions must be found.

A **revent** pipe, also called an auxiliary vent, attaches to the drain line near the fixture and runs up and over to the main vent. It may attach directly behind the fixture (sink, below) or to the horizontal drain line (revent alternative, opposite).

If two fixtures are on opposite sides of a wall, they may tie into the stack with a sanitary cross; this is called a **common vent** (back-to-back sinks, opposite).

When a fixture is close enough to a stack, a wet vent (tub, below) may be allowed by

code. In this case the tub's drain empties into a pipe through which water flows.

If a sink is freestanding in the middle of a room, a **loop vent** (opposite) may be allowed by code.

If reventing is difficult and wet-venting is not allowed, it may be necessary to install a separate vent. This requires running a separate vent pipe through the roof (see *page 171*).

The "critical distance"

Can you install a wet vent, or do you have to install a revent or a separate vent? Finding the answer can involve fairly complicated calculations, based on formulas that can

TYPICAL VENTING ALTERNATIVES

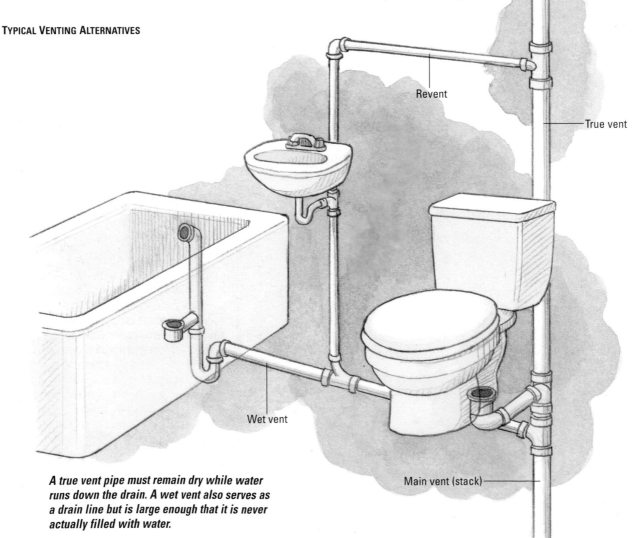

Revent

True vent

Wet vent

Main vent (stack)

A true vent pipe must remain dry while water runs down the drain. A wet vent also serves as a drain line but is large enough that it is never actually filled with water.

vary from one building department to another. The size of the vent pipe, the type of fixture, and the number of fixtures that are already wet-vented into the pipe are three factors that determine the "critical distance"—how far the fixture can be from the vent pipe. Measure the pipes carefully and consult with a plumbing inspector to determine whether wet-venting is possible.

Installing vent pipes

Vent pipes are often smaller in diameter than the drainpipes they serve. They need not slope like drainpipes. Normally they run either level or plumb, unless there is an obstacle to work around.

Vent pipes must be installed so that they stay dry when water runs through the drain line. That means that they should emerge from the top of the drainpipe, either straight vertically or at no less than a 45-degree angle from horizontal, so that water cannot back up into the vent.

The horizontal portion of a revent pipe must be at least 6 inches above the fixture's "flood level"—the highest point to which water can rise. (On a sink, the flood level is the sink rim or overflow hole.)

The main drain

Plan drain lines to minimize the possibility of clogs. The general rule is that smaller pipes—1¼ inch for bathroom sinks and 1½ inch for kitchen sinks, for instance—lead to larger branch drains. These in turn lead to the main stack, which is the largest pipe of all—typically 4 inches. Besides being large, the main stack is vertical, so it will rarely clog.

The main stack leads down into the ground and then out toward the municipal sewer. The underground horizontal pipe, or main drain, that runs toward the sewer line can sometimes get clogged, especially if it is an old drain made of clay pipe. (For how to clear a clogged main, see *pages 52–53*).

OTHER VENTING OPTIONS

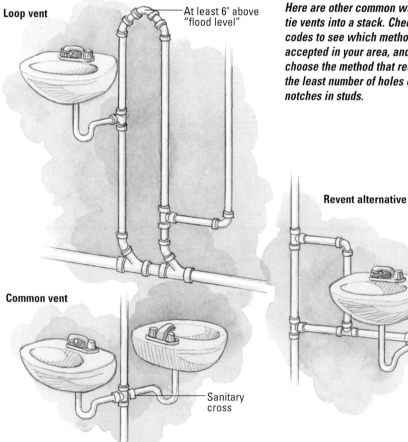

Loop vent

At least 6" above "flood level"

Common vent

Sanitary cross

Revent alternative

Here are other common ways to tie vents into a stack. Check local codes to see which methods are accepted in your area, and then choose the method that requires the least number of holes or notches in studs.

Catch basin

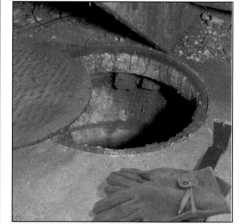

Many people pour grease down a kitchen sink. In time, this can lead to clogged drain lines. In some older homes, the kitchen sink has its own stack, and the drain line runs out to a catch basin—a container that traps grease. Occasionally the grease must be removed from the catch basin. A catch basin typically is located behind the house and has a large metal cover. In many cases, however, the catch basin has been bypassed and is no longer in use. There may also be a rectangular grease trap under the kitchen sink. This needs to be cleaned regularly.

SEPTIC SYSTEMS AND WELLS

If your home is outside a city or suburb, it probably has its own septic system rather than a municipal sewage system. Or if your home was built before municipal sewer lines were run, there may be an old, inactive septic system in your yard; you probably don't need to remove it.

How it works

In a typical septic system, wastewater flows from the house downhill to the septic tank, which may be made of concrete or plastic. Solid sludge sinks to the bottom of the tank and scum rises to the top. Baffles trap the scum so only liquid effluent leaves the tank. Bacteria slowly breaks down solid waste. Not all of the solids can be broken down in the tank. The gradual buildup must be pumped out.

Effluent flows out from a pipe into a distribution box. From there it flows into perforated pipes of clay or plastic. The pipes run through a leach field. As effluent leaches out into the soil, it is further broken down by microbes in the soil. Some of the effluent evaporates, and the rest provides nutrient-rich liquid that nourishes plants.

Avoiding septic system problems

If too much water runs into the tank, waste may be pushed out before it has been completely broken down. To avoid problems, fix dripping faucets and encourage family members not to use too much water. Use plain white toilet paper that is approved for septic systems. Avoid flushing bulky, inorganic items that could clog the system.

Be careful what you pour down the drain. Products that can inhibit the breakdown of waste include bleach, drain cleaners, paint thinner, motor oil, and any hazardous liquid.

A garbage disposer produces sludge that can clog a septic system. Using one is forbidden by many local codes. Do not drive a car or heavy machinery over the leach field; you could damage the pipes.

Additional tanks

To reduce the volume of waste flowing into a septic system, a kitchen sink's drain may run directly into a catch basin, which captures cooking grease. A catch basin (also called a grease trap) must be serviced separately from the septic tank (page 15).

In some systems, water from the washing machine runs into a seepage pit, which is either a hole filled with rocks or a pit lined with unmortared concrete blocks. If you have a seepage pit, be sure to use environmentally safe detergent.

Aerobic systems

Most septic systems are anaerobic, meaning that waste water stays underground. In areas with poor soil drainage, an aerobic lagoon is sometimes used. In this system, waste runs into a small pond (which should be fenced off), where it is digested by both bacteria and algae.

Other areas may require an aerobic tank system, which must be pumped regularly.

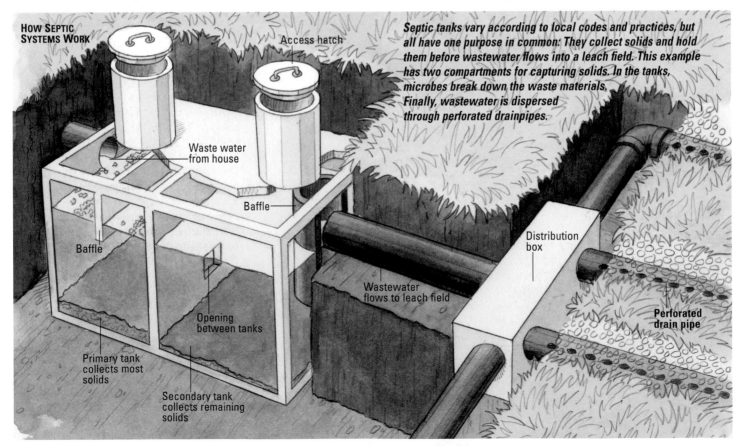

HOW SEPTIC SYSTEMS WORK

Access hatch

Waste water from house

Baffle

Baffle

Opening between tanks

Primary tank collects most solids

Secondary tank collects remaining solids

Wastewater flows to leach field

Distribution box

Perforated drain pipe

Septic tanks vary according to local codes and practices, but all have one purpose in common: They collect solids and hold them before wastewater flows into a leach field. This example has two compartments for capturing solids. In the tanks, microbes break down the waste materials. Finally, wastewater is dispersed through perforated drainpipes.

Regular maintenance

If the septic system is large enough and properly installed, it will require only occasional attention.

■ Once a year, use a sludge pole to check the sludge level. If the tank is almost half filled, have the tank pumped. Usually, a tank must be pumped every three or four years.

■ If the leach field starts to smell bad or if water backs up out of drains, contact a septic company immediately. There may be a clog that can be cleared if dealt with quickly.

■ If necessary, take steps to ensure that the leach field does not become saturated with water in the spring; a soaked field will not absorb effluent. You may need to redirect a gutter downspout, for instance.

■ Usually, bacteria remains in the tank and continues to work. However, if you suspect that the bacteria has been killed (by dumping chemicals down the drain, for example), you can buy an enzyme additive that will colonize the tank with microbes; just pour it down a drain.

Is the system large enough?

Codes determine how large a system must be—both the tank and the field—based on the number of people in the household. However, if the toilets and faucets will be in constant use, you may need a system larger than what is required. Adding new plumbing may require a larger septic system. If water backs up during wet periods, even when the tank is not full, the leach field may be too small. Consult with a septic service firm to see if you need a larger tank or field.

Gray-water irrigation

Some homes in areas with dry climates have a system that directs "gray water"—waste from clothes washers, bathtubs, and sinks—to an irrigation system that waters the lawn or specific plants. This system usually has only a very basic filter to keep out lint and hair. Be sure you use detergents that will not harm plants and do not pour chemicals down the drains.

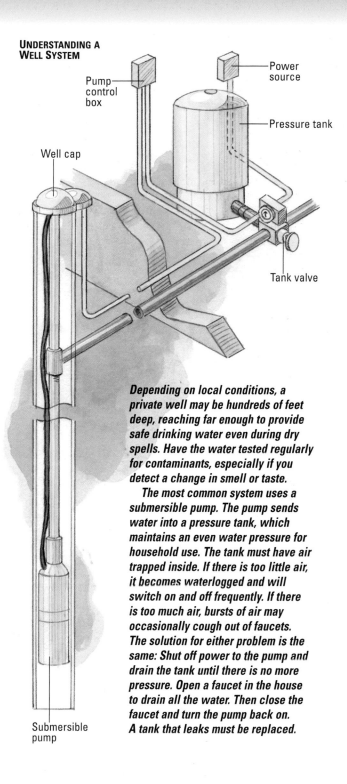

UNDERSTANDING A WELL SYSTEM

Power source

Pump control box

Pressure tank

Well cap

Tank valve

Submersible pump

Depending on local conditions, a private well may be hundreds of feet deep, reaching far enough to provide safe drinking water even during dry spells. Have the water tested regularly for contaminants, especially if you detect a change in smell or taste.

The most common system uses a submersible pump. The pump sends water into a pressure tank, which maintains an even water pressure for household use. The tank must have air trapped inside. If there is too little air, it becomes waterlogged and will switch on and off frequently. If there is too much air, bursts of air may occasionally cough out of faucets. The solution for either problem is the same: Shut off power to the pump and drain the tank until there is no more pressure. Open a faucet in the house to drain all the water. Then close the faucet and turn the pump back on. A tank that leaks must be replaced.

PLUMBING TOOLS

For a modest amount of money—probably less than a single visit from a plumber—you can assemble a tool kit that will tackle most jobs in your house. Invest in quality tools. They will stand up to tough tasks and be more comfortable to use.

General plumbing tools

These tools are useful no matter what material your pipes are made of. An **adjustable wrench** adjusts to grab nuts and bolts. A **locking adjustable wrench** is a handy variation on the same theme that quickly tightens on or releases nuts and bolts. A pair of **groove-joint pliers** is useful for tightening and loosening all sorts of joints. A **14-inch pipe wrench** is the ideal size for most projects. (To add to its persuasive force, slip a 1¼-inch steel pipe over the handle to increase the leverage.) If you will be working on steel pipe, buy a pair of pipe wrenches (add an 18-inch size).

To clear clogs in sinks, toilets, and tubs, first try a **flanged plunger**, whose funnel-like flange extends to fit snugly into a toilet. To plunge a sink or tub, fold up the flange. A **pressure plunger**, which expels a burst of water, sometimes can clear clogs standard plungers can't. If the clog is in a sink trap, you can often pull the hair and gunk out with a **ribbed plastic declogger.**

When those measures do not clear a clog, use a **hand-crank auger,** also called a snake. A **toilet auger** fits into the toilet and has a sleeve to protect the toilet bowl's porcelain finish.

Pressure plunger

Flanged plunger

Adjustable wrench

Putty knife

Locking adjustable wrench

Pipe wrench

Groove-joint pliers

Hand-crank auger

Ribbed plastic declogger

Toilet auger

A **putty knife** scrapes away old putty and other types of hardened debris. You'll need both **phillips** and **slot screwdrivers** to disassemble fixtures and fittings—a **4-in-1** combines both types. Use a **wire brush** to clean parts and encrusted pipe threads. A **strainer wrench** helps you twist out the upper part of the drain assembly in a sink or tub. To remove a large nut like that beneath a kitchen sink basket strainer, a **lock-nut wrench** is easier to use than groove-joint pliers. When repairing a faucet, you may need to get at the seat, a small part located inside the faucet body. Use a **seat wrench**. A **basin wrench** reaches into small spaces to loosen or tighten hold-down nuts. Without this tool, removing a kitchen or bathroom faucet is nearly impossible.

Tools for plastic pipe

You can use just about any saw to cut plastic pipe—a hacksaw, a standard backsaw, an ordinary handsaw, a circular saw, or even a power miter box. However, an inexpensive **plastic pipe saw** (also known as a PVC saw) cuts easily and leaves few burrs. Use it along with a **miter box** to ensure straight cuts. After cutting, burrs must be removed completely; a **deburring tool** does the job better and more quickly than a utility knife. To cut supply pipe (1 inch and smaller), you can also use a scissors-type **plastic pipe cutter**. Be sure to get a heavy-duty model made for PVC pipe. For PEX and other flexible tubing, a **plastic tubing cutter** makes a quick, clean cut.

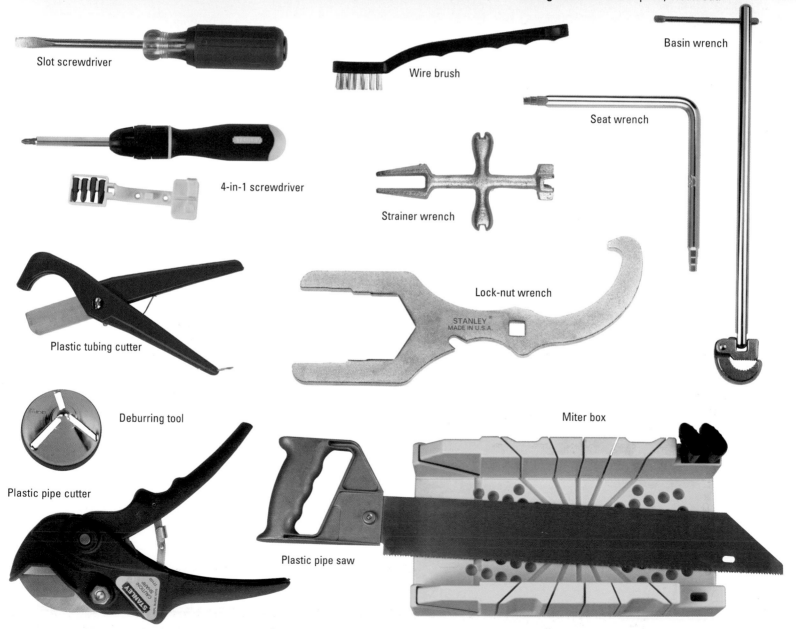

Slot screwdriver

Wire brush

Basin wrench

4-in-1 screwdriver

Seat wrench

Strainer wrench

Plastic tubing cutter

Lock-nut wrench

STANLEY
MADE IN U.S.A.

Deburring tool

Miter box

Plastic pipe cutter

Plastic pipe saw

PLUMBING TOOLS *(continued)*

Tools for copper pipe
A **tubing cutter** cuts copper pipe cleanly, quickly, and without bending the pipe out of round. For working in tight spots, you might need a **small tubing cutter** as well. (A hacksaw can cut copper pipe; but a dull blade may cause you to dent the pipe, making it very difficult to add fittings.)

To bend flexible pipe without crimping, use a **tubing bender.** Choose the size that tightly slips onto the pipe. A **flaring tool** may be needed for certain types of compression fittings, particularly in outdoor installations. A **handle puller** smoothly detaches faucet handles without strain or damage.

To sweat copper pipe and fittings, buy a **propane torch.** A model with an **electric igniter** is easiest—and safest—to use. To protect flammable surfaces from the propane torch flame, use a **fiber shield** or prop an old cookie sheet behind the joint being heated.

The ends of copper pipe and the insides of fittings must be burnished before soldering. A **multiuse wire brush** does both jobs. Or buy a **reamer brush** for the fittings and a roll of **plumber's emery cloth** for the pipe ends. Before joining pipes, paint **flux** on the pipes using a **flux brush.**

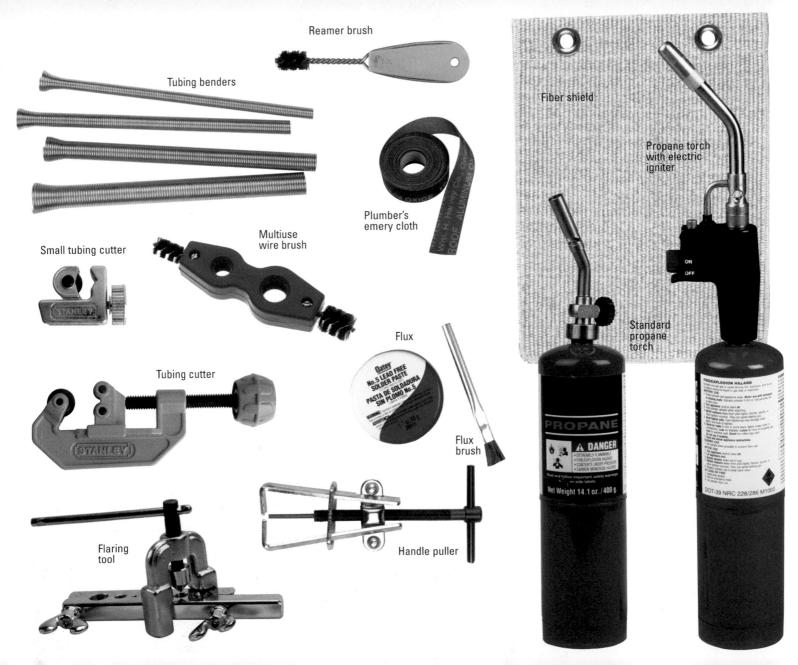

Reamer brush

Tubing benders

Fiber shield

Propane torch with electric igniter

Small tubing cutter

Multiuse wire brush

Plumber's emery cloth

ON
OFF

Standard propane torch

Tubing cutter

Flux

Flux brush

Flaring tool

Handle puller

PROPANE

⚠ DANGER
• EXTREMELY FLAMMABLE
• FIRE/EXPLOSION HAZARD
• CONTENTS UNDER PRESSURE
• CARBON MONOXIDE HAZARD

Net Weight 14.1 oz. / 400 g.

DOT-39 NRC 228/286 M1003

CARPENTRY TOOLS

When running new plumbing lines, much of your time will be spent cutting and drilling to clear a path for the pipes. This work must be done with precision so the house's framing will not be compromised. So in addition to plumbing tools, have on hand a set of general carpentry tools, including a **hammer** and **tape measure.** A **flat pry bar** will enable you to disassemble most nailed-together framing members. Occasionally you may need a longer pry bar. Demolition chores may require small or

large **sledge hammers.** Horizontal drainpipes must slope slightly. To check the slope, use a **carpenter's level** for long sections of pipe and a **torpedo level** for short sections.

Use a standard ⅜-inch **drill** to bore holes in 2× lumber. For installing screws, buy a **magnetic sleeve** and several screw heads. If you have to drill more than 10 holes, consider renting or buying a heavy-duty, ½-inch drill. Buy several **spade bits**—they wear out quickly. Attach spade bits to a **bit extender** when extra reach is needed.

A **quick-change sleeve** speeds switching **twist bits.** Make finder holes with a **long bit.** For cutting holes larger than 1 inch in diameter, buy a **hole saw.** A **right-angle drill** makes it possible to drill straight holes in tight places—handy when running pipe.

If you need to cut away a small amount of concrete or masonry, a hammer and **cold chisel** may be all you need. Renting or buying a **hammer drill** will speed tough-to-bore holes in concrete.

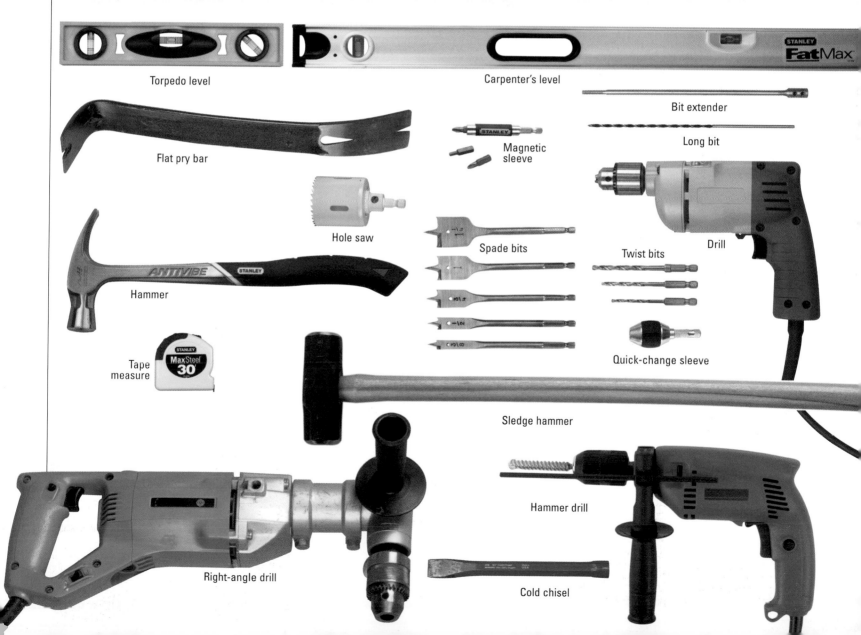

Torpedo level

Carpenter's level

Bit extender

Long bit

Flat pry bar

Magnetic sleeve

Hole saw

Spade bits

Drill

Twist bits

Hammer

Tape measure

Quick-change sleeve

Sledge hammer

Right-angle drill

Hammer drill

Cold chisel

CARPENTRY TOOLS (continued)

To get to pipes inside a wall, you'll need to cut through drywall or plaster. For small jobs a **drywall saw** is adequate. A full-size **hacksaw** is useful for cutting steel and copper pipes and for removing rusted fittings and old sections of pipe. Have a **close-work hacksaw** for working in tight areas. Most use full-size hacksaw blades as well as shorter metal cutting blades. A **stand-up flashlight** makes it easier to work in cramped, dark quarters.

For cutting access panels and opening area of flooring, use a **saber saw**. It can also be used for cutting holes in subflooring for drains and close bends. A **handsaw** is useful anytime you're altering framing or cutting access holes.

To chisel out a large area, rent an **electric jackhammer**, also known as a chipper. You can choose from several different types of **jackhammer chisels** to suit the job at hand.

Should your project call for cutting through subflooring or notching framing members, a **reciprocating saw** is indispensible. It reaches in to cut boards in tight and awkward spots and can even slice through nails and screws. You can also use it to cut into galvanized steel drain and supply lines. Several types of blades are available, including metal-cutting blades. Buy several; they often bend or break.

Use a **circular saw** for notching studs and, with a metal-cutting blade, for cutting cast-

Drywall saw

Handsaw

Utility knife

Close-work hacksaw

Hacksaw

Saber saw

Reciprocating saw

Jackhammer chisel

Stand-up flashlight

Electric jackhammer

iron pipe. You'll also need it if you revise existing framing to suit a new installation.

For large projects a **power miter box** (or chopsaw) with a fine-cutting blade does a quick and precise job of cutting PVC pipe. Make sure long pipes are supported to make a square cut and avoid binding.

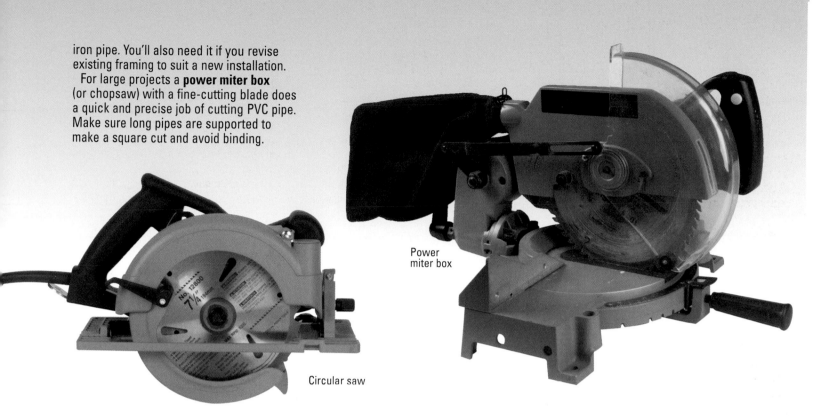

Power miter box

Circular saw

SAFETY FIRST
Tools that protect

Whenever doing work that creates sparks or flying debris, wear **safety goggles**. And preserve your hearing when using power tools—or even a simple hammer—with **ear protectors.**

Protect your hands with **leather gloves** when working with rough framing or cut pipes. When clearing clogs, you may get spattered with caustic chemicals; wear long clothes and **heavy-duty rubber gloves.**

Plug power tools into a **GFCI-protected extension cord,** which will shut off the moment it senses danger from exposure to water. (Cordless tools are safest.) When sweating joints have a **fire extinguisher** nearby.

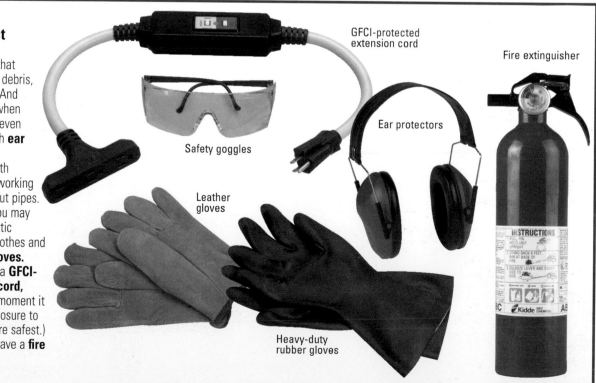

GFCI-protected extension cord

Fire extinguisher

Safety goggles

Ear protectors

Leather gloves

Heavy-duty rubber gloves

PIPES

The new pipes you install will probably be either copper supplies or PVC drainpipes. However, it's also likely that you'll encounter other types of pipe, such as galvanized steel and even cast-iron. If you have only a short run to make, you may choose the original material type. However, most inspectors would prefer that you use copper or PVC, which are less expensive and easier to install.

Cast iron

Most homes built before the 1960s have cast-iron vertical stacks and perhaps cast-iron horizontal drainpipes as well. This material is strong and usually durable; a pipe in good condition can be expected to last for decades. However, it can rust. It's not unusual for one or two sections to rust through while the rest of the pipe remains in good shape. Sections of cast-iron pipe can be replaced using plastic pipe with transition fittings.

In older cast-iron installations, each pipe has a bell-shaped "hub" at one end (below) into which the next pipe's straight end fits. The joint is sealed by packing it with oakum—a kind of oily fiber—and then pouring in molten lead. Newer cast-iron pipe is joined with "no-hub" fittings, comprised of neoprene sleeves tightened with stainless-steel clamps.

Plastic

Plastic pipe is inexpensive and easy to use. Joints are glued together using primer and cement made for the particular type of plastic *(page 32)*.

Black **ABS** (acrylonitrile-butadiene-styrene) pipe was the first plastic pipe to be used in homes. It is no longer permitted in many areas because its joints occasionally come loose, but normally it can be expected to last. (For how to install or add on to ABS, see *page 101*.)

White or cream-colored **PVC** (polyvinyl-chloride) pipe is now the most common choice for drainpipes. It lasts nearly forever, is strong, and is impervious to most chemicals. Stamped printing on the pipe tells the pipe size, as well as its "schedule," an indication of strength. Schedule 40 is considered strong enough for most residential drain lines.

Schedule 80 PVC is sometimes used for cold-water supply lines, though many inspectors disapprove of it. It definitely should not be used for hot-water supply, because it shrinks and expands with changing temperature. **CPVC** (chlorinated polyvinyl-chloride) pipe has the strength

Hub

Cast iron

PVC

ABS

Pipe sizes

Material	Outside Circumference	Inside Diameter
Copper		
	2"	1/2"
	2 3/4"	3/4"
	3 1/2"	1"
Steel (galvanized or black)		
	2"	3/8"
	2 3/8"	1/2"
	3 1/8"	3/4"
	4"	1"
	4 3/4"	1 1/4"
	5 1/2"	1 1/2"
	7"	2"
Plastic (PVC, CPVC, or ABS)		
	2 3/4"	1/2"
	3 1/2"	3/4"
	4 1/4"	1"
	5 1/8"	1 1/4"
	6"	1 1/2"
	7 1/2"	2"
	10 1/2"	3"
	14"	4"
Cast iron		
	7"	2"
	10 1/8"	3"
	13 3/8"	4"

of PVC and is also heat resistant, so many codes allow its use for interior supply lines *(pages 102–103)*.

New **PEX** supply pipe has a hoselike flexibility and joins with compression fittings, making it very easy to install *(pages 104–105)*. However, it is expensive and is not allowed by many codes.

Steel pipe

Many older homes have **galvanized steel** pipe for supply lines, and possibly for branch drain lines as well. It is a dull gray when old and slightly shiny when new.

Galvanized pipe is strong—it's very difficult to drive a nail through it—but don't expect it to last more than 50 years. Joints develop rust and, even worse, the insides can become clogged with mineral deposits, causing low water pressure.

Black steel pipe is used for gas lines only. It should not be used for water supply because it rusts more quickly than galvanized steel. (An exception: In some areas black steel is used for water supply lines leading into a boiler, steam lines, and air lines.)

Steel pipe is joined to fittings by first wrapping the threads with pipe-thread tape or covering them with pipe joint compound (which may be either gray or white) and then tightening. The joints must be very tight; inadequately tightened joints may eventually leak.

Copper

Copper pipe is extremely long lasting and resists corrosion, making it ideal for supply pipes. It is more expensive than plastic but still reasonably priced.

Rigid copper pipe comes in three thicknesses: The thinnest, rated "M," is usually considered strong enough for most residential applications. Thicker pipes, rated "L" or "K," are used outdoors and for drains.

Rigid copper pipe is joined to fittings by "sweating"—soldering the pieces together. A well-soldered joint should be wiped smooth; if there is a visible drip, the joint may not be strong *(pages 98–99)*.

Flexible copper tubing is often used to supply an icemaker, dishwasher, or other appliance. It is easily bent to make fairly tight turns. If it gets kinked, however, there's no way to fix it; the piece must be replaced. It is joined to fittings and valves using compression fittings *(page 117)* or soldered.

 **PRO TIP**

Finding the inside diameter

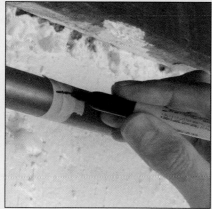

To find out a pipe's "ID"—inside diameter—first wrap a piece of tape or a strip of paper around the pipe, then make a mark to indicate the outside circumference of the pipe. Then use the Pipe Sizes chart opposite to find the inside diameter of the pipe.

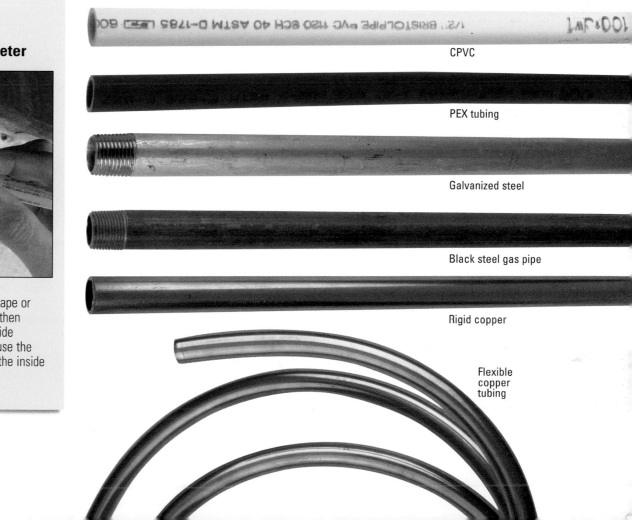

CPVC

PEX tubing

Galvanized steel

Black steel gas pipe

Rigid copper

Flexible copper tubing

SUPPLY PIPE FITTINGS

Whatever the material, most fittings fall into four categories: couplings, which join pipes in a straight line; elbows, which turn corners; tees, Ys, and crosses, which allow pipes to branch out into new lines; and caps, which seal the ends of pipes between roughin and the final installation of fixtures and appliances.

Always buy more fittings than you think you need—they're cheap, and people tend to undercount while planning. You'll save yourself extra trips to the home center

Copper fittings
A brass **drop-ear elbow**, or **stubout**, has two wings which can be screwed tightly against a wall. Some can be sweated (adding a length pipe sealed with a **cap**); some have **threaded** ends. Copper supply elbows (also called ells) are available in 90- and 45-degree angles. A **standard elbow** has two female openings of the same size; a **street elbow** has one female and one male end and is useful in tight spots. A **reducer elbow** makes the transition between one pipe size and another.

A **straight tee** fitting has three openings all the same size. A reducer tee has one smaller opening to accommodate a smaller pipe. Usually the two openings opposite each other are larger, and the perpendicular one is smaller.

Couplings simply join pipes in a straight line. A copper or plastic slip coupling, also known as a repair coupling, has no central indentation and can slide all the way onto one pipe, allowing you to join two pipes that

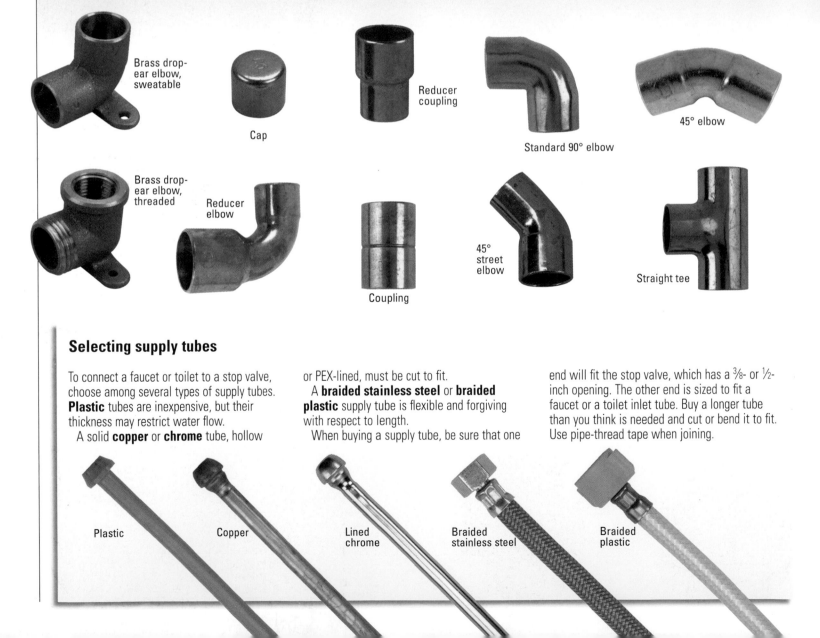

Brass drop-ear elbow, sweatable

Cap

Reducer coupling

Standard 90° elbow

45° elbow

Brass drop-ear elbow, threaded

Reducer elbow

Coupling

45° street elbow

Straight tee

Selecting supply tubes

To connect a faucet or toilet to a stop valve, choose among several types of supply tubes. **Plastic** tubes are inexpensive, but their thickness may restrict water flow.

A solid **copper** or **chrome** tube, hollow or PEX-lined, must be cut to fit.

A **braided stainless steel** or **braided plastic** supply tube is flexible and forgiving with respect to length.

When buying a supply tube, be sure that one end will fit the stop valve, which has a ⅜- or ½-inch opening. The other end is sized to fit a faucet or a toilet inlet tube. Buy a longer tube than you think is needed and cut or bend it to fit. Use pipe-thread tape when joining.

Plastic

Copper

Lined chrome

Braided stainless steel

Braided plastic

are rigidly held in place. A **reducer coupling** makes a transition to a smaller pipe size.

Steel fittings

Threaded steel pipe (both galvanized and black gas pipe) can be assembled moving in one direction only because all the threads are clockwise. Threaded steel fittings cover the same range of types as copper fittings: **Caps, couplings, elbows,** and **tees.** Threaded drop-ear elbows

(opposite) are fastened to framing and used to support a stop valve and supply tube.

To break into a line, use a special coupling called a **union,** which has three parts; it allows you to dismantle and join pipes from either side.

When changing pipe material, be sure to use the correct transition fitting. Use a dielectric fitting *(page 107)* when joining copper to steel. It has a plastic seal that stops the ionization process that would otherwise corrode the joint. Plastic-to-steel

and plastic-to-copper transition fittings are also available. Always use pipe-thread tape *(page 106),* when joining steel pipe. White tape is rated for water pipes, yellow for gas.

Other pipe materials

Flexible supply pipe is an increasingly accepted alternative to copper and steel. Using nylon and brass compression fittings, it is ideal for remodeling and installs much more quickly than traditional supply pipes (see *pages 104–105).*

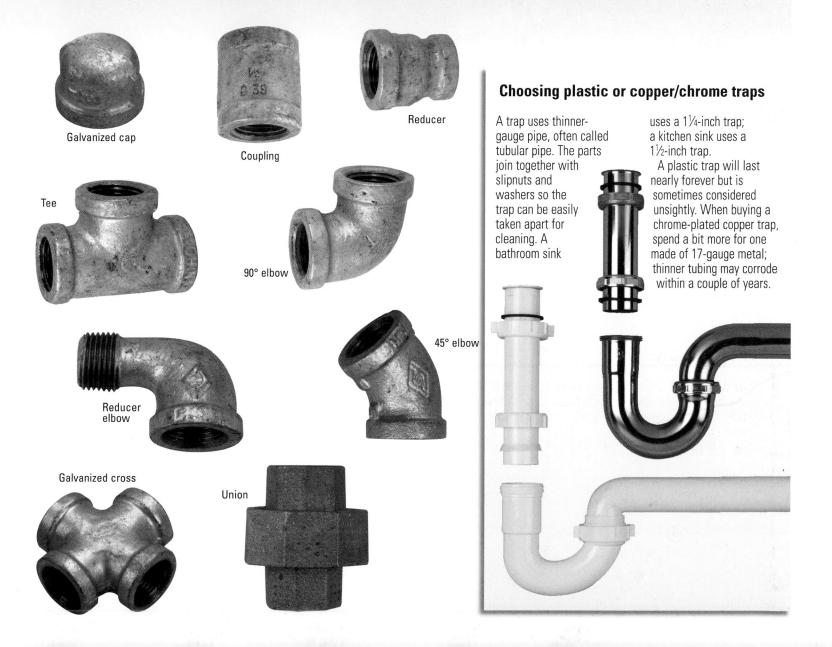

Galvanized cap

Coupling

Reducer

Tee

90° elbow

45° elbow

Reducer elbow

Galvanized cross

Union

Choosing plastic or copper/chrome traps

A trap uses thinner-gauge pipe, often called tubular pipe. The parts join together with slipnuts and washers so the trap can be easily taken apart for cleaning. A bathroom sink uses a 1¼-inch trap; a kitchen sink uses a 1½-inch trap.

A plastic trap will last nearly forever but is sometimes considered unsightly. When buying a chrome-plated copper trap, spend a bit more for one made of 17-gauge metal; thinner tubing may corrode within a couple of years.

DRAIN AND VENT FITTINGS

A plumbing inspector will pay close attention to DWV fittings, so be sure to list them in detail in your plan. Drain fittings make gradual turns to reduce the chance of clogs; vent fittings can make sharper turns. The dimension of the drains and vents vary according to use. A toilet typically requires 3–inch drain fittings and 2-inch vent fittings, while a sink will use 2-inch drain with a 2– or 1½-inch vent. On the other hand, an upflush toilet *(pages 219–221)* uses a 2-inch drain but needs a 3-inch vent because the force of expelling water upwards requires a lot of compensating air. Here are some of the common drain and vent fittings your project may call for.

A **waste cross** (sometimes called a "sanitary cross") and a **double-Y** have two branch openings. A **reducer** or a **reducer bushing** connects different size pipes.

A 90-degree drain elbow is called a sweep or a quarter bend. **Quarter bends** are available in short, medium, or long radii; when in doubt, use the **long radius elbow** if you have the room.

When working in a tight place, you can choose among a number of elbows, including a 60-degree, a 45-degree (or eighth bend), and a 22½-degree (or sixteenth bend).

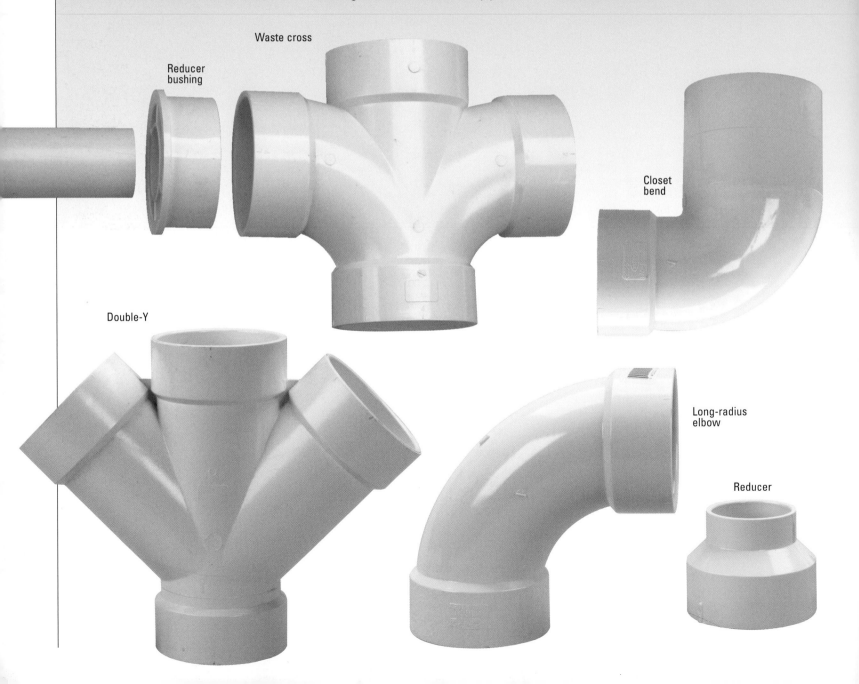

Waste cross

Reducer bushing

Closet bend

Double-Y

Long-radius elbow

Reducer

When running a line for a toilet, be sure to use a special **closet bend.** Its large end accepts a toilet flange, installed after the finished floor surface is completed.

When coming out of the wall for a sink drain, use a **trap adapter;** the trap can be screwed directly onto it.

Tees and **single-Ys** of all sizes are available. The two openings opposite each other in a straight line are called the run openings; the other opening is the branch opening. When describing a tee, the run size is given first, then the branch size. For instance, a **2×2×1½ tee** has two 2-inch run openings and one 1½-inch branch opening. Always buy **waste tee** (sometimes called a "sanitary tee"), which has a curved rather than an abrupt bend.

Codes require drain lines to have **cleanouts** at regular intervals. Install a Y with a cleanout plug or attach a cleanout plug to the end of a pipe.

To make a transition from galvanized steel to plastic drainpipe, use a plastic **male-to-threaded PVC coupling**.

To join plastic to cast iron, use a special adapter fitting with a **neoprene sleeve.** Reinforced with a stainless-steel sheath, it tightens around both types of pipes to make a permanent joint.

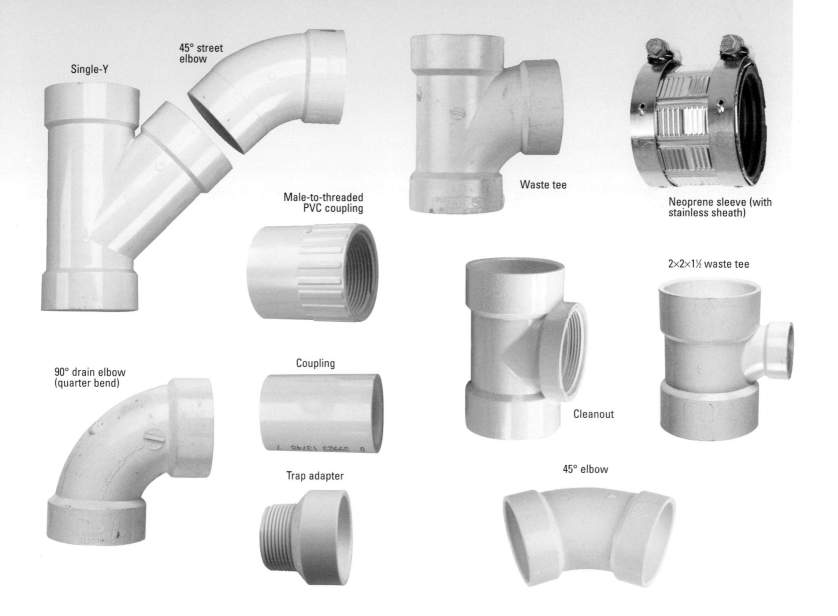

Single-Y

45° street elbow

Male-to-threaded PVC coupling

Waste tee

Neoprene sleeve (with stainless sheath)

2×2×1½ waste tee

90° drain elbow (quarter bend)

Coupling

Coupling

Cleanout

Trap adapter

45° elbow

MAPPING A HOME SYSTEM

Before attempting a major plumbing project, know your home's system. It may first appear to be a tangled web of hidden pipes, but you can soon learn where all the pipes go and what they do. Start by consulting the illustration on *pages 11 and 13*, which have an overview of how plumbing systems work.

If you are fortunate enough to have a set of architectural drawings of your house that includes the plumbing, the job may be already done. However, plumbers often deviate from plans, so take some time to compare the plans to the actual pipes. If you have architectural drawings that do not show plumbing, make several copies and sketch in the existing plumbing. If you have no drawings, sketch your own. Later turn rough sketches into orderly drawings; *pages 38–39* show how.

Tips for finding pipes

If you still can't find all the pipes after following the steps at right, try these methods:

■ If an interior wall is thicker than the other walls (the usual thickness is 4 to 4½ inches), chances are good that it is a "wet wall" through which the main stack runs.

■ To find pipes in walls, turn on water and hold a stethoscope or a drinking glass against the wall surface. Supply pipes will hiss, and drainpipes will gurgle.

■ Turn off any intermediate shutoff valves and test to see which rooms they control.

■ If it is safe, climb onto your roof and run a hand-crank auger down through a vent pipe. Have a helper listen as you wiggle the auger. In this way you can map both the main and secondary vents.

■ If you have hot-water heat, map heating pipes separately. In older homes radiator pipes are usually larger than supply pipes, though they may resemble drainpipes. In a newer home, copper heat pipes (which carry water to convectors or to radiant-heat lines) may be ½- or ¾-inch copper and look just like supply pipes.

DWV map

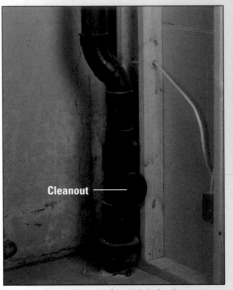

Locate the main stack, which is the largest-diameter pipe in a home. It should have a cleanout (near the floor in older homes, about 42 inches up in newer), which you can use to clean out the main drain line. The stack usually runs straight up to the roof but it may have an offset.

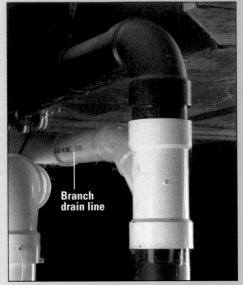

A secondary stack is a feature of most homes and often serves the kitchen. It also extends up through the roof, and it should have a cleanout. From a basement or crawlspace, you may be able to look up and see branch drain lines entering the stack.

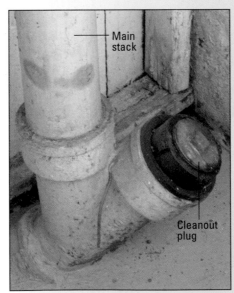

The main stack in an older home is a thick cast-iron pipe. It almost certainly travels straight up to the roof. It may have a cleanout plug like the one shown, or there may be a cleanout hub on the floor.

A secondary stack in an older home is cast iron. Unlike the main stack, it may go around obstacles. Belowground, it may join directly with the main drain, or it may run to a common catch basin (see *page 15*).

To follow the course of the supply lines, start where the main line enters the house, and find the main shutoff *(page 8).* Near the water heater, note where the single pipe branches off into hot and cold and how the hot/cold pairs branch off supplying different areas of the house.

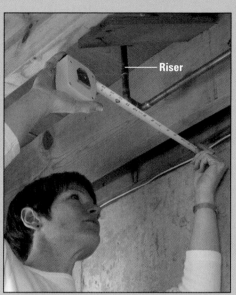

To trace the supply pipes further, determine where they enter the floor above. A supply pipe may run vertically with the wall (called a riser). However, it's not unusual for the supply pipe to turn and run horizontally. Keep in mind that supply pipes must end up near drainpipes.

You'll likely find an access panel in the wall directly behind a shower (shown) or bathtub's faucet. Remove the panel to expose the plumbing—it will provide valuable clues about how supply lines are routed.

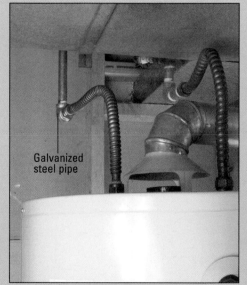

Older supply pipes are made of galvanized steel. If you see extensive rust at the joints, plan to replace the pipes. If water pressure is low in all or part of the house, mineral buildup may be the problem.

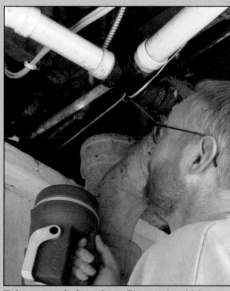

Take note of pipe sizes. Risers should be ¾ inch, but in many old homes they are only ½ inch, which can lead to low water pressure, especially if the pipes are galvanized steel.

You may find an access panel in a place other than behind a tub. Chances are such a panel was installed when a plumber had to make a repair.

PLUMBING CODES

Plumbing is the most complicated aspect of most bathroom and kitchen remodeling projects. It is essential that all the plumbing conform to code. Do-it-yourself plumbing that is done without the benefit of inspections often turns out to be not only faulty, but also dangerous and unhealthy.

The National Uniform Plumbing Code applies generally to the entire country, but local codes—which may be more stringent—most concern you. At the beginning of the planning process, visit or call your building department and obtain any printed information about local plumbing codes. Have the plans approved before starting work and perform all work to the satisfaction of the inspector (see opposite). Draw a detailed plan *(pages 38–39)* that includes a list of all materials.

Common codes

The first priority is venting. Can you revent, or do you need to send a new vent pipe up through the roof? Drainpipes that are not properly vented will run sluggishly and may release noxious fumes into the house. See *pages 14–15* for solutions to most venting problems. Here are some other important code considerations:

■ Fixtures must not be placed too close together. This is critical in a bathroom where space may be at a premium. See *pages 162–163* for clearances.

■ Determine the correct pipe sizes for drains, vents, and supply lines (see *page 35*).

■ Most inspectors will accept rigid copper pipe for supplies and PVC for drains.

■ To ensure adequate water pressure, you may need to replace an existing globe shutoff valve with a "full bore" ball or gate valve *(page 34)*, which does not impede the flow of water. If pressure is very low, you may need a booster pump. Where pressure is too high, you may need a pressure-reducing valve.

■ The installation of plumbing must not weaken the structure of a house. The inspector may require that you reinforce joists that have been cut to accommodate pipes. Other requirements include the use of fire caulking around pipes and placement of protective plates over pipes.

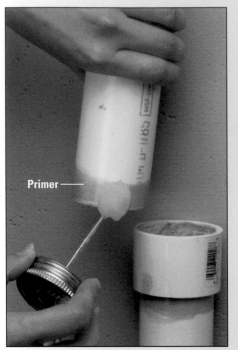

Use purple primer when joining PVC pipes so the inspector can quickly tell that the pipes have been primed. Pipes that are glued without primer will eventually leak.

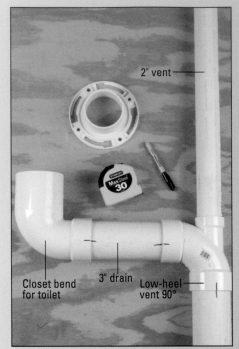

Purchase the right fittings by listing them in detail on your plan. Be sure to use special drain fittings (like the closet bend shown) so wastewater can flow smoothly. Inspectors will have very specific fitting requirements for different fixtures.

CORRECT SLOPE FOR DRAINPIPE

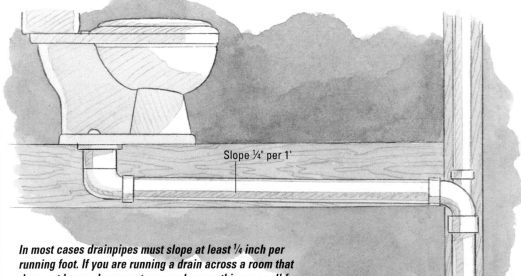

In most cases drainpipes must slope at least ¼ inch per running foot. If you are running a drain across a room that does not have a basement or crawlspace, this may call for careful calculations. Codes may require that vent pipes slope at ⅛ inch per foot, or they may permit you to install them level.

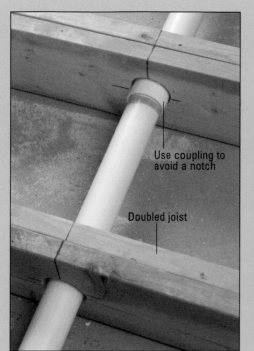

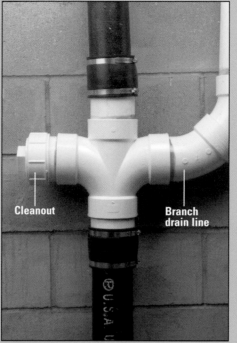

Cutting a notch in a joist greatly weakens it. So whenever possible, bore holes through joists instead. This calls for careful work; holes for drainpipe must be at slightly different levels so the pipe will slope. Whether notched or bored, long spans may need doubled joists (shown).

Codes call for cleanouts at various points so drains can be easily augered in case of a clog. To be safe, install a cleanout whenever you tap into a drain line unless there is already one nearby.

Once the drain lines are assembled, an inspector will probably test to make sure they do not leak. Some inspectors will simply pour water through the pipes. Other inspectors require that the line be plugged with an inflatable drain plug (shown) and the system filled with water.

STANLEY PRO TIP: **Working with the building department**

Though it may seem a bother, working with your municipal building department ensures safe and reliable plumbing. When you sell your house, prospective buyers may be put off if they discover that work was done without inspection and may therefore be out of code. Many departments prefer to work with professionals and are skeptical of homeowners' ability to tackle advanced plumbing tasks. Here are some tips for getting off to the best possible start:

■ Find out if your building department requires a licensed plumber to run new plumbing lines. Some departments require a homeowner to pass a written or oral test before doing certain types of work.

■ The inspector's job is not to help plan but to inspect. An inspector may be willing to offer advice but don't ask, "What should I do?" Instead propose a plan and present it for feedback.

■ Draw up professional-quality plans, along with a complete list of materials (*pages 38–39*). Make an appointment with the inspector to go over your plans. Listen carefully and take notes. Be polite and respectful but don't be afraid to ask questions if you do not understand.

■ Schedule inspections and be prepared for them. There will probably be two: one for the rough plumbing and one for the installation of fixtures. Don't make an appointment until the work is done—inspectors dislike coming back for a reinspection.

Above all, do not cover up any rough plumbing until the inspector has signed off on it. Doing so runs the risk of having to tear out brand-new walls to revise the plumbing.

WHAT IF...
You have a septic system?

If you live in a rural area, wastewater may drain into a septic system in the yard rather than flowing into a municipal sewage system. A typical septic system has three parts. Water flows first into a watertight septic tank, which retains the larger solids. Liquid with suspended smaller particles travels to a distribution box, which in turn sends the waste out to a series of perforated pipes. Waste liquid percolates through the pipes and into the ground.

If the system backs up, the tank may need to be pumped by a special service. Be sure you know where the tank is located; its lid may be buried.

If grass becomes very dark near the tank, the tank has probably cracked and needs to be replaced.

PLUMBING CODES *(continued)*

Valves, fixture controls, cleanouts, and compression pipe fittings must not be covered by a wall or floor surface. If you may need to work on the plumbing in the future, install an access panel. The most common location is behind a tub or shower *(page 31).*

When changing pipe materials, use the correct transition fitting. Without a dielectric union (shown), the joint between galvanized and copper pipe would quickly corrode. Use the approved fitting when changing from plastic to copper, cast iron to plastic, and ABS to PVC.

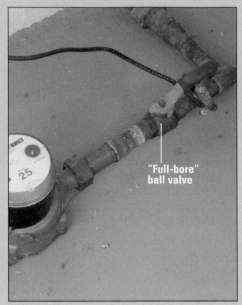

"Full-bore" ball valve

Old plumbing can usually remain; however, new plumbing needs to meet code. If old galvanized pipes and gate valves cause low water pressure, you may need to change them in order to supply the new pipes with enough pressure. As shown, a newer ball valve has replaced a gate valve.

Hammer arrester

Codes may require a water hammer arrester near appliances such as a washing machine (shown), and perhaps at every faucet. Supply pipes may need to be cushioned wherever they run through or up against a framing member.

In addition to the main shutoff valve for a house, codes may require shutoff valves that control a portion of the house. A hose bib should have an interior shutoff valve. All faucets and toilets must have individual stop valves (see *page 8).* This corroded old valve will need replacement or repacking.

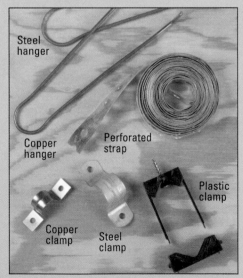

Steel hanger

Copper hanger

Perforated strap

Plastic clamp

Copper clamp

Steel clamp

Use approved clamps or straps to secure pipes. According to most codes, copper supply pipe must be supported every 6 feet; galvanized or black steel pipe every 12 feet; PVC or ABS drainpipe every 4 feet; cast-iron pipe every 5 feet. To be safe, install more supports than are required.

Water distribution pipes

Distribution pipes carry water from the main supply line to the rooms in the house, where they connect to branch lines.

Branch pipes
These pipes run from the distribution pipes to the fixtures. As a general rule, you can run ½-inch pipe to most fixtures; run ¾-inch pipe to a hose bib or a water heater.

Different fixtures place a different demand on supply pipes. Each fixture has a demand rating based on fixture units (see charts, right).

Supply tubes
These are the flexible lines that run from the stop valve to a faucet, fixture, or appliance. As a general rule, run ½-inch supply lines to all fixtures except toilets and bathroom sinks, which use ⅜-inch tubes.

DETERMINING SUPPLY FIXTURE UNITS

Add up the total number of fixture units in your house using this chart, then estimate how far the pipes travel inside your house.

Fixture	Units
Toilet	3
Bathroom sink	1
Tub/shower	2
Dishwasher	2
Kitchen sink	2
Washing machine	2
Hose bib	3

DETERMINING SUPPLY SIZE

Once you've totaled your home's fixture units, use this chart to check the minimum required size for the distribution pipes. Note that this chart is for estimating only. Local codes may vary, depending in part on the water pressure supplied by the utility.

Size of pipe from street	Size of distribution pipe	Length of pipe run/number of units			
		40'	60'	80'	100'
1"	1"	36	31	27	25
1"	¾"	33	28	25	23
¾"	1"	29	25	23	21
¾"	¾"	18	16	14	12
¾"	½"	6	5	4	4

Sizing drainpipes

Use the chart at right to count the number of fixture units that will be connected to a drain line, then see the chart at far right for the minimum drainpipe size. NOTE: If a toilet connects to a drainpipe, the pipe must be at least 3 inches. Check local building codes.

Fixture trap size
A bathroom sink uses a 1¼-inch trap. Showers and floor drains use 2-inch traps. All other sinks and appliances use 1½-inch traps.

DETERMINING DRAIN FIXTURE UNITS

Fixture	Units
Shower/Tub	2
Bathroom sink	1
Toilet	3
Kitchen sink	2
Kitchen sink with disposer	3
Washing machine	2
Laundry sink	2
Floor drain	2

DETERMINING DRAINPIPE SIZE

Pipe size	Maximum units, horizontal drainpipe	Maximum units, vertical drain stack
1¼"	1	2
1½"	3	4
2"	6	10
3"	20	30
4"	160	240

ACCESSIBLE INSTALLATIONS

In the past, kitchens and bathrooms often presented obstacles to the elderly or people with disabilities. But a growing list of plumbing products engineered for easier use plus some simple design changes now can be combined to create accessible kitchens and baths in any home. Often these changes benefit everyone in a household, as well as relatives and guests.

Available resources

The Americans with Disabilities Act (ADA) of 1991 establishes accessibility standards for commercial and public facilities. Some of these regulations pertain directly to plumbing fixtures and the design of bathrooms and kitchens.

The ADA standards are not required for private residences, but they are a valuable source of information. Visit the ADA web site at www.usdoj.gov/crt/ada/.

Your local building department should be able to help you design kitchens and baths that are universally accessible. Some plumbing companies carry a line of accessible products. Other companies specialize in ADA-approved sinks and other fixtures, which include those with pedal-operated controls.

Customize your plan

Don't just follow the rules; make sure your layout and fixtures will be useful for everyone in your family for now and in the future. Whenever possible test a product or layout ahead of time to make sure it can be used easily by a person in a wheelchair or walker.

Purchase ADA-approved grab bars and position them with these two purposes in mind: A grab bar should enable a person to easily enter and exit an area; there should be a grab bar at a convenient location so a person can reach it in case of a slip or fall. Be sure to anchor grab bars with screws driven deeply into studs.

Planning an accessible kitchen

This sink has a specially designed enclosure below, which covers all plumbing, electrical, and mechanical parts. If you install an ADA-approved unit, you will be assured easy access. A typical enclosure is made of vinyl. It is usually not possible to install a garbage disposer inside this type of unit. A "one-touch" faucet with a pull-out sprayer is often preferred.

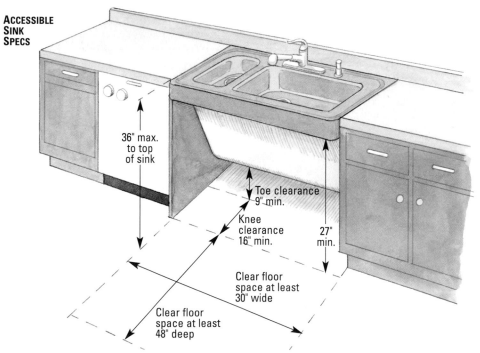

ACCESSIBLE SINK SPECS

36" max. to top of sink

Toe clearance 9" min.

Knee clearance 16" min.

27" min.

Clear floor space at least 30" wide

Clear floor space at least 48" deep

In front of the sink, provide a clear area 48 inches by 30 inches. Test with a wheelchair to make sure the entry and turnaround area are large enough. Make sure it is possible for a person to wheel up to the sink, operate the handles, and reach the sink's drain plug.

The top of the sink should be no higher than 34 inches—2 inches lower than a standard

countertop. Check for the height that works best; you may go as low as 28 inches.

The area under the sink should be free of obstructions, such as electrical cables or a garbage disposer.

Provide a counter space for food preparation, with a countertop at the correct height and no cabinet below.

Planning an accessible bathroom

A bathroom sink should have the same sort of accessibility as a kitchen sink (opposite).

There should be room to wheel into the bathroom and to move easily from one fixture to another. ADA-recommended clearances vary depending on the shape of the bathroom and the position of fixtures; shown here are some typical dimensions.

There should be a space at least 56 inches by 60 inches around a toilet. The space extending in one direction from the center of the toilet should be at least 42 inches.

Provide a stable, ADA-approved seat in a bathtub. Usually, it's best to have a detachable handheld shower unit, so the person can wash while sitting.

A shower usually provides easier access than a tub. However, the stall must be extra large— at least 36 by 60 inches—and must have a solid seat. A shower curtain is usually easier to operate than a shower door.

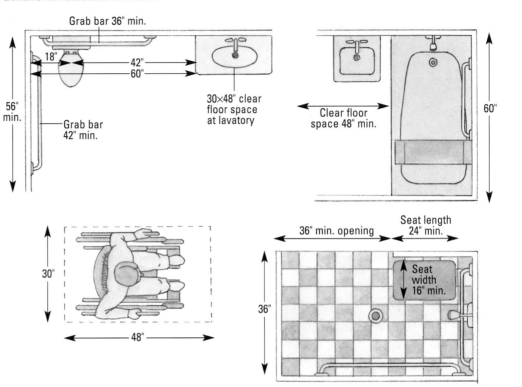

PLANNING AN ACCESSIBLE BATHROOM

Grab bar 36" min.

18"

42"

60"

56" min.

Grab bar 42" min.

30×48" clear floor space at lavatory

Clear floor space 48" min.

60"

30"

48"

36"

36" min. opening

Seat length 24" min.

Seat width 16" min.

The sink shown above has large, easy-to-use handles and roll-under space beneath. The tub and shower unit at right has solid, well-placed grab bars, a stable and slip-resistant seat, and a handheld shower unit.

MAKING DRAWINGS

You may think that a rough sketch of a plumbing project is all you need. After all, you can figure out the details as you work, right? Even professional plumbers have to make on-the-fly changes after they start doing the work. The framing they find may differ from what they expected, or they may discover that their plan was faulty. Pros usually map a job in painstaking detail to avoid as many surprises as possible.

It's fairly easy to produce plan views and riser drawings that use official plumbing symbols. The effort expended making detailed drawings will save time and expense later. The drawing process helps you think through the project in detail. That may enable you to spot a mistake you might otherwise overlook. It will almost certainly minimize extra trips to the plumbing supply store. Also a clear, professional-quality plan will make your initial meeting with the building department more pleasant.

Getting started

A plan for a new plumbing service starts with a map of the existing plumbing; (see *pages 30–31*). Use color codes when drawing a plan to indicate the function of each pipe.

If you have architectural drawings, make several photocopies of them. If you have no architectural drawings, make several copies of an accurate scale drawing of the room.

The necessary tools are simple: a gridded straightedge like the one shown opposite will help you draw parallel lines. You'll also need colored pencils, an eraser, and a 30-60-90-degree triangle.

Use grid paper so it's easy to establish a scale, like ½ inch to 6 or 12 inches. Such a scale makes it easy to note any problems with the layout and is a useful guide for estimating materials.

Final drawings

To make a plan drawing, first draw all fixtures to precise size and make sure they are not too close together (see *page 162*). Then put in the drain lines with fixtures; then the supplies. Make riser drawings as well.

Use the drawing to make a list of materials. Indicate the exact type of every fitting so the inspector can approve them. Indicate pipe sizes, including valves to match the pipe dimension.

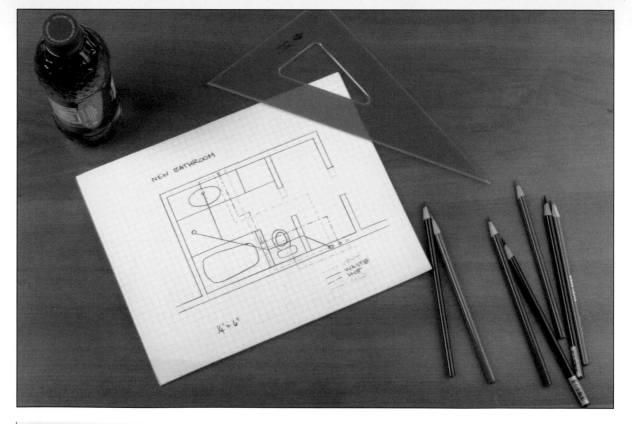

Solid lines indicate drainpipes, and broken lines indicate hot and cold water lines. Because this is an overhead view, notes must indicate any vertical runs. Different colored pencil lines make clear the function of each pipe. All pipe sizes are shown with a curled leader line to avoid confusion. Expect to make several versions of your plan—better to make your mistakes on paper than on the job site.

Photocopy the floor plan
For complex projects, draw your floor plan, then make several photocopies. This allows you to sketch out several trial plans.

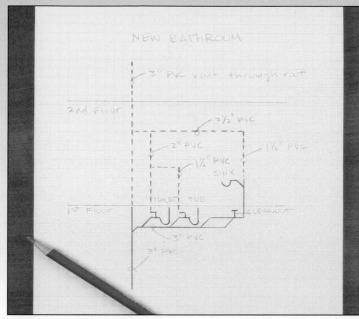

A DWV elevation describes the upward path of the stack, vents and revents, the length of drainpipe runs, and traps. Its primary purpose is to show how the fixtures will be vented. It doesn't have to be drawn over an architectural drawing.

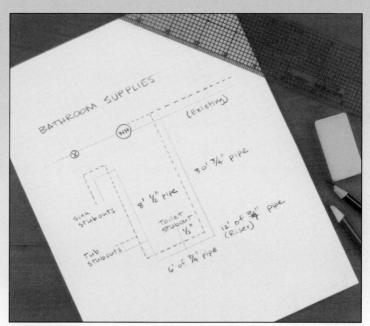

A supply drawing indicates the estimated length of supply pipes. The main purpose is to determine the minimum size of the pipes (see the chart on *page 35*).

Plumbing symbols

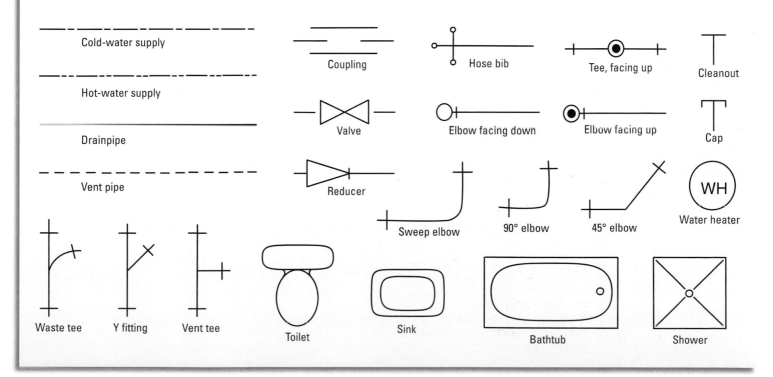

Cold-water supply

Hot-water supply

Drainpipe

Vent pipe

Waste tee Y fitting Vent tee

Coupling

Valve

Reducer

Toilet

Hose bib

Elbow facing down

Sweep elbow

Sink

Tee, facing up

Elbow facing up

90° elbow   45° elbow

Bathtub

Cleanout

Cap

Water heater

Shower

DEALING WITH CLOGGED PIPES

If a drain runs sluggishly or is stopped up, the plumbing is probably fine, though it's likely clogged with grease, soap, hair, or a small object. If you have children, the culprit may be a small toy.

Preventive measures

Always use the toilet, not the sink, to dispose of semisolid waste. However, even a toilet cannot handle large objects: Sanitary napkins, tampons, and big wads of toilet paper can clog it.

Equip sinks and tubs with strainers, and regularly clear away hair and gunk.

Food that has been ground up in a garbage disposer can form a thick paste, especially if grease is part of the mix. Keep grease out of the sink whenever possible. Use cold water when running the disposer, then run hot water for a few seconds to clear the trap.

Diagnosing and unclogging

If only one fixture is sluggish or stopped up, the clog is probably in the fixture's trap or in the branch drain line. If more than one fixture is affected, the problem is farther down the line—most likely in a drainpipe or even the stack. If all the fixtures on the first floor are clogged, the main drain may need to be augered— a job for professionals.

This chapter describes basic unclogging methods, beginning with the simplest. Start by plunging. If that doesn't work, move on to dismantling a trap and possibly replacing the trap. If the problem is farther down the line, use an auger.

Bathtubs, bathroom drains, and kitchen strainers all call for special solutions, described on *pages 48–55*.

For low water pressure in a faucet or showerhead, *pages 42–43* show how to increase the flow.

Working safely

Chances are you will get splashed while unclogging a drain. If drain cleaner has been poured down the drain, unclogging it can be dangerous (see box opposite). When working with drain cleaner, wear plastic gloves, long sleeves, and safety goggles. Cover the work area with an old rug or a drop cloth before starting work.

CHAPTER PREVIEW

Clogged and sluggish pipes can usually be cleared using simple techniques and a few basic tools.

Clearing aerators and showerheads
page 42

Clearing clogs by plunging
page 44

Dismantling a trap
page 46

Bathroom sink drain
page 48

A bright flashlight that stands upright frees your hands and does not pose a shock hazard.

A drop cloth, a rug, or even an old pillow makes a tough job more comfortable.

Working under a sink can be downright miserable. Make the work site as comfortable as possible by adding a drop cloth, a rug, and even an old pillow, especially where the edge of the cabinet can dig into your back. Place tools so they are easily reached, and set up a flashlight.

Kitchen basket strainer
page 50

Clearing drain lines
page 52

Clearing sinks, tubs, or toilets
page 54

CLEARING AERATORS AND SHOWERHEADS

An aerator screws onto the end of a faucet. It typically has two screens through which water passes, creating a mixture of water and air that produces a smooth flow and minimizes splash.

Tiny particles caught in an aerator's screens reduce the water flow. The solution is usually simple: Just unscrew and take apart the aerator, flush the particles out of the screens, reassemble, and screw it back on.

If aerators clog regularly, your water system may be at fault. If your home has old galvanized steel pipes, particles are probably flaking off the inside of the pipes and may need to be flushed *(pages 140–141)*. If your home has copper supply pipes, the problem may be that the water delivered by the utility company is impure; try installing a water filter.

If water flows slowly into a washing machine, shut off the stop valves and unscrew the hoses. You'll find a screen at the end of the hose; if it is stopped up with particles, clean it out.

PRESTART CHECKLIST

☐ **TIME**
Just a few minutes to clean out an aerator or showerhead. If mineral deposits are severe, soak the parts overnight.

☐ **TOOLS**
Groove-joint pliers, screwdriver, old toothbrush, straight pin

☐ **SKILLS**
No special skills needed

☐ **PREP**
Cover the sink or shower drain so small parts can't accidentally slip down

☐ **MATERIALS**
Vinegar, lime-deposit cleaner

Aerators

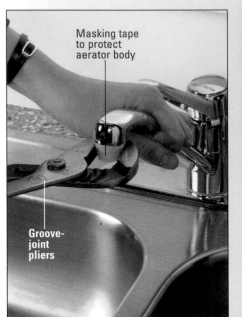

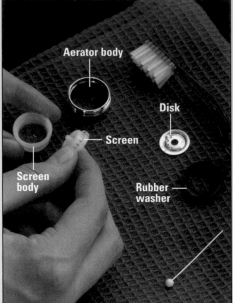

1 You may be able to unscrew an aerator with your fingers. If not, wrap masking tape around the aerator to protect it from scratching, and unscrew it with groove-joint pliers. Turn the faucet on and off several times to flush out any additional debris.

2 Disassemble the aerator with your fingers or use a small screwdriver. Note how the pieces go together. If the aerator is damaged, buy a replacement. Clean the screens with a toothbrush and pin, and rinse. If the minerals are caked on, soak them in vinegar overnight and clean again.

AERATOR TYPES

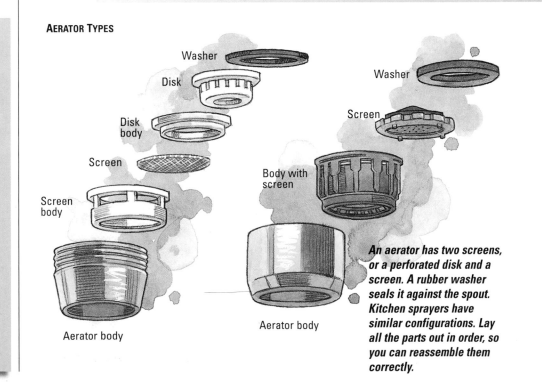

An aerator has two screens, or a perforated disk and a screen. A rubber washer seals it against the spout. Kitchen sprayers have similar configurations. Lay all the parts out in order, so you can reassemble them correctly.

Showerheads

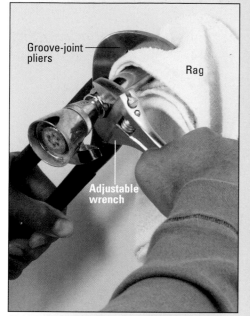

Groove-joint pliers

Rag

Adjustable wrench

1 Unscrew the showerhead collar with an adjustable wrench. If the shower arm turns while you are doing this, grip it with groove-joint pliers while you unscrew the showerhead. Wrap a cloth around the shower arm to keep from damaging it.

Straight pin

2 Run water backward through the showerhead and poke the spray outlets with a pin or brush to flush out the debris.

3 If the debris does not flush out easily, soak the showerhead overnight in a solution of vinegar and lime-deposit cleaner and try again. You may need to disassemble the showerhead and clean all the parts individually. If the showerhead is damaged, buy a new one.

TWO TYPES OF SHOWERHEADS

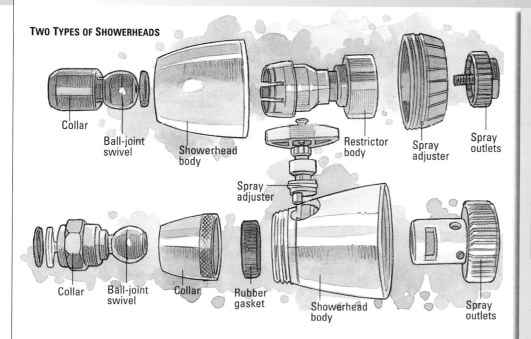

Collar

Ball-joint swivel

Showerhead body

Restrictor body

Spray adjuster

Spray outlets

Spray adjuster

Collar

Ball-joint swivel

Collar

Rubber gasket

Showerhead body

Spray outlets

As you dismantle a showerhead, lay the parts out in order so you can easily reassemble them later.

Check the flow restrictor

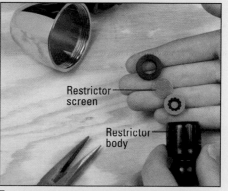

Restrictor screen

Restrictor body

To conserve water, many newer showerheads have built-in flow restrictors. If the water pressure in the shower is low, check to see if the restrictor is clogged with mineral deposits. Dismantle the restrictor and soak its parts overnight in a bowl of lime-deposit cleaner.

CLEARING CLOGS BY PLUNGING

If a sink or tub is clogged, try running hot water through it. Check the strainer (if there is one) and clean out any hair or debris that may have collected. If water still drains slowly, the next step is plunging.

To use a flanged plunger on a sink or tub, fold the flange into the body of the plunger. For small sinks, you may find that a regular plunger works best.

Plunging works in two ways: by pushing a clog through to the stack, and by pulling debris back up into the sink.

For tough jobs, you may want to try a pressure-type plunger, which looks a bit like an accordion *(page 89)*. It generates greater pressure than a standard plunger.

Before plunging, make sure the water has only one exit point—through the drain. Plug overflow holes and clamp connecting hoses before you begin.

Sometimes plunging works easily, with little mess. Other times, water sprays all over the place. Be prepared to wipe up substantial amounts of water.

PRESTART CHECKLIST

☐ **TIME**
About half an hour to prepare and plunge a sink, tub, or toilet

☐ **TOOLS**
Regular, flanged, or pressure-type plunger

☐ **SKILLS**
No special skills needed

☐ **PREP**
Block any alternate passageways through which plunged water may flow

☐ **MATERIALS**
No special materials needed

1 If a drain is sluggish, wait for most of the water to drain out. If the drain is clogged, bail out the water. For best results, there should be about 2 inches of standing water in the sink—just enough to cover the plunger.

2 Often hair and gunk caught on the stopper is the cause of the clog. Remove the stopper and clean it off. (If the stopper does not pull out easily, see *page 48*.) If the sink still does not drain readily, the real clog is farther down the line.

WHAT IF...
A double-drain sink is clogged?

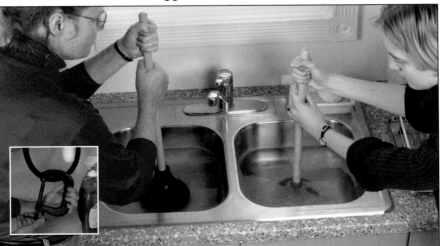

Before plunging a kitchen drain connected to a dishwasher, tightly clamp the drain hose (inset), usually attached to a garbage disposer under the sink. If the sink has two bowls, have a helper block one drain with a second plunger while you plunge the other.

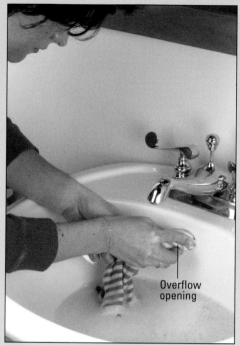

Overflow opening

3 Stuff a wet rag into the overflow opening so water cannot spurt through it as you use the plunger. A helper may need to hold the rag in place as you plunge.

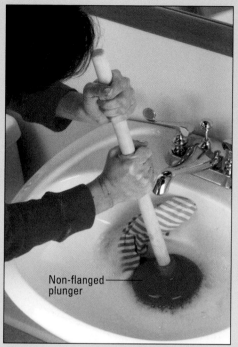

Non-flanged plunger

4 Make sure the plunger forms a tight seal around the drain hole. Work the plunger with a steady, firm, up-and-down motion. You'll feel the water pushing and pulling through the drain. If the clog does not clear immediately, don't give up. Make at least several attempts.

Pull out debris

5 If the water suddenly drains out, the clog has passed out of the drainpipe and into the stack, or the plunger has sucked debris back into the sink. If the drain remains clogged after numerous attempts at plunging, move on to dismantling the trap *(pages 46–47)*.

Plunging a tub

Stuff overflow opening with a rag.

Before plunging a bathtub, remove the drain assembly *(pages 54–55)* and stop the overflow hole with a wet rag. Remove the strainer and bail or add water until there is just enough water to cover the plunger.

Plunging a toilet

Flange

To plunge a toilet, use a flanged plunger with the flange pulled out. Fit the flange into the drain hole, seat the body of the plunger firmly around the hole, and push and pull vigorously.

STANLEY PRO TIP

Pushing through with water pressure

Use an expansion nozzle (also called a balloon or blow bag) to blast a blockage through to the stack. Attach the nozzle to a garden hose, insert it into the drain, and turn on the hose. The nozzle will expand to seal around the drain. Pressure builds until a burst of water is released to clear the clog. **Check your local codes to make sure the use of this tool is allowed in your area.**

DISMANTLING A TRAP

A trap not only seals out gases *(page 10)*, it also provides a bottleneck that prevents clogs from traveling farther down the line. That's why most clogs are found in a trap bend.

To clear a clog, dismantle the trap and clean it out. You'll probably need to replace some rubber washers—they get brittle with age. It's not unusual to find that the entire trap needs replacing. If even one component is leaky, replace the entire trap rather than a single piece—one worn component is likely to mean wear in others. Less expensive chrome-plated traps are notoriously short-lived. They may look okay on the outside, but squeeze the bottom of the bend with your fingers. If you feel it give, even slightly, the metal is corroded. For durability, buy a plastic trap or a chrome-plated trap that is made of heavy-gauge brass.

Bathroom traps are 1¼ inches in diameter; kitchen drains are 1½ inches.

PRESTART CHECKLIST

☐ **TIME**
About an hour to dismantle and reinstall a trap

☐ **TOOLS**
Groove-joint pliers, screwdriver, toothbrush, hacksaw, sandpaper

☐ **SKILLS**
Dismantling and connecting parts with washers and nuts

☐ **PREP**
Prepare a comfortable work site *(page 41);* have a bucket or dishpan and a drop cloth in place

☐ **MATERIALS**
Washers, pipe tape, perhaps a new trap

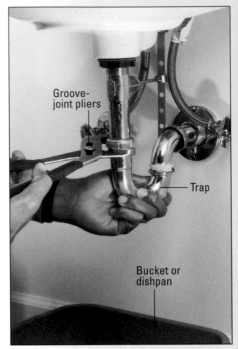

Groove-joint pliers

Trap

Bucket or dishpan

1 Place a bucket under the trap. Loosen the nut on each side of the curved piece with groove-joint pliers. Slide the nuts out of the way and pull the curved piece off.

2 Use a toothbrush to remove hair and other debris that has collected in the trap. If the trap is in good shape, replace the washers and reassemble it. If any parts are damaged, install a new trap (Steps 3–5).

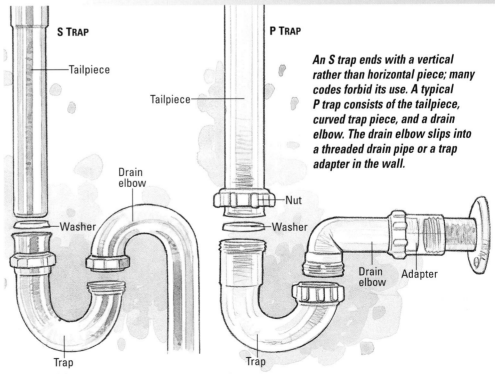

S TRAP

Tailpiece

Drain elbow

Washer

Trap

P TRAP

Tailpiece

Nut

Washer

Drain elbow

Adapter

Trap

An S trap ends with a vertical rather than horizontal piece; many codes forbid its use. A typical P trap consists of the tailpiece, curved trap piece, and a drain elbow. The drain elbow slips into a threaded drain pipe or a trap adapter in the wall.

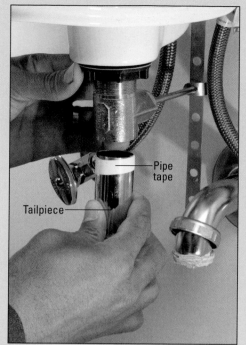

3 Take the old parts to a home center or hardware store to find replacements. Make sure the new pieces will fit exactly; you may need to cut the tailpiece or drain elbow. Begin assembly by wrapping pipe tape clockwise around the threads of a tailpiece, and screw it onto the drain body.

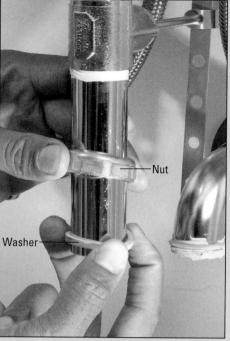

4 With the tailpiece installed, dry-fit all the pieces to make sure they join together with ease. If you have to force a connection, it may leak. For each joint, slide on the nut, then the washer.

5 Assemble the pieces and hand-tighten all the nuts. Then go back and tighten the nuts with groove-joint pliers. To test the drain for leaks, stop up the sink, fill it with water, and open the stopper. Watch carefully for any leaks as the water flows through. Tighten joints where necessary.

CUT THE TAILPIECE
Cutting trap components

To cut a chrome-plated trap piece, place it in a miter box and cut with a hacksaw. To avoid denting the pipe, exert gentle pressure as you cut. After cutting, remove any burrs with sandpaper.

STANLEY PRO TIP

Plastic vs. metal traps

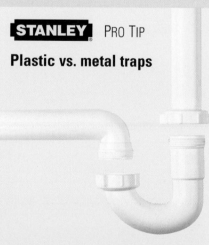

Metal usually is associated with durability, but in the case of sink traps, plastic is the long-lasting choice. Usually you can replace a chrome trap with a plastic one; just make sure it's the right size for the sink and the wall pipe. If appearance is important, choose a chrome-plated brass trap.

Trap with a cleanout plug

Some heavy-duty traps are equipped with a cleanout, a plug that can be removed. Place a bucket under the trap, unscrew the plug, and let the water run out. Reach inside with an auger to remove debris.

BATHROOM SINK DRAIN

The pop-up assembly on a bathroom drain has several moving parts that wear out over time. If the unit is made of thin metal or plastic that is easily bent or broken, repairs may not last; consider buying a new faucet and drain assembly.

Troubleshooting

■ If a stopper is loose and won't stay open, tighten the pivot ball retaining nut.

■ If a stopper is difficult to raise, loosen the pivot ball retaining nut. If that doesn't work, remove the pivot rod, clean out the opening in the drain body, and replace worn gaskets or washers.

■ If the stopper does not seat all the way into the drain body when you pull up on the lift rod, adjust the pivot rod.

■ If a stopper does not hold water, remove it and clean the rubber seal. If there is an O-ring, replace it, or replace the stopper.

■ If water leaks from the pivot rod, tighten the nut. If that doesn't work, remove the pivot rod and replace the gaskets.

PRESTART CHECKLIST

☐ **TIME**
An hour or so for most repairs

☐ **TOOLS**
Groove-joint pliers, screwdriver, long-nose pliers

☐ **SKILLS**
No special skills needed

☐ **PREP**
Make the work area comfortable; place a bucket under the assembly to catch water

☐ **MATERIALS**
Plumber's putty, replacement 1¼-inch rubber or plastic washers, perhaps new gaskets, perhaps a new drain assembly

Adjusting the stopper

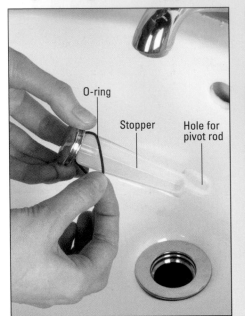

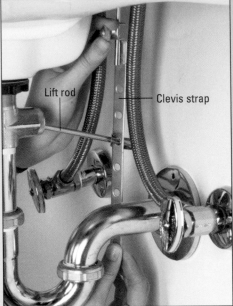

1 Some stoppers can be removed simply by pulling up. With others you twist a quarter-turn or so, then lift up. A third type has a hole through which the pivot rod passes (shown); remove the pivot rod first. Check the O-ring for damage; remove and replace it if necessary.

2 To adjust a stopper up or down, loosen the lift rod nut with your fingers or with a pair of long-nose pliers if it is corroded. Slide the clevis strap up or down as needed, tighten the nut, and test.

BATHROOM DRAIN ASSEMBLY

A pop-up assembly only looks complicated. A pivot rod, connected to the lift rod with a clevis strap, raises and lowers the stopper.

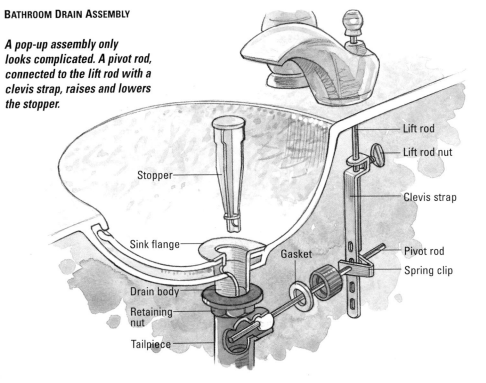

Replacing a drain body

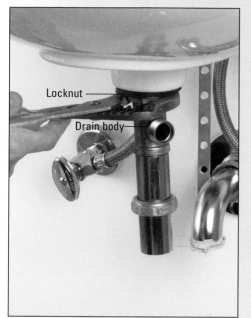

Locknut

Drain body

Sink flange

Locknut

Drain body

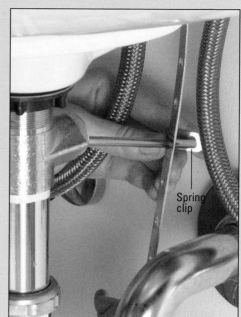

Spring clip

1 Disconnect the trap *(page 46)*. Slide the clevis strap off the pivot rod, loosen the retaining nut, and remove the pivot rod. Insert a screwdriver into the drain opening in the sink to keep it from turning, and loosen the locknut with pliers.

2 Unscrew the locknut. Push down on the sink flange with one hand while you unscrew the drain body with the other.

3 Buy a new drain assembly with a lift rod that fits through your faucet, or buy a new faucet and drain body. Slip the sink flange through the hole in the sink and screw on the drain body. Tighten the locknut, install the pivot rod, attach it to the clevis strap with the spring clip, and adjust.

STANLEY PRO TIP

Easy fix for a leaking drain body

You may need to tighten the retaining nut on a pivot rod from time to time, either to seal a leak or to keep a stopper from falling down when it's supposed to stay up.

REFRESHER COURSE
Dismantling a trap

Use a pair of groove-joint pliers to loosen the slip nuts on the curved trap piece. Slide the nuts and rubber washer out of the way and pull the pieces apart. Unless the rubber washers are in pristine condition, replace them. If the trap is damaged, replace it.

WHAT IF...
There is no rubber gasket?

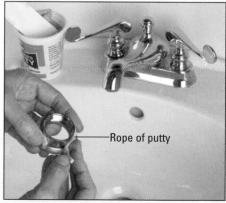

Rope of putty

A bathroom sink flange may come with a rubber gasket that seals it to the sink. If not, apply a rope of plumber's putty to the underside of the flange before installing it. Excess putty will squeeze out as you tighten the locknut.

KITCHEN BASKET STRAINER

If water leaks from under the sink, the basket strainer may not be tightly sealed. To test, close the stopper, fill the sink with water, and inspect from underneath with a flashlight and a dry rag.

If the strainer leaks, try tightening the locknut using groove-joint pliers or a spud wrench (opposite page). If that doesn't solve the problem, remove the strainer, following the steps on these pages. Either clean the drain hole and reinstall the strainer or install a new strainer.

A cheap strainer made of thin metal or plastic may soon fail to seal water. Spend a little more for a better quality strainer that will last longer.

Installation is the same no matter what the sink material—stainless steel, cast iron, or acrylic.

PRESTART CHECKLIST

☐ **TIME**
About 2 hours to remove a basket strainer and install a new one

☐ **TOOLS**
Groove-joint pliers, spud wrench, plastic putty knife, hammer

☐ **SKILLS**
Dismantling and reinstalling a trap (pages 46–47)

☐ **PREP**
Make the work site under the sink comfortable; position a bucket to catch water

☐ **MATERIALS**
New basket strainer, plumber's putty, replacement 1½-inch rubber or plastic washers

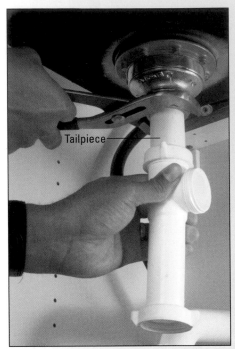

Tailpiece

1 Unscrew the slip nuts at the bottom and top of the tailpiece. Gently pull the tailpiece down from the strainer and remove it. Unless the washers are in very good condition, buy replacement washers. If any part of the trap is damaged, replace it as well.

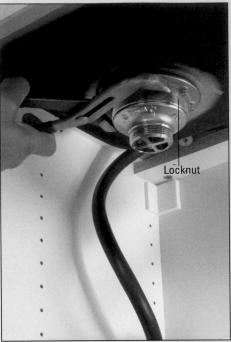

Locknut

2 Loosen the locknut with groove-joint pliers or a spud wrench (opposite). Remove the nut, and pull out the strainer. Scrape the old putty away from around the sink hole, and clean with a rag.

KITCHEN SINK STRAINERS

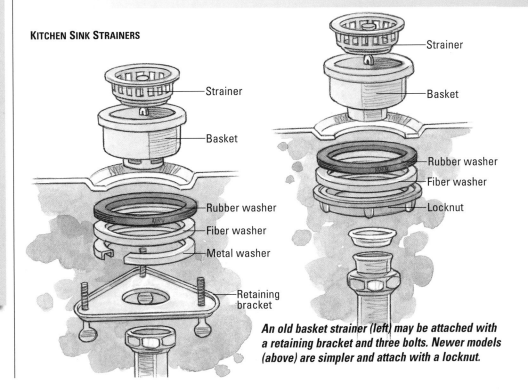

Strainer

Basket

Strainer

Basket

Rubber washer

Fiber washer

Metal washer

Retaining bracket

Rubber washer

Fiber washer

Locknut

An old basket strainer (left) may be attached with a retaining bracket and three bolts. Newer models (above) are simpler and attach with a locknut.

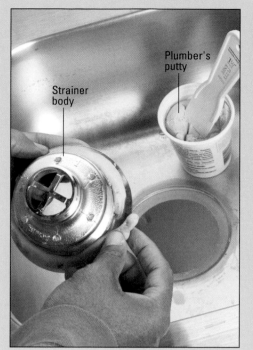

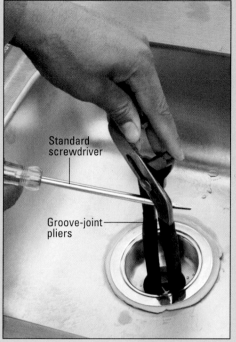

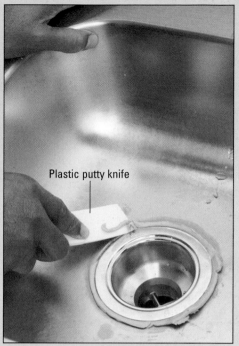

3 Make a rope of plumber's putty (do not use putty that has started to dry), and place it around the sink hole or under the lip of the strainer body. Press the strainer body into the hole and center it.

4 Have a helper hold the strainer in place while you slip on the rubber washer, the cardboard washer, and the locknut. To keep the strainer from spinning while you tighten the locknut, insert the handles of a pair of pliers into the holes and brace them with a screwdriver.

5 Tighten the locknut as tight as it will turn. Scrape away the squeezed-out putty with a plastic putty knife to avoid scratching the sink. Reattach the tailpiece. To test for leaks, close the stopper, fill the sink, then pull out the stopper.

WHAT IF...
There is a leak from the garbage disposer?

A garbage disposer comes with its own strainer. If water leaks from above the disposer (that is, at the point where the disposer attaches to the sink), tighten the mounting ring screws. If that doesn't solve the problem, remove the disposer, disconnect the flange, clean the hole around the sink, and install a new rope of putty.

If water leaks from the connection where the drain meets the disposer, tighten the two screws. You may need to replace the rubber gasket inside. If water seeps from the disposer itself, replace the disposer.

Got a disposer?
For instructions on installing a new trap and disposer for a kitchen sink, see *pages 204–205*.

Get a grip with a spud wrench

Tightening and loosening a basket strainer's locknut is difficult because the nut is large and hard to reach. A pair of groove-joint pliers does the trick but may be cumbersome. A spud wrench (below) or a special basket-strainer wrench makes the job easier.

If the nut is very tight, place the tip of a screwdriver against one of its lugs and tap with a hammer until it loosens.

CLEARING DRAIN LINES

When a sink, toilet, or tub becomes clogged, first try plunging. Bail out most of the water but leave a couple of inches so the plunger can seal tightly around the drain opening. Seal any openings—such as the overflow openings of a bathroom sink or a tub—by firmly pressing a wet rag into the opening. When plunging a double-bowl sink, seal the drain hole of the other bowl. If you have a dishwasher, clamp its drain hose tightly before plunging so you won't force water back into the dishwasher.

If plunging doesn't work, try hand augering, dismantling a trap, or forcing pressurized water into the drain. These techniques will almost certainly clear a clog for an individual drain.

If more than one drain is stopped or runs slowly, take more aggressive steps. Auger through an intermediate cleanout or trap. If that doesn't solve the problem, you may need to auger the main drain. Call on a plumbing company that specializes in clearing clogs or rent a power auger and do it yourself.

PRESTART CHECKLIST

☐ **TIME**
With a rented power auger, an hour or two to run it through a main drain

☐ **TOOLS**
Hand-crank or power auger, adjustable wrench, pipe wrench, groove-joint pliers, perhaps a hammer and chisel

☐ **SKILLS**
Identifying and opening traps and cleanouts

☐ **PREP**
Clear the area and prepare for cleaning up afterward

☐ **MATERIALS**
Pipe-thread tape, replacement cleanout plug, bucket

Unclogging a house line

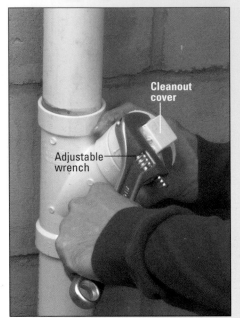

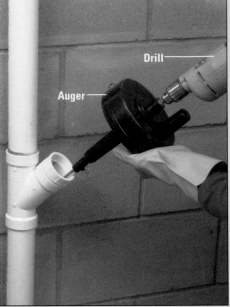

1 Remove a cleanout plug using an adjustable wrench or a pipe wrench. A cleanout usually provides access to the main or secondary stack.

2 Many hank-crank augers like this one have a shaft that attaches to a standard power drill (opposite). The resulting tool is more powerful and easier to use than a plain hand-crank auger (below).

TYPES OF TRAPS

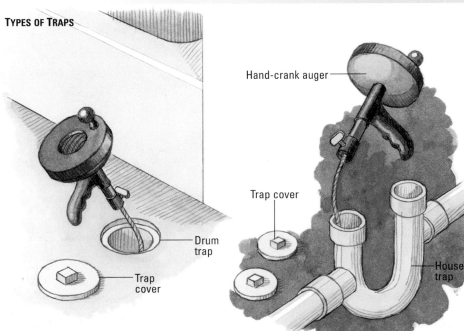

A single drain cover on a bathroom floor opens to a drum trap. A house trap typically has two trap covers near each other on the floor. Both can be augered.

Augering a main drain

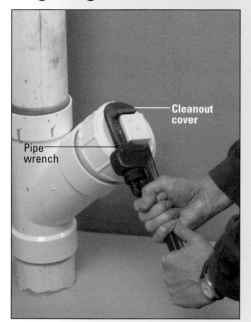

Pipe wrench

Cleanout cover

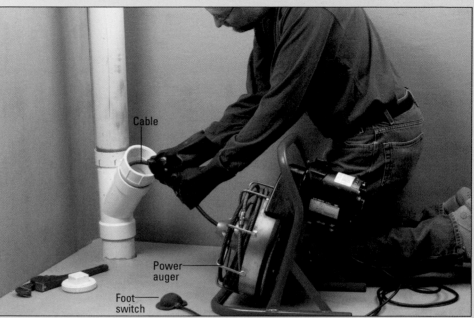

Cable

Power auger

Foot switch

1 The main drain—the line coming from the street to your house—may be clogged by tree roots that have grown into it. (Many old drain lines are made of clay or have permeable joints.) Open the cleanout plug. If you have a metal cleanout plug, you may have to loosen it with a hammer and chisel.

2 Rent a power auger with several bits to handle various obstructions. Rental staff can advise on which bit to use. Select the bit and attach it with the setscrew provided on the cable end. Position the auger close to the pipe to minimize the length of exposed cable. **Make sure**

machine or drop cords are not lying in water. Plug in the auger. Wear heavy rubber gloves. Push the cable into the drain until you hit an obstruction. Switch on the auger and use the foot switch to start the cable rotating. Let it run for a while, then turn off the auger and push the cable in farther.

WHAT IF...
You have a brass plug?

Almost every cast-iron cleanout has a brass plug, often painted over. Try to remove it with a pipe wrench. (If you reuse the brass plug, first wrap the threads with pipe-thread tape.) If it won't budge, attack it with a hammer and cold chisel. Install an expandable rubber replacement cleanout.

AUGERING FROM THE ROOF

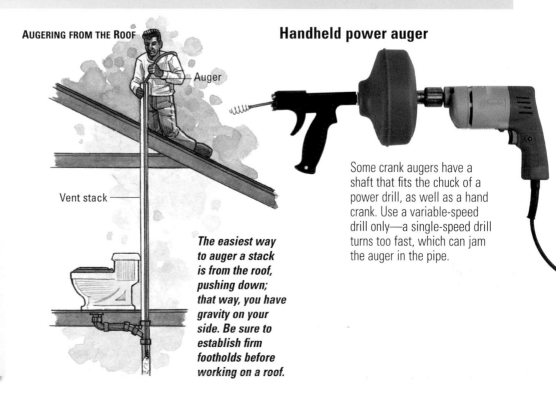

Auger

Vent stack

The easiest way to auger a stack is from the roof, pushing down; that way, you have gravity on your side. Be sure to establish firm footholds before working on a roof.

Handheld power auger

Some crank augers have a shaft that fits the chuck of a power drill, as well as a hand crank. Use a variable-speed drill only—a single-speed drill turns too fast, which can jam the auger in the pipe.

CLEARING SINKS, TUBS, OR TOILETS

An inexpensive hand-crank auger clears most household clogs. It consists of a snakelike cable made of metal, with a widened tip that grabs or pushes debris. Power-operated augers work quicker but are a bit dangerous; if the clog is solid, a fast-turning auger is likely to get stuck so tightly you cannot extract it.

Before use, check that the tip of the auger is in good shape. If it is broken or has come unwound, buy a new auger.

You may choose to run an auger through the sink and into the trap, rather than dismantling the trap. However, before doing so on a bathroom sink, you'll need to remove the pivot rod *(page 48)*. It's usually not possible to auger a kitchen sink, because of the garbage disposer and because the drain assembly for a double-bowl sink has too many turns.

If a tub drains sluggishly, hair and soap sludge may be stuck to the drain/overflow assembly. A plunger type assembly (right) is less complicated and less likely to clog than a pop-up assembly (opposite), but both need occasional cleaning.

A toilet auger (opposite) is the solution when plunging fails. Otherwise, remove the toilet to auger out the clog *(page 89)*.

PRESTART CHECKLIST

☐ **TIME**
About 2 hours to dismantle a trap and auger a branch line

☐ **TOOLS**
Groove-joint pliers, hand-crank auger

☐ **SKILLS**
Dismantling and reinstalling a trap

☐ **PREP**
Make the work site comfortable; place a bucket under the trap to catch spills

☐ **MATERIALS**
Replacement washers for the trap

Augering a sink trap

Drain opening

Hand-crank auger

1 Dismantle the trap. Loosen the auger setscrew and pull out about a foot of cable. Push the cable through the pipe until it stops. You've probably run into a bend in the pipe, rather than the obstruction. Tighten the setscrew. Crank clockwise until the cable moves forward.

2 Loosen the setscrew, push the cable until it stops, tighten the setscrew, and crank again. The auger may grab rather than push the obstruction. If so, pull out the auger, clean away any hair and gunk, and push the auger in again to remove more of the obstruction.

WHAT IF...
You must auger a tub?

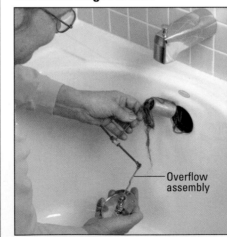

Overflow assembly

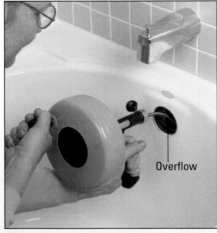

Overflow

1 To auger a bathtub, first check to see whether there is a drum trap in the bathroom *(pages 52, 152)*. If so, auger from there. Otherwise remove the overflow assembly *(pages 152, 156)*.

2 Run the auger down through the overflow, using the techniques shown.

Cleaning a pop-up (rocker-arm) type assembly

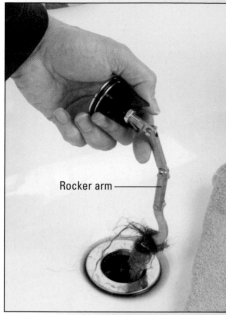

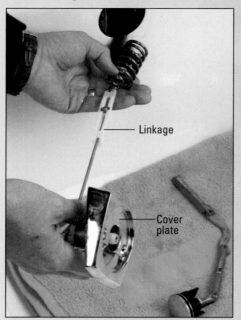

Linkage

Cover plate

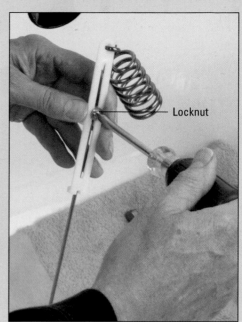

Locknut

1 If the tub has a pop-up assembly, flip the trip lever up to raise the stopper. Gently pull the stopper and the rocker arm up and out of the tub. Clean away any debris.

Rocker arm

2 Remove the cover plate screws and pull out the cover plate with the linkage connected to it. Clean away any hair, coagulated soap, and other debris that might be attached to the linkage.

3 If the stopper does not seal completely, loosen the locknut and twist the threaded rod so it rises up about ⅛ inch. Tighten the locknut. Reinstall and test.

WHAT IF...
The auger gets stuck?

If you suspect that an auger is in danger of getting stuck, pull it out rather than pushing and turning further. It may take four or five attempts before the clog is removed or pushed through the pipe.

If an auger does get stuck, tighten the setscrew and turn the crank counterclockwise. This usually frees it. If that doesn't work, push and pull rapidly back and forth.

It may take some time, but these measures almost always work. If the auger will not come loose after repeated tries, call a professional plumber for help.

TOILET AUGER

A toilet auger has a rubber sleeve to protect the porcelain from scratches. It's just the right length and shape to get at clogs inside and just beyond a toilet.

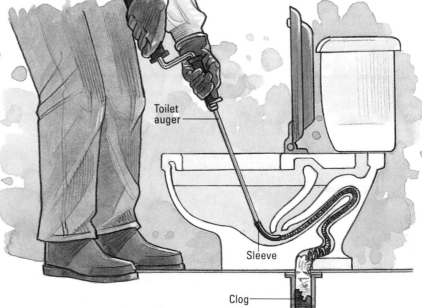

Toilet auger

Sleeve

Clog

FAUCETS

A leaky faucet is the most common household plumbing problem. A house call by a professional plumber will cost plenty, so it makes sense to fix it yourself. This chapter explains how to stop sink and bathtub faucets from dripping from the spout or oozing water from the base of the handle.

Shut off the water

The first step is to stop the flow of water to the faucet (see *pages 8–9*). If there is a pair of stop valves under a sink, turn them off. If there are no stop valves, look for intermediate shutoff valves elsewhere in the house. Failing that, you may have to shut off water to the entire house.

Some bathtub faucets have integrated shutoffs. Look for an access panel behind the tub; shutoff valves may be inside. If not, you'll need to shut off intermediate valves or water to the whole house.

After shutting off the water, open the faucet and wait for the water to stop running. If the faucet is on the first floor of a multistory house, you may have to wait a minute or so for the water to drain.

If the house has old galvanized pipes, shutting the water off and turning it back on will probably dislodge debris inside the pipes, clogging aerators in faucets and showerheads throughout the house; see *pages 42–43* for how to clean them.

Finding the right parts

You may spend more time finding the correct parts than working on the faucet. To prevent multiple shopping trips, remove the worn parts—perhaps even the whole faucet—and take them with you to the store.

The faucets shown in this chapter are the most common types. Chances are good that yours will look and work much like one of them. However, hundreds of faucet types have been made, so you could have an unusual model with parts that are hard to find.

A helpful and competent salesperson can save you plenty of time. Some home centers have knowledgeable people. The staff at a local hardware store may have more expertise. Plumbing supply stores, which cater to professionals, can be impatient with do-it-yourselfers, but they have a wide selection of parts as well as knowledgeable personnel.

If your faucet has a brand name inscribed on its body, look for a repair kit to match. Otherwise, dismantle the faucet to find out its type. Read the relevant repair instructions *(pages 58–75)* to determine which parts need replacement.

In some cases, only inexpensive O-rings and washers are needed. Other times, a main part—a cartridge, stem, or ball, for instance—needs to be replaced. Usually replacing the inner workings results in a faucet that works as smoothly and is as durable as a new faucet.

Fix or replace?

If parts are hard to find or expensive, or if the faucet is unattractive, you may be better off replacing the whole faucet rather than repairing it; *pages 80–85* show how. Depending on the type and age of the faucet, replacing may take less time.

Other leaks

If water leaks below the sink, the problem may be a leaky stop valve or supply tube *(pages 122–123)*. If the leak is at the point where the supply tube enters the faucet, try tightening the nut. If that doesn't solve the problem, replace the supply tube.

If you can find the parts, most faucet repairs are easy. Otherwise consider installing a new unit.

CHAPTER PREVIEW

Sink faucet repairs
page 58

Tub and shower faucet repairs
page 70

Diverters
page 76

Tub spouts
page 77

At a hardware store or home center, you will find a rack of repair kits that cover the most common faucet types. If you don't find the right parts, they can probably be ordered. Failing that, consider replacing the entire faucet set.

Repair kit

Replacement O-ring

Replacement washer

Worn washer

Before installing a new rubber part, check that it is an exact duplicate of the old part. Worn washers (above) or O-rings are the most common cause of run-on faucets. They come in a wide variety of shapes and sizes, even within the same brand, so always bring the worn part along when you're shopping for a replacement.

Installing a flex-line shower unit
page 78

Kitchen sprayers
page 79

Installing a kitchen faucet
page 80

Installing a bathroom faucet
page 84

STEM (COMPRESSION) FAUCETS

Most older two-handle faucets have stems that move up and down when a handle is turned. A rubber washer at the bottom of the stem presses against a seat in the faucet body to seal out water. If the washer or the seat becomes worn, water seeps through and drips out of the spout. If water seeps below the handle or the base of the faucet, an O-ring or the packing probably needs to be replaced.

Getting the parts

All-purpose repair kits for stem faucets contain washers and O-rings of various sizes. To make sure you have a perfect match, take the stem along when buying the repair kit. An older type of faucet may need a packing washer or string packing. If the stem itself is worn, replacing the rubber parts will not solve the problem. You can replace the stem, but it may be hard to find; replacing the faucet is usually the best option.

PRESTART CHECKLIST

☐ **TIME**
Less than an hour for most repairs

☐ **TOOLS**
Screwdrivers, adjustable wrench, groove-joint pliers, possibly a handle puller, seat wrench, or seat grinder

☐ **SKILLS**
Shutting off water, dismantling a faucet, installing small parts

☐ **PREP**
Shut off the water, close the sink stopper, place a rag in the sink to catch any parts

☐ **MATERIALS**
Washer, O-rings, packing, silicone grease

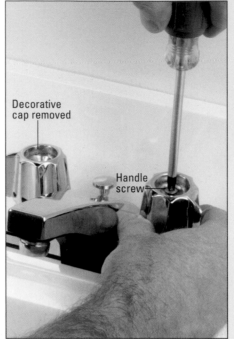
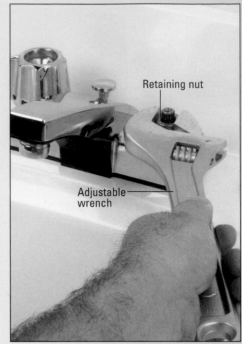

1 Shut off the water and open both handles until water stops running. Pry off the decorative cap (if any), remove the handle screw, and gently pry off the handle. If the handle is stuck, try tapping and prying on one side, then the other, or use a handle puller *(opposite)*.

Decorative cap removed
Handle screw

Retaining nut
Adjustable wrench

2 Use an adjustable wrench to loosen and remove the retaining or packing nut. A sleeve may also cover the stem. Grab the stem with a pair of pliers and pull it out.

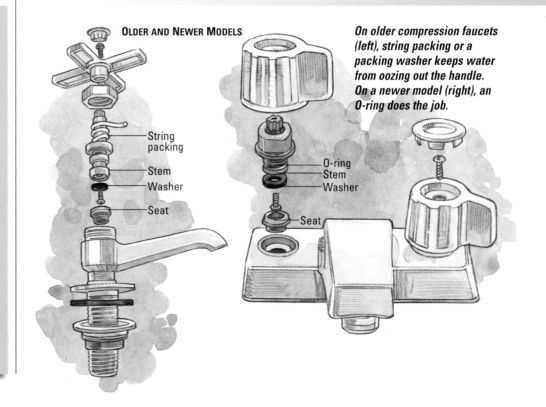

OLDER AND NEWER MODELS

String packing
Stem
Washer
Seat

O-ring
Stem
Washer
Seat

On older compression faucets (left), string packing or a packing washer keeps water from oozing out the handle. On a newer model (right), an O-ring does the job.

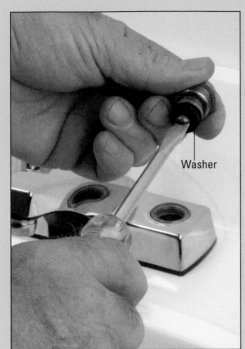

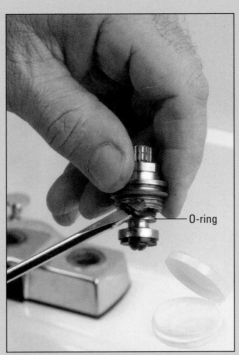

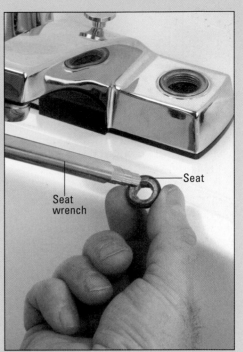

3 If water drips out the spout when the handle is turned off, you probably need to replace a worn washer. Remove the screw and install an exact replacement. If this doesn't solve the problem, or if washers wear out quickly, replace the seat (Step 5).

4 If water seeps out below the handle, replace a worn O-ring or any other rubber part on the stem. Gently pry out the O-ring with a knife or small screwdriver. Rub silicone grease on the replacement O-ring and reinstall it.

5 If the seat is pitted or scratched, remove it using a seat wrench *(page 19)*. Install an exact replacement. If you can't find a new seat, you may be able to grind a worn seat to smooth it.

WHAT IF...
The handle is stuck?

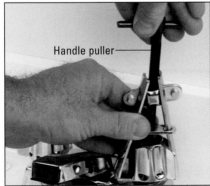

Handles on older two-handle faucets may be stuck tight. If tapping and prying with moderate pressure does not remove a handle, avoid the temptation to pry hard—you may crack the handle or the faucet body. A handle puller grasps the handle from underneath at two sides and slowly draws the handle off the stem.

STANLEY PRO TIP

Use packing on old stems

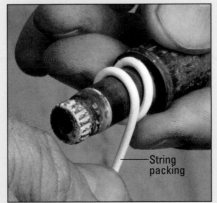

An older faucet may have a rubber packing washer or string packing under a packing nut. If water leaks out the handle, clean out the old packing and install a new packing washer, or wrap string packing around the stem and cram it up into the packing nut.

GRIND A WORN SEAT
Using a seat grinder

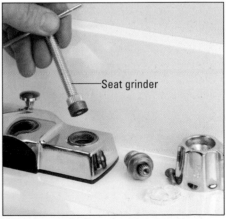

If you cannot obtain a new seat, try using a seat grinder to smooth the existing seat. Keep the tool stable while you grind; if it wobbles, you may make matters worse. The seat should be smooth and even when you're done.

REVERSE-COMPRESSION FAUCETS

This two-handle faucet looks like a stem faucet but operates by opening and closing in the opposite direction. The seat is attached to the bottom of the stem body. The washer attaches to the bottom of the spindle and faces upward. When the faucet is opened, the spindle moves downward, creating a gap between the seat and the washer.

Getting the parts

Chicago (shown in Steps 1–5) and Crane (shown on *page 61*) are among the companies that make this type of faucet. Be sure to get parts made specifically for your model. Washers may be different in shape, so a standard stem washer may appear to fit, but it will not properly seal. Repair kits typically have O-rings, seats, and washers, so you can replace all the non-metal parts. Often, however, all you need is the washer.

PRESTART CHECKLIST

☐ **TIME**
Less than an hour for most repairs

☐ **TOOLS**
Screwdrivers, adjustable wrench, groove-joint pliers, possibly a handle puller

☐ **SKILLS**
Shutting off water, dismantling a faucet, installing small parts

☐ **PREP**
Shut off the water, close the sink stopper, place a rag in the sink to catch any parts

☐ **MATERIALS**
Washer, seat, and O-rings for your faucet

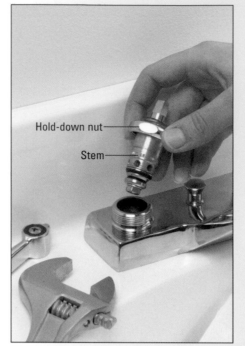

Hold-down nut

Stem

1 **Shut off the water** and open both handles until water stops flowing. Remove the handle *(pages 58–59)*. Use an adjustable wrench to loosen the hold-down nut. Unscrew and remove the stem.

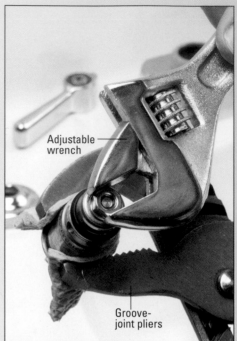

Adjustable wrench

Groove-joint pliers

2 Grasp the stem with groove-joint pliers, using a cloth in the jaws to prevent scratches. Use an adjustable wrench to loosen and remove the nut at the bottom; the seat will not slide out. On models with no bottom nut, twist the seat to remove it.

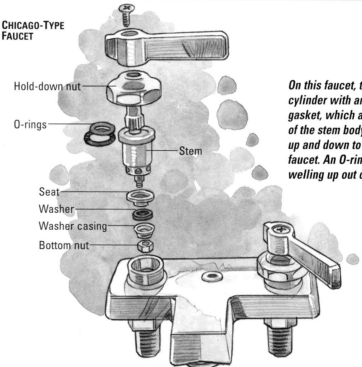

CHICAGO-TYPE FAUCET

Hold-down nut

O-rings

Stem

Seat

Washer

Washer casing

Bottom nut

On this faucet, the seat is a thin brass cylinder with an integrated rubber gasket, which attaches to the bottom of the stem body. The washer moves up and down to close and open the faucet. An O-ring keeps water from welling up out of the handle.

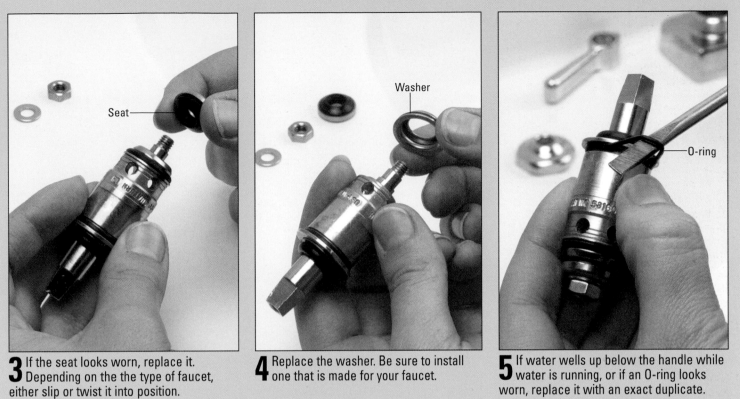

3 If the seat looks worn, replace it. Depending on the the type of faucet, either slip or twist it into position.

4 Replace the washer. Be sure to install one that is made for your faucet.

5 If water wells up below the handle while water is running, or if an O-ring looks worn, replace it with an exact duplicate.

WHAT IF...
You have a Crane reverse-compression faucet?

1 The other prominent maker of reverse-compression faucets is Crane. Remove a Crane stem as you would a Chicago model. Twist the top portion to unscrew it from the bottom portion.

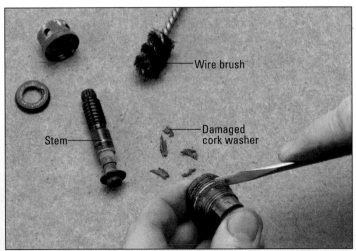

2 Clean away debris with a toothbrush or soft wire brush. Remove rubber and cork parts. Install exact replacements (the replacement for a cork ring may be made of rubber). Rub silicone grease on the large threads before reassembling.

TWO-HANDLE CARTRIDGE (DISK) AND DIAPHRAGM FAUCETS

Many newer two-handle faucets, including models made by Price-Pfister, Sterling, Kohler, and Moen, use either individual cartridges or diaphragm stems. Both types are long-lived and easy to repair.

An individual cartridge is similar to a single-handle cartridge *(page 68)*. It contains a plastic or rubber valve that opens and closes to permit or stop the flow of water.

Fixing a leaky faucet may require replacing the cartridge or replacing O-rings and seals, depending on the manufacturer and model.

PRESTART CHECKLIST

☐ **TIME**
Less than an hour for most repairs

☐ **TOOLS**
Screwdrivers, adjustable wrench, groove-joint pliers, possibly a socket wrench, and a handle puller

☐ **SKILLS**
Shutting off water, dismantling a faucet, installing small parts

☐ **PREP**
Shut off the water, close the sink stopper, place a rag in the sink to catch any parts

☐ **MATERIALS**
Repair kit for your faucet model, silicone grease

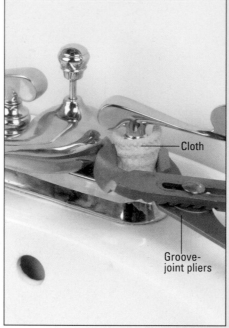

Cloth

Groove-joint pliers

1 **Shut off the water.** Turn the handles on to drain out any water. The handle may be held with a top screw *(page 58)*, or it may twist off. Wrap the handle with a cloth before twisting it with groove-joint pliers.

Socket wrench

2 Pull the cartridge up and out. With some types, it is important to note which direction the cartridge is facing so you can reinstall it facing the same direction. You may need to use a socket wrench, pliers, or even a special pulling tool made for certain brands of stems *(page 69)*.

PRICE-PFISTER, STERLING/ROCKWELL TYPES

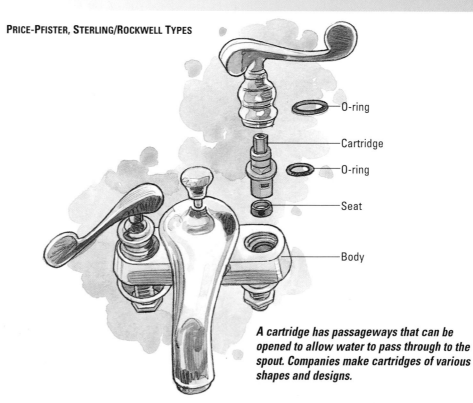

O-ring

Cartridge

O-ring

Seat

Body

A cartridge has passageways that can be opened to allow water to pass through to the spout. Companies make cartridges of various shapes and designs.

Seat

3 If the cartridge is metal, replacing the rubber parts usually fixes the problem. Pry off the rubber seat at the bottom.

Valve open

O-ring

4 Twist the cartridge spindle so the valve opens. Wash out any debris. If the internal parts are worn, replace the cartridge. Replace the rubber seat and any O-rings. Rub the parts with silicone grease.

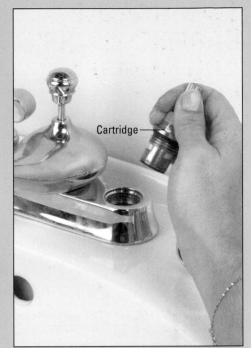

Cartridge

5 Install the cartridge and the handle and test. If you cannot turn the water on or off, remove and reorient the cartridge.

Diaphragm faucet

A diaphragm faucet has two stems similar to those in a standard stem faucet *(pages 58–59)*. However, the stem has a neoprene cap, called a diaphragm, at the bottom instead of a washer. Usually you can simply pry off the diaphragm and slip on a new one. If that does not fix a leak, replace the stem or the faucet.

Stem

Diaphragm

Seat

Two-Handle Disk Faucet

A two-handle disk faucet uses disk assemblies similar to one in a single-handle disk faucet and also has springs similar to those in a ball faucet.

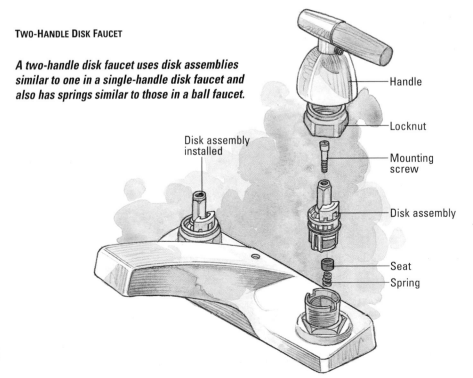

Disk assembly installed

Handle

Locknut

Mounting screw

Disk assembly

Seat

Spring

SINGLE-HANDLE DISK (CERAMIC DISK) FAUCETS

A single-handle disk faucet made by American Standard, Peerless, and Reliant, among others, is made with a pair of ceramic or plastic disks encased in a cylinder. The upper disk rotates when you turn the handle. Water flows when the inlets of the upper and lower disks line up.

Getting the parts

If water wells up around the handle or drips out of the spout, replace the seals with exact duplicates. If that does not solve the problem, replace the entire cylinder—you cannot open it up to replace disks. If water flow is slow or erratic, particles of rust and minerals may be clogging the inlets. Cleaning them solves the problem.

PRESTART CHECKLIST

☐ **TIME**
Less than an hour for most repairs

☐ **TOOLS**
Screwdriver, adjustable wrench, groove-joint pliers, hex wrench, cleaning brush

☐ **SKILLS**
Shutting off water, dismantling a faucet, installing small parts

☐ **PREP**
Shut off the water, close the sink stopper, place a rag in the sink to catch any parts

☐ **MATERIALS**
Repair kit with seals and O-rings, silicone grease

1 **Shut off the water.** Turn the faucet on until the water stops running. To remove the handle, you'll probably need to unscrew a setscrew using a hex wrench or small screwdriver. Lift off the handle and remove the dome housing.

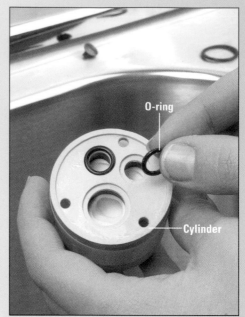

2 Pull out the cylinder that contains the disks and take it to a home center or hardware store to find replacement parts. The O-rings can be pried out of the cylinder using your fingers.

AMERICAN-STANDARD TYPE

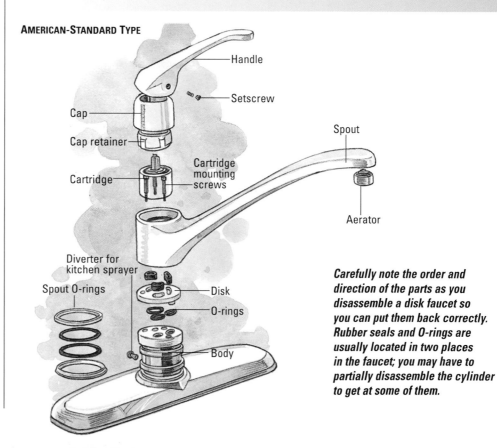

Carefully note the order and direction of the parts as you disassemble a disk faucet so you can put them back correctly. Rubber seals and O-rings are usually located in two places in the faucet; you may have to partially disassemble the cylinder to get at some of them.

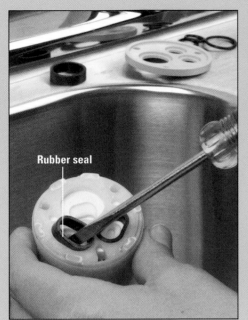

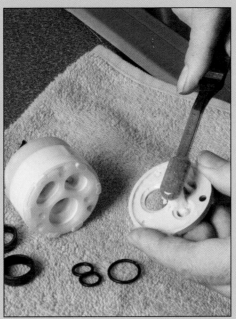

3 On some models, removing the bottom plate reveals the rubber seals. Remove them with a small screwdriver, taking care not to nick the plastic housing. If the cylinder is cracked or scored, replace it. Otherwise buy a kit with the rubber seals and O-rings.

4 Before replacing the rubber parts, gently clean away scum and debris from the seats, using a toothbrush or a nonmetallic abrasive pad. Rub a little silicone grease on the rubber parts.

5 Reassemble the cylinder. Install the cylinder so it faces the same direction as it did before.

Disk faucet with gaskets

Instead of individual O-rings or rubber seals, some disk faucets use a rubber or nylon gasket. This way only one part is needed rather than two or three separate parts. To repair, simply replace the worn gasket.

WHAT IF...
The faucet leaks at the base?

Some single-handle disk faucets have large rubber rings at the base of the spout. These may wear out. Remove the worn rings with a standard screwdriver or knife. Take the old ring with you to find an exact replacement.

Clean away any debris, coat the replacement parts with silicone grease, and reinstall.

To repair the diverter and the kitchen sprayer, see *page 79*.

If water drips below the faucet and you find wet spots in the cabinet floor, feel with your hand and check with a flashlight to find the highest wet spot. You may need to tighten a supply tube where it hooks to the faucet.

BALL FAUCETS

On the outside, this single-handle faucet (made by Delta and others) looks a lot like a disk faucet, but it has a narrower cylinder under the handle. Inside is a metal or plastic ball with grooves and holes. When the handle turns, the grooves or holes line up with rubber-sealed inlets in the faucet body to allow water to flow.

This type of faucet can become clogged by small particles. If water flow is slow or erratic, disassemble and clean the inlets.

Getting the parts

If water seeps out below the handle or drips out the spout, tighten the cap or the cap-adjusting ring. If that does not solve the problem, buy a rebuild kit for your model.

If water seeps out the base of the faucet, replace the O-rings. If water drips from the spout, replace the seats and springs. Less commonly, a ball is damaged and needs to be replaced.

PRESTART CHECKLIST

☐ **TIME**
Less than an hour for most repairs

☐ **TOOLS**
Screwdriver, adjustable wrench, groove-joint pliers, hex wrench

☐ **SKILLS**
Shutting off water, dismantling a faucet, installing small parts

☐ **PREP**
Shut off the water, close the sink stopper, place a rag in the sink to catch any parts

☐ **MATERIALS**
Repair kit (including O-rings, seats, springs, and other plastic parts), perhaps a new ball

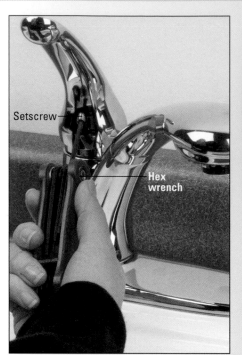

Setscrew

Hex wrench

1 **Shut off the water** and turn the faucet on until water stops running. Loosen the handle setscrew with a hex wrench, sometimes included in a repair kit. Lift off the handle and unscrew the cap.

Ball

Plastic cam

2 Remove the plastic cam and lift out the ball. If the ball is worn, replace it along with the seats and springs.

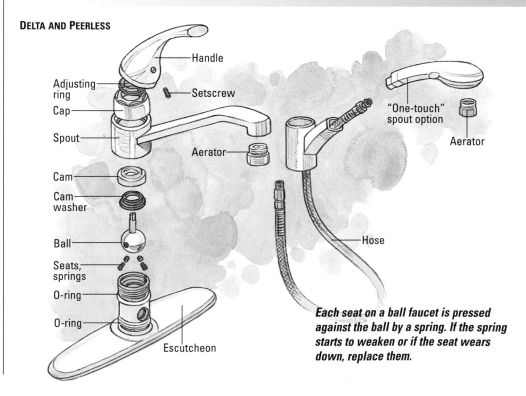

DELTA AND PEERLESS

Handle

Adjusting ring

Setscrew

Cap

Spout

Aerator

Cam

Cam washer

Ball

Seats, springs

O-ring

O-ring

Escutcheon

"One-touch" spout option

Aerator

Hose

Each seat on a ball faucet is pressed against the ball by a spring. If the spring starts to weaken or if the seat wears down, replace them.

Seat

3 Carefully insert the tip of a screwdriver into a seat and pull it out. This may take a couple of tries for each seat.

Spring

4 Use the same technique to remove the springs. Clean or flush out debris in the faucet body. Purchase springs and seats for your faucet model.

5 Replace the springs and seats, and press them into place with your finger. Insert the ball so it sits snugly. Add the washer and screw on the adjusting ring. You may need a special wrench to tighten the ring. If the faucet still leaks, tighten the ring further.

WHAT IF...
You find debris?

If small particles partially clog the inlets, first wipe away as much as you can. Slowly turn the water back on to flush out more particles. If you have old galvanized pipes, you may need to do this regularly.

O-rings at the base

To cure a leak at the base of the faucet below the handle, pull or twist off the spout. Pry or cut off the old O-rings, coat the faucet body lightly with silicone grease, and slip on the new O-rings. When you reattach the spout, make sure it slides all the way down.

STANLEY PRO TIP

Metal or plastic ball?

An inexpensive plastic ball is easily scratched, so it may wear out in less than a year, especially if your water contains debris. A metal ball is worth the extra cost because it lasts longer.

CARTRIDGE FAUCETS

Several manufacturers, including Moen, Price-Pfister, Delta, Peerless, and Kohler, make single-handle cartridge faucets. Each model has a cartridge of a slightly different design. A cartridge may have a cylinder with grooves, or it may be tapered so water can pass through when it is turned.

Getting the parts

If water leaks out the spout, you'll have to replace or repair the cartridge. If a leaky faucet's cartridge is plastic, replace it; if it is metal, you may need to replace only the O-rings. If water wells up below the handle, replace the O-rings around the faucet body. Many repair kits contain both the cartridge and the O-rings.

PRESTART CHECKLIST

☐ **TIME**
Less than an hour for most repairs

☐ **TOOLS**
Screwdrivers, adjustable wrench, groove-joint pliers, hex wrench

☐ **SKILLS**
Shutting off water, dismantling a faucet, installing small parts

☐ **PREP**
Shut off the water, close the sink stopper, place a rag in the sink to catch any parts

☐ **MATERIALS**
Replacement cartridge or repair kit for your model, silicone grease

Hex wrench

1 Shut off the water. Turn on the faucet until the water stops running. To remove the handle, pry off the decorative cap and remove the screw, using a hex wrench or screwdriver as needed. Lift off the handle.

Handle attachment mechanism

2 Unscrew the cap or retaining ring. If you find a handle-attachment mechanism like the one shown, note how it is attached so you can replace it correctly.

DELTA AND PEERLESS TYPES

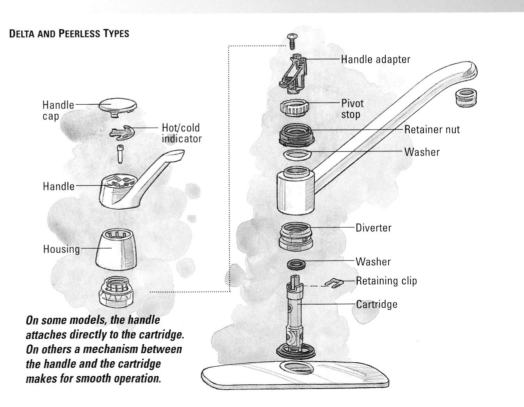

Handle cap
Hot/cold indicator
Handle
Housing

Handle adapter
Pivot stop
Retainer nut
Washer
Diverter
Washer
Retaining clip
Cartridge

On some models, the handle attaches directly to the cartridge. On others a mechanism between the handle and the cartridge makes for smooth operation.

3 Many cartridges can be removed simply by pulling up with pliers. If it is stuck, you may need to buy a stem puller designed for your faucet.

4 Remove the spout. Pry off any damaged O-rings and replace them with duplicates. Apply a thin coat of silicone grease and replace the spout.

5 Replace either the O-rings on the cartridge or the entire cartridge. If the cartridge is not already greasy, apply a thin coat of grease and push it into position.

STANLEY PRO TIP

Special pullers

Some faucets have cartridges that can be removed only with a manufacturer-specific pulling tool. Trying to remove the cartridge without the proper tool can damage the cartridge and faucet.

Other cartridges

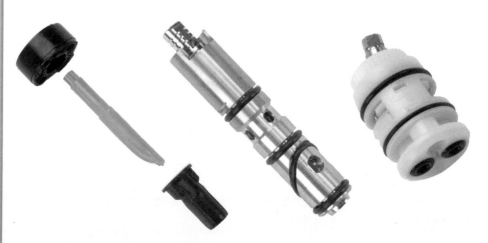

A plastic cartridge made by Kohler (left) slips into a cartridge casing; make sure it is well greased. If hot and cold are reversed after installing it, remove the cartridge and turn it 180 degrees. A brass cartridge (center) requires several O-rings of two different sizes. Another type (right) uses O-rings as well as rubber seats.

TUB AND SHOWER STEM COMPRESSION FAUCETS

Tub and shower faucets work much like sink faucets, but they are oriented horizontally rather than vertically. In addition, their parts are usually larger. A two-handle stem shower faucet has a stem with a washer that presses against a seat to seal off water, just like the faucet shown on *pages 58–59*. A three-handle unit adds a stemlike diverter to direct water up to the shower or down to the tub spout.

Getting the parts

Often leaks can be fixed simply by replacing the washers. Even if you need to replace the seats or stems, it usually makes sense to repair rather than replace an old shower faucet, because replacement requires opening up the wall. If parts are hard to find, special order them at a plumbing supply store.

PRESTART CHECKLIST

☐ **TIME**
An hour or two for most repairs

☐ **TOOLS**
Screwdrivers, adjustable wrench, groove-joint pliers, perhaps a stem socket wrench, seat wrench

☐ **SKILLS**
Shutting off water, dismantling a faucet, installing small parts

☐ **PREP**
Shut off the water, close the tub stopper, place a rag in the tub to catch any loose parts

☐ **MATERIALS**
Washers, O-rings, perhaps new stems

1 **Shut off the water**. Turn both handles on until water stops flowing. Pry off the handle cap, remove the screw, and pry off the handle. You may need to use a handle puller *(page 59)*. Unscrew the stem sleeve and pull off the escutcheon.

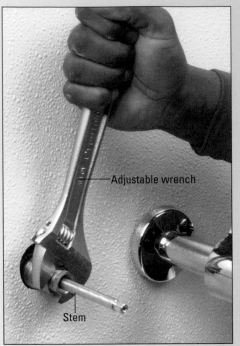

2 If the stem protrudes far enough past the wall surface, loosen it with an adjustable wrench or groove-joint pliers. If the stem is recessed, use a stem wrench.

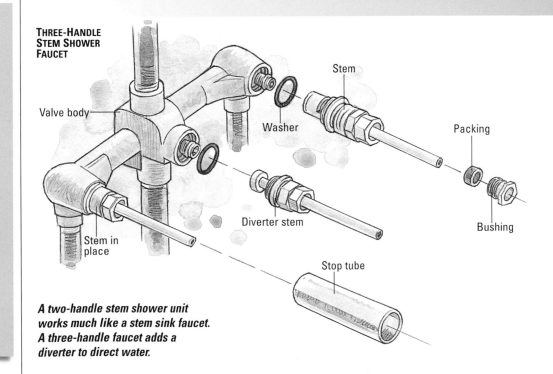

THREE-HANDLE STEM SHOWER FAUCET

A two-handle stem shower unit works much like a stem sink faucet. A three-handle faucet adds a diverter to direct water.

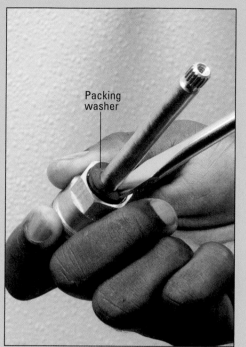

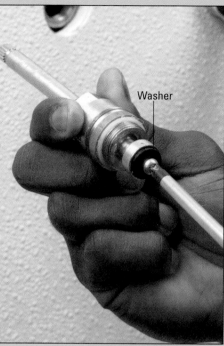

3 If water seeps out around the handle, replace a worn packing washer or stuff thread packing around the stem and into the cavity behind the packing nut *(page 59)*.

4 If water drips out the spout or the showerhead, replace a worn washer with an exact duplicate.

5 If replacing the washer does not stop the leak or if washers wear out quickly, remove the seat with a seat wrench and replace it. Or grind the seat smooth with a seat grinder *(page 59)*.

RECESSED
Using a stem wrench

If the stem nut is behind the wall, you won't be able to unscrew the stem with an adjustable wrench or pliers. Use a stem wrench, a deep socket wrench made to fit a bathtub stem.

Repairing a diverter

The diverter on a three-handle tub faucet is essentially a stem. When its washer presses against the seat, water cannot rise up to the showerhead and is diverted to the tub spout.

You repair a diverter in much the same way as you do a hot or cold stem. Replace the washer at the bottom and replace any O-rings and other removable parts.

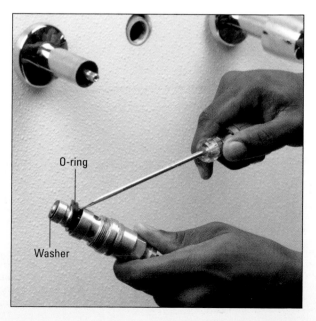

TUB AND SHOWER CARTRIDGE FAUCETS

O nce you shut off the water and remove the handle and escutcheon, you can quickly determine whether your single-handle tub and shower faucet is a cartridge, ball, or disk type *(pages 72–75)*.

Getting the parts

Tub cartridge faucets work just like sink cartridge faucets *(pages 68–69)*. Usually the faucet only turns water on and off; a diverter valve on the spout directs water to the showerhead or the spout. A number of manufacturers make cartridges of varying designs, so take the cartridge with you when you shop for parts. You may need to replace the entire cartridge. Follow the steps as shown to remove it.

PRESTART CHECKLIST

☐ **TIME**
An hour or two for most repairs

☐ **TOOLS**
Screwdriver, adjustable wrench, groove-joint pliers, hex wrench, cartridge puller

☐ **SKILLS**
Shutting off water, dismantling a faucet, installing small parts

☐ **PREP**
Shut off the water, close the tub stopper, place a rag in the tub to catch any parts

☐ **MATERIALS**
Cartridge or repair kit for your faucet model, silicone grease

1 **Shut off the water** and turn the faucet on until water stops running. To remove the handle, you may need a hex wrench, which is sometimes included in a repair kit. Remove the screws holding the escutcheon and slide out the escutcheon.

2 If there is a chrome sleeve, unscrew it or pull it out. Use a small screwdriver to pry out the retaining clip that holds the cartridge in place.

MOEN, KOHLER/BRADLEY TYPE

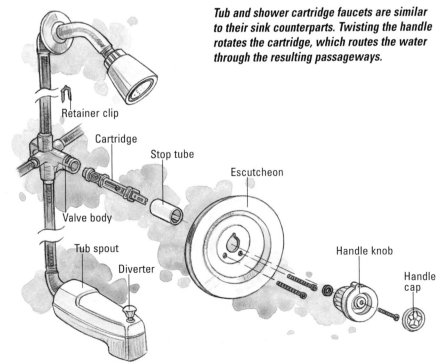

Tub and shower cartridge faucets are similar to their sink counterparts. Twisting the handle rotates the cartridge, which routes the water through the resulting passageways.

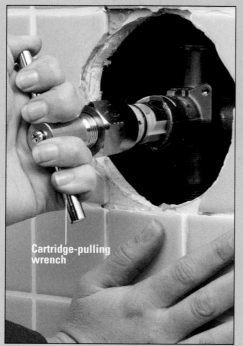

3 Some cartridges can be removed easily with pliers; others require a special cartridge-pulling wrench (usually available at hardware stores or home centers) made for a specific brand of faucet.

O-ring

4 If the cartridge is in good shape, replace the O-rings and any other replaceable parts. (Often, however, it doesn't cost much more to replace the cartridge.) Rub the O-rings with a thin coat of silicone grease.

Retaining clip

5 Insert the new or repaired cartridge into the faucet body, oriented as it was originally. Slide in the retaining clip and replace the handle and escutcheon.

WHAT IF...
You find this cartridge?

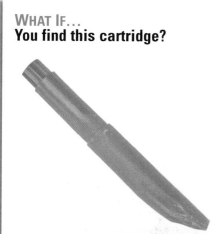

This cartridge works by virtue of its tapered shape, rather than a series of grooves. Take careful note of the cartridge's orientation when you remove it so you can put it back the same way. If hot and cold water are reversed after you reinstall the cartridge, twist it 180 degrees.

Antiscald faucets

A short burst of scalding water can be painful and even dangerous, especially for young children. That's why plumbing codes may require new tub and shower faucets to have a mechanism that prevents the passage of very hot water. Some temperature-balancing or antiscald faucets may prevent cold water from being turned off; others may have a thermostatic device that closes the hot-water valve when it senses the water is too hot.

It's hard to tell from just looking at a faucet whether it is an antiscald model. Sometimes by rocking the faucet you'll hear a click that indicates the unit has an antiscald valve. In some cases, you can replace an older standard cartridge with an antiscald cartridge.

TUB AND SHOWER BALL FAUCETS

A ball faucet has a metal or plastic ball with grooves that allow the passage of water *(page 66)*. Small springs press rubber seats against the ball to control the flow of water. Replacing the seats and springs usually will stop a leak. The ball itself may also need to be replaced.

Sometimes a leak can be fixed simply by tightening the adjusting ring with a pair of pliers or with a special tool designed for that particular model of faucet. If water flow is slow or erratic, remove the seats and springs and run water to flush out any debris.

PRESTART CHECKLIST

☐ **TIME**
An hour or two for most repairs

☐ **TOOLS**
Screwdrivers, adjustable wrench, groove-joint pliers

☐ **SKILLS**
Shutting off water, dismantling a faucet, installing small parts

☐ **PREP**
Shut off the water, close the tub stopper, place a rag in the tub to catch any parts

☐ **MATERIALS**
O-rings, seats, and other rubber parts, silicone grease, perhaps a new cylinder

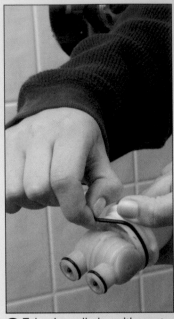

1 **Shut off the water.** Turn the faucet on until it drains. Remove the handle and escutcheon. Pry off any retaining clips, unscrew the retaining ring, and pull out the cylinder.

2 Take the cylinder with you to buy replacement parts. Most O-rings can be removed easily with your fingers. Replace all rubber parts. With a rag under the faucet body, slowly turn on the shutoff to flush out debris.

Adjusting ring

3 Rub silicone grease over the rubber parts. Reinsert the cylinder, reattach the retaining clip (if there is one), and screw on the adjusting ring. If the faucet leaks, tighten the ring.

DELTA/PEERLESS TYPE

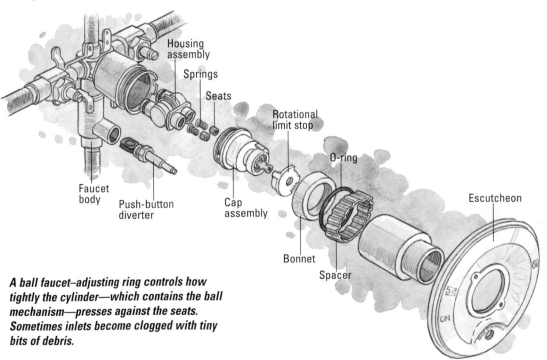

Housing assembly · Springs · Seats · Rotational limit stop · O-ring · Faucet body · Push-button diverter · Cap assembly · Bonnet · Spacer · Escutcheon

A ball faucet–adjusting ring controls how tightly the cylinder—which contains the ball mechanism—presses against the seats. Sometimes inlets become clogged with tiny bits of debris.

TUB AND SHOWER DISK FAUCET

This faucet works exactly like a sink cartridge faucet (*pages 68–69*). Repairs are done much the same.

If water drips out the spout or seeps out around the handle, buy a kit and replace all the rubber parts. Inspect the cylinder that contains the disks and replace it if you see signs of wear. If your model has plastic rather than ceramic disks, replace the entire unit.

Depending on the model, you may need to partially disassemble the cylinder to access all the rubber parts.

PRESTART CHECKLIST

☐ **TIME**
An hour or two for most repairs

☐ **TOOLS**
Screwdrivers, adjustable wrench, groove-joint pliers, cleaning brush

☐ **SKILLS**
Shutting off water, dismantling a faucet, installing small parts

☐ **PREP**
Shut off the water, close the tub stopper, place a rag in the tub to catch any parts

☐ **MATERIALS**
Repair kit for your model of faucet, silicone grease

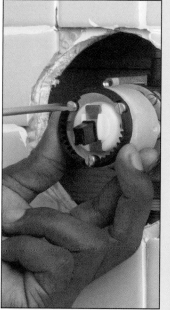

1 **Shut off the water** and turn the faucet on until water stops running. Remove the handle and the escutcheon. Unscrew three screws to remove the cylinder.

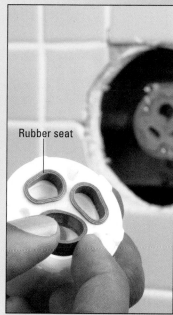

Rubber seat

2 Remove rubber seats with your fingers. Clean the openings with a toothbrush or an abrasive pad. Replace the rubber seats with duplicates. Rub a bit of silicone grease over the seats.

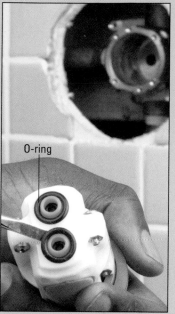

O-ring

3 Do the same for all other rubber parts. If you need to pry out an O-ring, you may need to use a small screwdriver. Work carefully to prevent nicking the plastic housing.

AMERICAN STANDARD, RELIANT TYPE

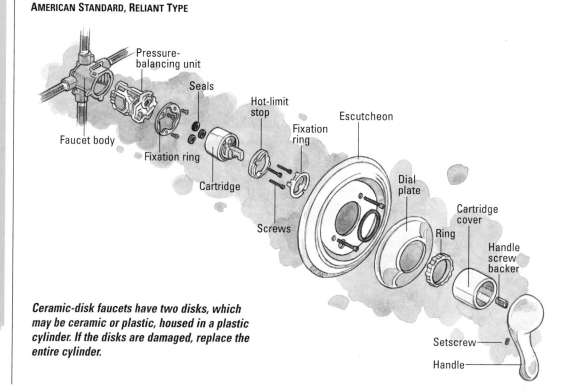

Pressure-balancing unit
Seals
Hot-limit stop
Escutcheon
Fixation ring
Faucet body
Fixation ring
Cartridge
Dial plate
Cartridge cover
Ring
Screws
Handle screw backer
Setscrew
Handle

Ceramic-disk faucets have two disks, which may be ceramic or plastic, housed in a plastic cylinder. If the disks are damaged, replace the entire cylinder.

DIVERTERS

Most single-handle shower faucets simply turn water on and off; a pull-up diverter valve on the spout determines whether water goes up or down. Some models, however, have a diverter built into the handle.

Getting the parts

You may be able to find repair parts in a kit made for a specific faucet. If not, O-rings and washers made for stem faucets may fit. In some cases, the seal is made with brass parts and no washers, in which case simple cleaning and light sanding may solve the problem.

An old diverter stem may be corroded, or its spring may weaken to the point that the stem needs to be replaced. If you cannot find an old diverter stem, the home center or plumbing supply house should be able to order it. While you are waiting for the part to arrive, wrap duct tape around the handle of the diverter to keep it from going in. This will allow you to use the shower while waiting for the replacement part.

PRESTART CHECKLIST

☐ **TIME**
Less than an hour for most repairs

☐ **TOOLS**
Screwdrivers, adjustable wrench, groove-joint pliers, toothbrush

☐ **SKILLS**
Shutting off water, dismantling a faucet, installing small parts

☐ **PREP**
Shut off the water, close the tub stopper, place a rag in the tub to catch any loose parts

☐ **MATERIALS**
Repair kit for your faucet model, or O-rings and washers to match

Push/pull type

1 **Shut off the water** and drain the system by turning on the faucet. Remove the handle and the escutcheon. Use groove-joint pliers or an adjustable wrench to remove the diverter unit.

2 Remove and replace any worn rubber parts. If the diverter itself is worn, you may be able to buy a replacement.

BUILT-IN DIVERTER

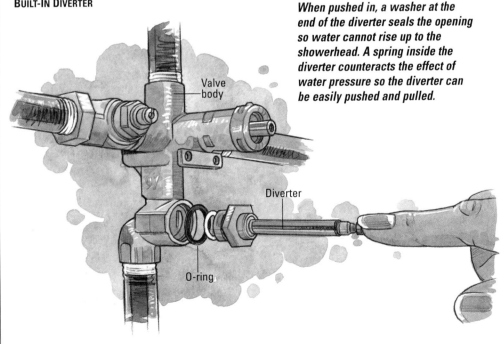

When pushed in, a washer at the end of the diverter seals the opening so water cannot rise up to the showerhead. A spring inside the diverter counteracts the effect of water pressure so the diverter can be easily pushed and pulled.

TUB SPOUTS

A tub spout may be screwed onto a threaded pipe, or it may be anchored to a nonthreaded pipe with a setscrew. Before you start to unscrew a spout, check underneath to see if there is a setscrew.

If water seeps from behind the spout, it may be attached to a threaded pipe that is not tight. Remove the pipe, wrap its threads with pipe-thread tape, and use a pipe wrench to tighten it.

If given a choice, spend a little more for a brass spout. It will last longer than a bargain-bin spout, which may be made of thin metal or even plastic that wears and stains quickly.

PRESTART CHECKLIST

☐ **TIME**
Less than an hour for most repairs

☐ **TOOLS**
Screwdrivers, hex wrench, groove-joint pliers, pipe wrench, caulk gun

☐ **SKILLS**
Unscrewing and reinstalling a spout

☐ **PREP**
There is no need to shut off the water. Place a towel in the bottom of the tub to catch any debris or caulk.

☐ **MATERIALS**
New spout, pipe-thread tape, tub-and-tile caulk

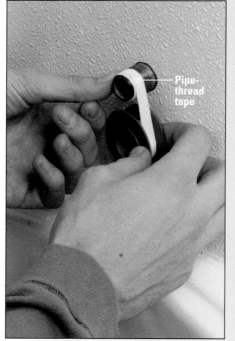

1 Use groove-joint pliers or a pipe wrench to remove an old spout that is threaded on. Clean the end of the pipe and scrape away any caulk on the wall. Wrap the pipe threads clockwise with two or three turns of pipe-thread tape.

2 Screw on the new spout by hand. Wrap masking tape or a cloth around the spout, or wrap electrician's tape around the jaws of groove-joint pliers, and tighten the spout firmly. If the pipe is copper, avoid overtightening, which can strip the threads.

SETSCREW
Removing a spout held with a hex-head screw

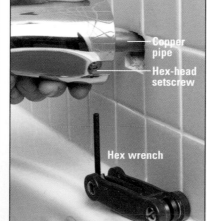

Some spouts attach with a setscrew. Loosen the screw with a hex wrench and slide off the old spout.

Spout retrofit kit

Not all spouts are created equal. Some are threaded where they meet the wall; others have threads deep in the body of the spout. You may be able to replace the pipe coming out of the wall, or purchase a retrofit kit (shown) that helps make the transition.

INSTALLING A FLEX-LINE SHOWER UNIT

If your bathtub has a spout but no showerhead, installing one would be a big job. The demolition, wall repair, and tiling would take much more time than the plumbing. One solution is a flex-line shower unit. It installs quickly, and its removable showerhead is a handy feature.

If you want to install a flex-line shower, the surrounding walls should be covered with tile or another water-resistant material. If you have an old claw-foot tub that does not abut the walls, purchase a circular shower curtain.

PRESTART CHECKLIST

☐ **TIME**
About an hour for most units

☐ **TOOLS**
Drill with masonry bit, screwdriver, hammer, groove-joint pliers

☐ **SKILLS**
Drilling holes in tile, assembling parts

☐ **PREP**
No need to shut off the water. Place a towel in the bottom of the tub to catch any parts.

☐ **MATERIALS**
Flex-line shower unit, pipe tape, plastic anchors

1 Remove the old spout and screw on the one that comes with the shower unit. See *page 77* for steps.

2 Hold the showerhead bracket or template in place, and mark for mounting holes. Press the tip of a nail on a mark, and tap with a hammer to make a small chip as a starter hole. Drill holes with a masonry bit.

3 Tap plastic anchors into the holes and attach the showerhead bracket with the screws provided. Snap on its decorative body. Screw the flex line to the tub spout and slip the showerhead into the bracket.

FLEX-LINE SHOWER UNIT

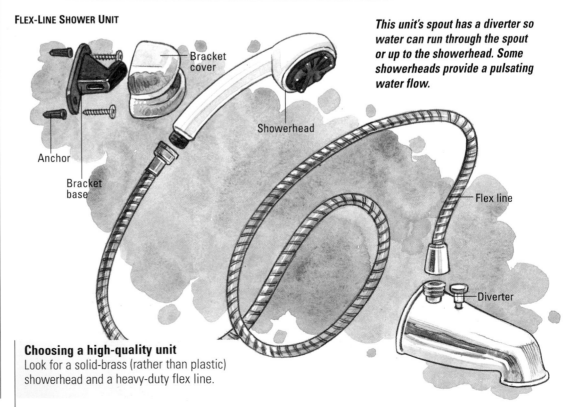

This unit's spout has a diverter so water can run through the spout or up to the showerhead. Some showerheads provide a pulsating water flow.

Choosing a high-quality unit
Look for a solid-brass (rather than plastic) showerhead and a heavy-duty flex line.

KITCHEN SPRAYERS

Kitchen sink sprayers are easy to repair. If you find that you spend a lot of time repairing the sprayer, you may want to consider purchasing a one-touch faucet *(page 83)*.

If pressure is low, check under the sink to make sure the hose is not kinked. If that's not the problem, disassemble and clean the sprayer. If that fails, turn off the water and check the diverter.

If water comes out of the sprayer even when its valve is not depressed, replace the sprayer body and valve.

PRESTART CHECKLIST

☐ **TIME**
An hour or two for most repairs

☐ **TOOLS**
Screwdriver, groove-joint pliers, long-nose pliers, knife, toothbrush

☐ **SKILLS**
Dismantling and reassembling a unit with small parts

☐ **PREP**
Shut the water off only to work on the diverter valve. Lay down a small towel for organizing small parts.

☐ **MATERIALS**
Replacement parts for the sprayer and diverter, perhaps a new sprayer, silicone grease

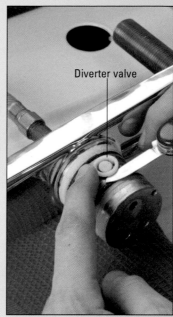
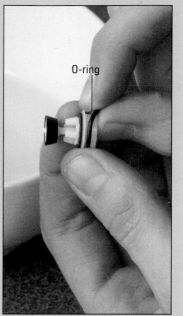

Diverter valve

O-ring

1 Pull the sprayer out and use pliers to dismantle the spout, keeping track of all its parts. Clean them with a toothbrush. If parts are caked with minerals, soak them overnight in vinegar.

2 If cleaning or replacing the sprayer does not solve the problem, **shut off the water.** Remove the spout and find the diverter valve. On this model, it is in the faucet body. Pry out the valve with a knife.

3 Replace worn parts or the entire diverter valve. Clean away any debris, and coat the rubber parts with silicone grease. Reinstall and test. If you still have problems, consider buying a new faucet.

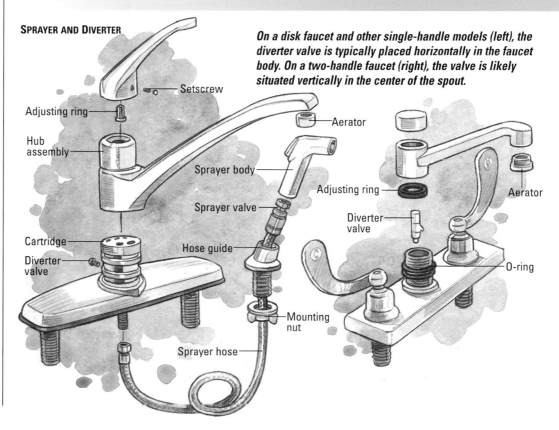

SPRAYER AND DIVERTER

On a disk faucet and other single-handle models (left), the diverter valve is typically placed horizontally in the faucet body. On a two-handle faucet (right), the valve is likely situated vertically in the center of the spout.

Setscrew
Adjusting ring
Hub assembly
Cartridge
Diverter valve
Aerator
Sprayer body
Adjusting ring
Sprayer valve
Hose guide
Diverter valve
Aerator
O-ring
Mounting nut
Sprayer hose

INSTALLING A KITCHEN FAUCET

The three holes in a kitchen sink accommodate most new kitchen faucets. There may be a fourth hole for a sprayer. If your faucet does not have a sprayer, consider installing a hot-water dispenser or a drinking-water faucet hooked up to a filter *(pages 206–208)*.

Installing a faucet would be easy if you didn't have to work in cramped conditions. If you are also replacing the sink, install the faucet before installing the sink *(pages 200–203)*. Otherwise do what you can to make the work site comfortable *(page 41)*.

Whether you reuse the old supply tubes or buy new ones, make sure they are long enough to reach the stop valves and that they have fittings of the correct size (⅜ inch or ½ inch) for the stop valves. If there are no stop valves under the sink, now is a good time to install them *(pages 124–125)*.

Choosing a faucet

Most people find single-handle faucets easier to use. Make sure the spout is the right length for your sink. A heavy, solid-brass unit will outlast a less expensive unit. The faucet should come with a warranty that includes the sprayer.

PRESTART CHECKLIST

☐ **TIME**
About 2 hours to install most faucets

☐ **TOOLS**
Screwdriver, adjustable wrench, putty knife, groove-joint pliers, basin wrench

☐ **SKILLS**
Shutting off water, working under a sink, attaching plumbing parts

☐ **PREP**
Shut off the water to the old faucet. If the drain trap is in the way, you may have to remove it.

☐ **MATERIALS**
New faucet, plumber's putty, pipe-thread tape, masking tape

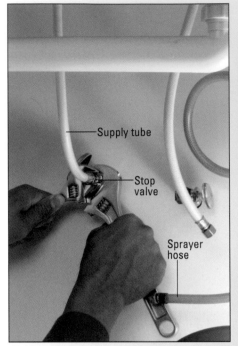

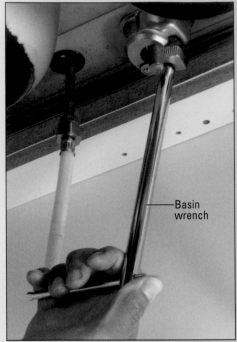

1 **Shut off the water** and open the faucet until the water stops running. From underneath, use a wrench or pliers to hold the stop valve still while you loosen the supply tube nut with another wrench or pliers. Disconnect the sprayer hose from the faucet, or simply cut the hose.

2 With a basin wrench, loosen the nut on the one or two mounting shanks. If there is a sprayer hose guide, loosen it from underneath with a basin wrench as well. On other types of faucets, you may need to loosen a center mounting nut.

ONE-HANDLE INSTALLATION

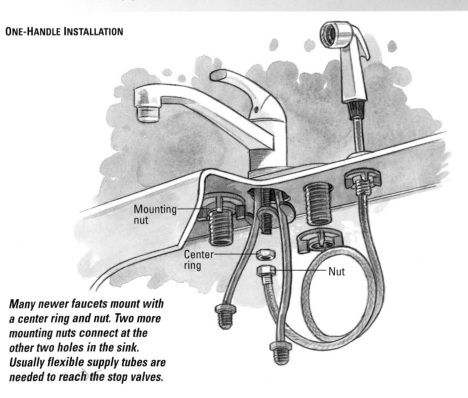

Many newer faucets mount with a center ring and nut. Two more mounting nuts connect at the other two holes in the sink. Usually flexible supply tubes are needed to reach the stop valves.

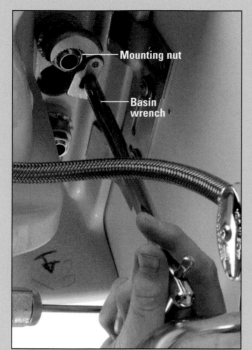

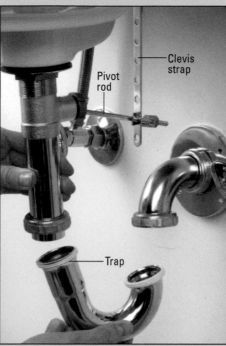

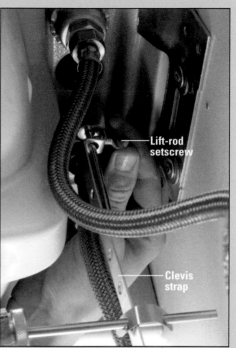

3 Have a helper hold the faucet straight while you tighten mounting nuts from below. If the faucet is not solidly attached after hand-tightening, use a basin wrench to tighten the nuts further.

4 You can use the existing drain body, or install a new one. With the stopper closed all the way, slide the clevis strap onto the lift rod and the pivot rod, using the spring clip to hold it in place. Tighten the setscrew that holds the strap to the lift rod. Install the trap *(pages 46–47)*.

5 Make sure the stopper seals water when the lift rod is pulled up and that it opens fully when the rod is pushed down. To adjust, loosen the setscrew and move the clevis strap up or down.

Installing a drain body

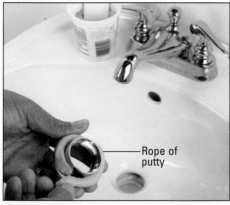

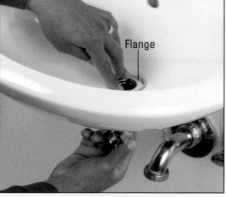

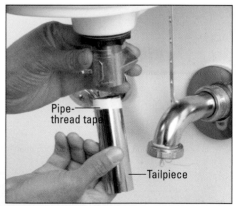

1 Loosen the slip nut to disconnect the drain body from the trap. Remove the locknut under the sink, and slide out the old drain body. Clean away caked-on putty. Place new rope of putty around the hole, slip the new drain flange through the hole, and press it into place.

2 Twist the locknut onto the drain body, and slip on the friction washer and the rubber gasket. Hold the flange with one hand while you hand screw the drain body into it. Tighten the locknut with groove-joint pliers, taking care that the drain body faces rear.

3 Install the pivot rod, and install the clevis strap (see Step 4 above). Apply pipe-thread tape to the threaded end of the tailpiece, and screw it onto the drain body. Install the trap *(pages 46–47)*.

TOILETS

Considering how often they are used—typically, thousands of times per year—most toilets are remarkably durable. The basic toilet is made of porcelain or vitreous china and lasts practically forever, as long as it doesn't get cracked. The mechanical inner workings, however, are somewhat complicated, so it is not surprising that they occasionally need repair. Fortunately no repair is too tough for a determined do-it-yourselfer.

Sanitary conditions

Many people are understandably reluctant to touch the water in a toilet. With a few precautions, however, contact with unsanitary water can be avoided.

Water from the toilet bowl cannot back up into the tank; water in the tank is just as clean as water from a faucet. If you clean the bowl and flush several times, even the water in the bowl will be clean.

When a toilet is clogged, sewage may back up and overflow onto the floor. Wear heavy-duty rubber gloves when cleaning.

You may need to insert a plunger into sewage to clear a clog. After doing so, clean the plunger thoroughly—inside and out—with hot water and detergent.

How it works

A toilet bowl has a built-in trap. When water rushes in from the tank through a series of openings under the bowl rim, the water in the bowl is pushed through the trap and into the sewer line. Some bowls have a jet opening located near the bottom for increased flushing power.

A wax ring seals the bowl to the toilet flange on the floor. Flushed water flows through a closet bend below the floor, and out to a large drain stack. This arrangement ensures that anything that makes it through the toilet will reach the stack and exit the house.

There are two mechanisms in the tank. The flush valve has a rubber flapper attached to a chain or, in older toilets, a rubber stopper attached to a lift rod. When the flapper or stopper rests on the flush valve seat, water is sealed inside the tank. When you push down on the flush handle, the flapper or stopper is raised, providing an opening for water to run out of the tank and into the bowl. When the tank is nearly empty, the flapper or stopper settles down onto the seat again, sealing the tank for filling.

The other tank mechanism is the fill valve assembly, which squirts water into the tank until the water reaches a certain level, then automatically shuts off. Most older toilets have a brass ballcock fill valve attached to a float ball; when the ball floats high enough, the water automatically shuts off. A diaphragm fill valve is also attached to a float ball. A float-cup fill valve replaces the float ball with a plastic cup that slides up and down its shaft as the water rises and falls.

If the fill valve fails to shut off, the excess water will flow down the overflow tube and into the bowl.

An emergency fix

If water starts welling up when you flush the toilet rather than swirling down into the bowl, you may be able to keep water from spilling onto the floor if you act quickly. Remove the tank lid, reach into the tank (remember, this water is clean), and push down on the flapper or stopper until it settles on the flush valve seat. Water will stop flowing. Take steps to clear the clog (page 89) before flushing the toilet again.

Nearly all toilet problems can be fixed quickly and inexpensively.

CHAPTER PREVIEW

Troubleshooting and repairs
page 88

Clearing a clog
page 89

Eliminating run-on
page 90

Installing a new float cup
page 91

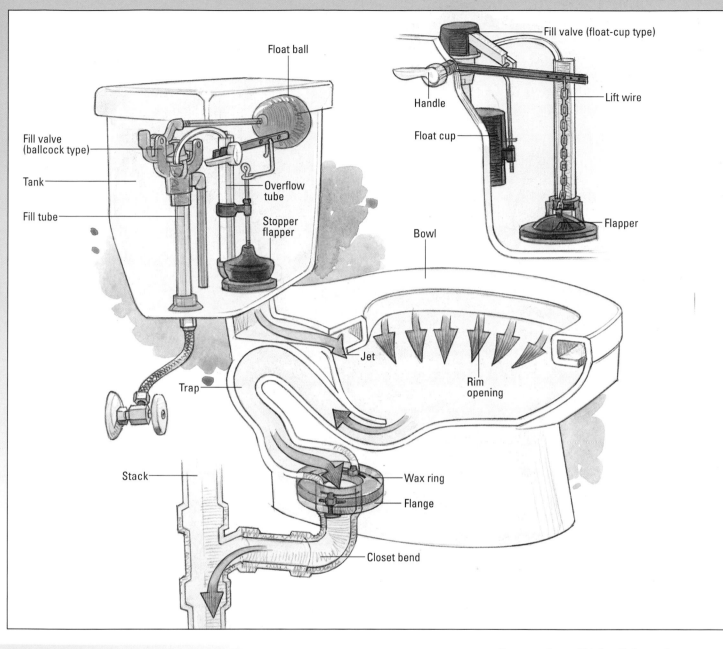

Float ball

Fill valve (float-cup type)

Handle

Lift wire

Fill valve (ballcock type)

Float cup

Tank

Flapper

Fill tube

Overflow tube

Stopper flapper

Bowl

Jet

Rim opening

Trap

Stack

Wax ring

Flange

Closet bend

Seeping and phantom flushes
page 92

Leaks from the tank
page 93

Replacing a toilet
page 94

No matter how old it is, all the moving parts in a toilet—the fill valve, the stopper, and the float—can be replaced, either with exact duplicate parts or with new mechanisms that perform the same duties reliably. If it's a leak, it can be fixed either by tightening a bolt or by replacing a gasket. In the most extreme instance, you will have to pull up the toilet and replace the wax ring. A clog can almost always be cleared with a plunger or auger. The only time you need to replace a toilet is if the tank or the bowl is cracked.

TROUBLESHOOTING AND REPAIRS

No matter how old or complicated a toilet may appear, replacement parts are readily available and usually are not difficult to install. In fact, the only reason to replace a toilet is if it is cracked—or simply out of style.

It's important to make the correct diagnosis before starting a repair. A look under the tank lid quickly reveals the cause of many problems. If flushes are incomplete, check that the water level reaches the proper height—an inch or less from the top of the overflow tube. If the toilet constantly hisses or if water seeps into the bowl, the tank water level may be too high. The excess water is slowly overflowing into the overflow tube and into the bowl. Adjusting the water level is usually a simple matter. In some cases, however, the fill valve may need to be repaired or replaced.

If the toilet is clogged, use a plunger or an auger to clear the problem.

If water seeps out the bottom of the bowl when the toilet is flushed, the wax ring needs to be replaced *(page 94–95)*.

Solutions to common toilet problems

Bowl overflows or will not flush freely: Clear a clog with a plunger, pressure plunger, or toilet auger *(page 89)*.

Toilet does not flush: Check that the handle is connected to the flapper via a chain or to the stopper via a lift rod *(page 92)*. Check that water is turned on and running into the tank.

Incomplete (short) flushes: Check the water level in tank and adjust the float ball, chain, or lift rod *(page 90)*. Flush the toilet and watch the flapper or the stopper; if it goes down too soon, replace it *(page 92)*.

Handle is loose or tight: Tighten the nut holding the handle to the tank. Check the handle's connection to the wire or the lift rod *(page 90)*.

Water sprays out of the tank: Reattach the refill tube to the overflow tube *(page 91)*.

Run-on: Adjust the float ball, stopper, or cup. Replace a leaky float ball or stopper *(page 90)*. If these measures do not bring the water level below the top of the overflow tube, repair or replace the fill valve *(page 91)*.

Water seeps continuously into the bowl, making it necessary to jiggle the handle; occasional "phantom flushes": Clean the flush valve seat and adjust the flapper or stopper. You may need to replace the flapper or stopper *(page 92)*.

Leak from the tank: Check and tighten water supply connection. Tighten tank bolts. If the tank is cracked, replace it *(pages 94–95)*.

Leak from the base of the bowl: Remove the toilet, replace the wax ring, and reinstall the toilet. If the bowl is cracked, replace it *(pages 94–95)*.

PRESTART CHECKLIST

☐ **TIME**
Less than an hour for most repairs

☐ **TOOLS**
Screwdriver, groove-joint pliers, adjustable wrench, toilet plunger, toilet auger, locking pliers, small mirror, bottle brush

☐ **SKILLS**
Making simple plumbing corrections

☐ **PREP**
Place a drop cloth on the floor; set the tank lid where it won't get damaged

☐ **MATERIALS**
Repair parts, perhaps a new float-cup assembly

THREE TYPES OF FILL VALVES

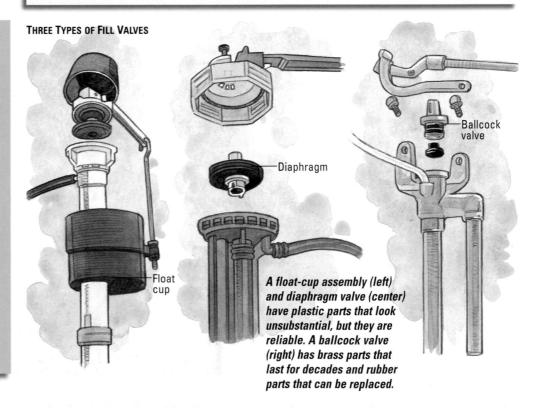

Float cup

Diaphragm

Ballcock valve

A float-cup assembly (left) and diaphragm valve (center) have plastic parts that look unsubstantial, but they are reliable. A ballcock valve (right) has brass parts that last for decades and rubber parts that can be replaced.

Clearing a clog

Plunger

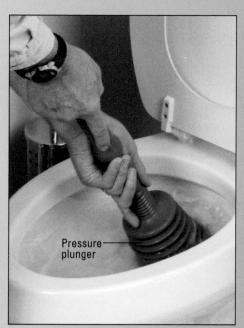

Pressure plunger

Toilet auger

1 You can usually clear a clog with a toilet plunger. Insert the plunger flange into the hole at the bottom of the bowl until it seals. Push and pull vigorously several times. Repeat the process as many as 10 times.

2 For tenacious clogs, this type of plunger exerts even greater pressure. Seat it firmly in the bowl hole, and pump it until you feel the pressure build. When the clog clears, you will feel a sudden loss of pressure.

3 If plunging does not clear a clog, use a toilet auger. Pull the auger's handle up, insert the auger, then crank while pushing down. The auger may push an obstruction through, or it may grab the obstruction so you can then pull it out (see *page 55*).

Water-saving toilets

U.S. codes require that new toilets use no more than 1.6 gallons of water per flush; older toilets use from 3 to 5 gallons. Many early 1.6-gallon models, made in the mid-1990s, do not flush well because the manufacturers simply reduced the tank size without changing the design. If yours is one of these, you may want to replace it with a newer model that flushes more completely.

Newer gravity-flush models increase pressure by virtue of different hole designs that maximize water flow.

For even more flushing power, consider spending more for a pressure-assisted toilet, which uses pressurized air to make the water flow faster *(page 177)*. However, this design is noisy.

A pump-assisted toilet creates great pressure with less noise, but it is expensive, and has an electric pump that must be hooked up to power.

WHAT IF...
The clog is severe?

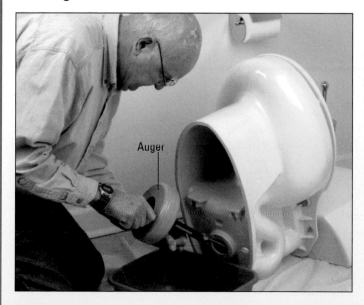

Auger

Occasionally a clog is too stubborn to be cleared by a plunger or auger. (Dumping construction materials, such as joint compound or tile-setting mortar, into a toilet can lead to this condition.) If you run into this problem, turn off the water, drain the tank, and remove the toilet *(page 94)*. Turn the toilet upside down and chip away any caked-on debris. Then run an auger through it backward.

Eliminating run-on

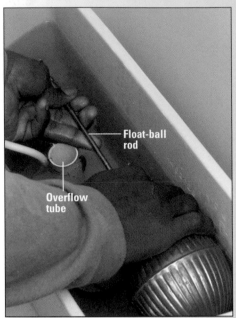

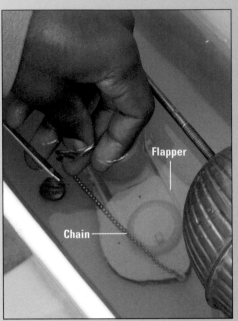

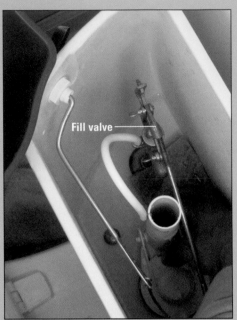

1 If water runs continuously, remove the tank lid and check the water level. If water is running over the top of the overflow tube, lower the level. If there is a float ball, bend its rod so the ball sits lower.

2 A kinked or tangled chain may cause run-on. Detach it from the handle arm, undo the kink or tangle, and reattach it so there is about ½ inch of slack in the chain when the flapper is seated.

3 If these measures do not solve the problem, the fill valve needs to be repaired or replaced. The tank must be emptied for this and other repairs. **Shut off water to the toilet** and flush the toilet to remove most of the water. Use a sponge to remove the rest of the water.

WHAT IF...
The float cup needs adjusting?

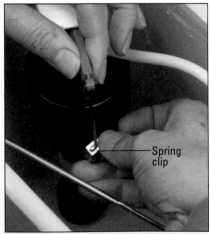

To adjust water level when there is a float-cup assembly, pinch the spring clip and slide the float cup up or down—up to raise the water level, down to lower it.

Adjusting the lift wire

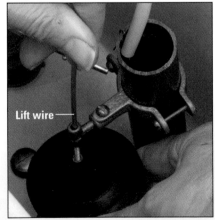

The lift wire attached to a stopper must slide smoothly. If it doesn't, straighten it. You may need to bend the wire that connects the lift wire to the handle. Work carefully and test thoroughly until the lift wire slides without interruption every time.

Making handle adjustments

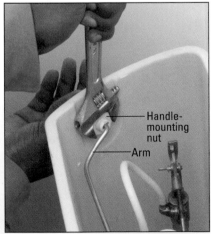

If a handle jiggles loosely, tighten the nut that connects it to the tank. Check the arm that connects to the flapper or stopper as well. Make sure it does not bump into any mechanisms in the tank.

Installing a new float cup

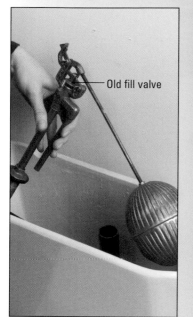

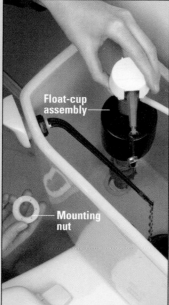

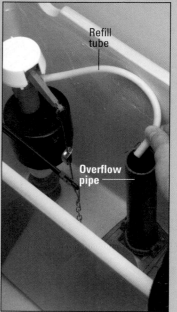

Old fill valve

Float-cup assembly

Mounting nut

Refill tube

Overflow pipe

1 **Shut off water at the stop valve.** Disconnect the supply tube. Clamp locking pliers onto the nut at the base of the old assembly. Under the tank, use an adjustable wrench to remove the nut. Lift the assembly out.

2 Insert the new float-cup assembly through the hole in the tank. Hold it in place with locking pliers and tighten the mounting nut under the tank. Make sure the cup will be clear of any obstructions.

3 Remove the flapper or stopper. Slide the new flapper down the overflow pipe and adjust it so it flops down onto the center of the flush-valve seat. Attach the chain to it so there is about ½ inch of slack.

4 Clip the refill tube to the overflow tube. Reattach the supply tube and turn the shutoff valve back on. Let the tank fill and check for leaks.

Repairing a ballcock valve

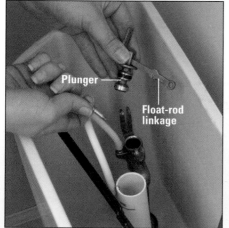

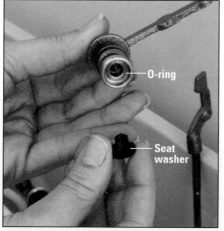

Plunger

Float-rod linkage

O-ring

Seat washer

1 If only the rubber parts of a ballcock valve are damaged, you can replace them. Remove the float-rod linkage, which is attached with two screws. Use pliers to pull out the plunger.

2 Clean away sediment in the valve, using a toothbrush or a soft wire brush. If the O-rings and the seat washer are worn, you may find it difficult to find replacements. In that case, buy a new float-cup assembly and replace the entire assembly.

WHAT IF...
There is a diaphragm valve?

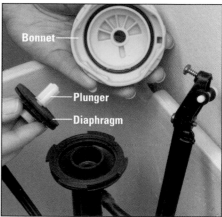

Bonnet

Plunger

Diaphragm

Remove the clip or screws from the top of a diaphragm fill valve and lift out the bonnet. Pull out the plunger. Clean away any debris or slime. If the plunger or the diaphragm is worn, replace it or replace the entire unit.

Seeping and phantom flushes

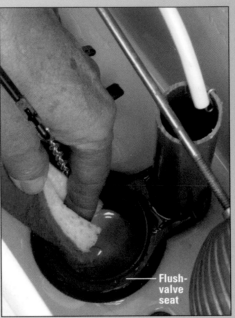

Flush-valve seat

Flapper

Water runs into bowl: If water sometimes gurgles into the bowl until you jiggle the handle, the handle may be loose or in need of adjustment. Metal handle arms can be adjusted by gentle bending. The lift rod or chain may be stuck or snagged—adjust or replace if needed.

Phantom flushes: If water slowly seeps into the bowl, you may or may not hear it. A faint, "phantom" flush may occur every so often. In this case, the flapper or stopper is not sealing tightly against the flush-valve seat. **Shut off the water** and flush; then clean the seat with a nonmetallic scrubbing pad.

Persistent problems: See whether the flapper or stopper is centered in the seat. Raising or twisting a flapper may solve the problem. If not, install a new one. Bring the old flapper to a home center so you can buy an exact replacement. If the new flapper does not seat tightly, try a different type.

WHAT IF...
The toilet has a weak flush?

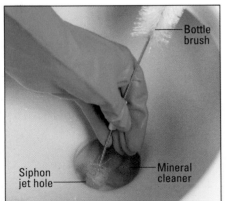

Bottle brush

Siphon jet hole

Mineral cleaner

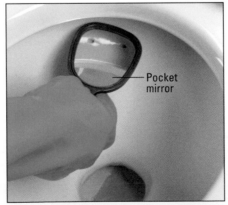

Pocket mirror

1 If water flows weakly into the bowl, partially blocked rim openings or a blocked jet may be the culprit. **Shut off the water** and flush; then pour mineral cleaner into the bowl. Clean the siphon jet with a bottle brush.

2 Brush the rim openings with the cleaner and allow several minutes for it to soak in; repeat several times. A mirror will help you see if any openings are clogged. Auger a rim opening with a piece of insulated wire or a very small bottle brush.

A replacement flapper kit

Replacement flappers are available for virtually every toilet. This kit is ideal if you're having trouble getting a flapper to seal. It comes with its own seat, which seals tightly on top of an existing seat.

Leaks from the tank

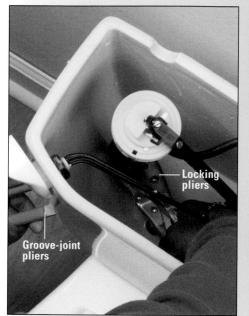

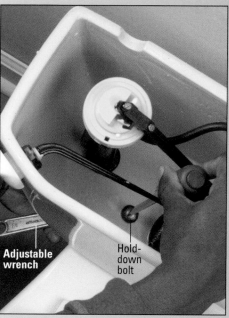

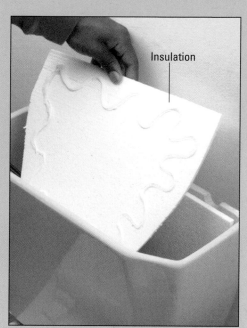

Leak at supply: If water leaks where the supply tube enters the tank, **shut off the water** and flush. Gently clamp locking pliers to the nut inside the tank and tighten the mounting nut under the toilet. If this doesn't solve the problem, you may need to replace the mounting-nut gasket inside the tank.

Leak between tank and bowl: Shut off the water and flush. With an adjustable wrench holding the nut under the tank, tighten the screw inside the tank. Don't overtighten; you may crack the tank. If this doesn't solve the problem, replace the rubber washers under the hold-down bolts.

Sweaty tank: If drops of condensation appear on the tank, buy a tank insulating kit. Drain and dry the tank. Cut each insulation piece to fit and attach it with the adhesive provided.

Replacing a toilet seat

To remove an existing toilet seat, pry up any caps at the back of the seat to reveal the screw heads. Clamp locking pliers to the nut below and unscrew. Some plastic nuts have wings, so you do not need the pliers.

If old metal bolts are rusted tight, spray them with penetrating oil. If necessary, cut through the bolts with a hacksaw.

Clean the top of the bowl. Hold the new seat centered over the bowl as you tighten the nuts.

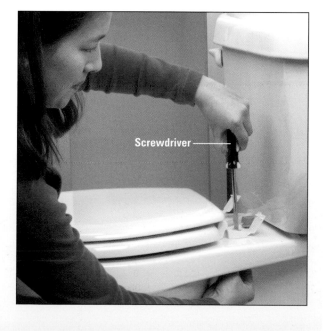

STANLEY PRO TIP

Water from the bowl means the toilet needs resetting

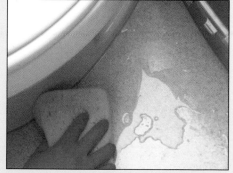

If water leaks from the bottom of the bowl when you flush, check the bowl for cracks. If there are none, the wax ring needs to be replaced. Follow the steps on *pages 94–95* to remove the toilet, install a new wax ring, and reinstall the toilet.

REPLACING A TOILET

Most new toilets come in two boxes, one for the bowl and one for the tank with all the moving parts installed. Attaching the tank to the bowl should take only half an hour or so.

The steps at right show how to assemble the tank and bowl, then how to install the toilet. You may choose to install the bowl first and then attach the tank. If the existing toilet is heavy, you may want to detach the tank from the bowl before removing it. Keep your back straight and lift with the legs. Arrange for a helper if possible. Follow these same steps if your toilet is leaking from the base and you need to replace the wax ring.

Choosing a toilet

You may choose a pressure- or pump-assisted toilet. Most toilets have mounting holes 12 inches from the back wall, but some are 10 inches away. Measure the old toilet carefully and buy a new one with the same dimensions.

PRESTART CHECKLIST

☐ **TIME**
About 2 hours to remove an existing toilet and install a new one

☐ **TOOLS**
Adjustable wrench, screwdriver, putty knife, hacksaw, utility knife

☐ **SKILLS**
Making simple plumbing connections, assembling a toilet

☐ **PREP**
Shut off water to the toilet, flush; use a sponge or rag to remove all the water you can from the tank and the bowl

☐ **MATERIALS**
Toilet, flanged wax ring, perhaps a nonflanged ring, flange bolts, plumber's putty

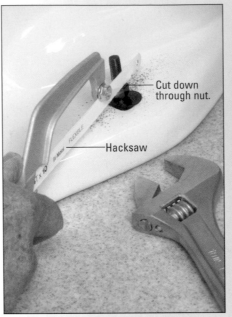
Cut down through nut.
Hacksaw

1 **Shut off water at the stop valve.** Disconnect the supply tube at the tank and wall. Pry off any decorative caps and unscrew the nuts holding the bowl to the floor. If the nuts are frozen, cut through them with a hacksaw.

Old putty

2 If there is a bead of caulk around the bowl at the floor, cut through it with a utility knife. If the toilet is old, check to see if the tank is bolted to the wall and remove the bolts. Grasp the toilet bowl on each side, pick it up, and set it on a drop cloth.

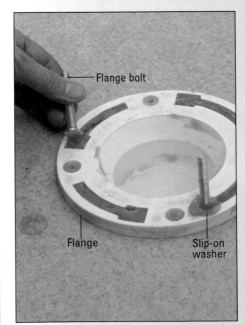
Flange bolt
Flange
Slip-on washer

6 If the new toilet does not include them, buy new flange bolts. Use slip-on plastic washers to hold them temporarily in place, pointing straight up. Remove the rag from the hole.

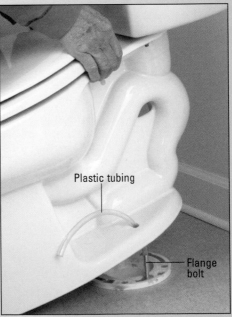
Plastic tubing
Flange bolt

7 Lower the toilet bowl so that the flange bolts poke through the holes. If it is difficult to line up the holes with the bolts, place a piece of plastic tubing over the bolt to guide it through the base as you lower the bowl.

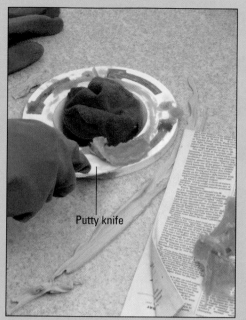

Putty knife

Mounting bolt

Spud gasket

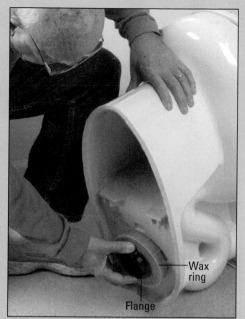

Wax ring

Flange

3 Place a large, damp rag in the hole to seal off sewer gas. Scrape away all putty and wax from the floor. Finish cleaning with a rag. If you are reinstalling the existing toilet, clean the bottom of its bowl in the same way.

4 Assemble the tank and the bowl of a new toilet, following the manufacturer's instructions. A large spud gasket seals the opening below the flush-valve seat. Place a rubber washer under the head of each mounting bolt. Do not overtighten the nuts.

5 Press a new wax ring, flange pointed out (or down), on the underside of the toilet bowl. (Not all toilets or drainpipes accept a flanged ring; wax rings without the flange are also available.)

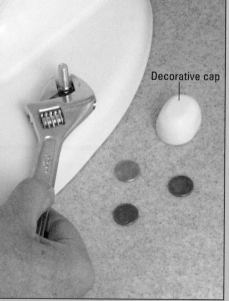

Decorative cap

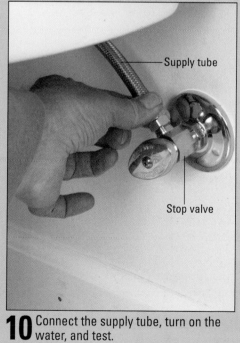

Supply tube

Stop valve

8 Press down on the bowl with both hands to seat the toilet firmly on the wax ring. Check the position of the toilet by looking at the toilet tank: it should be parallel to the wall and level.

9 Tighten the nut on each side of the bowl, alternating sides. If the floor is uneven, use pennies as shims. Avoid overtightening. Stop tightening when the bowl feels solid when you sit on it. Carefully cut off the tip of each bolt and cover with a decorative cap.

10 Connect the supply tube, turn on the water, and test.

WORKING WITH PIPE

Cutting and joining the various types of pipe—copper, plastic, and steel—calls for special techniques. These methods can be learned in an hour or two. This chapter teaches you how to work with the materials you choose.

Practice, practice

Though you may never learn to install plumbing as quickly as a professional plumber, with practice you can make joints that are every bit as strong and durable as those made by the pros. But these techniques take practice, so buy extra pipe and fittings and practice cutting until you can make straight cuts. Experiment to find out how far a pipe pokes into a fitting so you can measure accurately. Clamp a pipe to a vise on a workbench and join it to a fitting. Keep practicing until you are confident that your joints are tight and secure.

Preparing the work site

Working in tight spots is usually what makes plumbing difficult. Evaluate the working conditions and take time to make things as comfortable as possible. Remove all obstructions. Place a bucket under any pipe that might leak as it is disassembled. In confined spaces, have plenty of large towels on hand to soak up spilled water and to cushion your back, head, and knees. Protect floors with a thick drop cloth.

You may need to pull an existing pipe away from a wall or framing member in order to cut and join a new line to it.

Remove a clamp or strap or two and pull gently. Copper pipe can kink if you pull it too hard. Unscrewing a steel pipe fitting can stress corroded threads enough to cause a leak.

Before working on any project, practice the golden rule of plumbing: **Shut off the water** and test to make sure the water is off. When working on DWV pipes, shut off the water, flush all the toilets, and tell household members not to use the drainage system.

Make the job site safe. When sweating copper pipe, protect all flammable surfaces and have a fire extinguisher ready. When working on a drain line, keep the room ventilated in case noxious fumes escape. **Shut off a gas line before working on it.**

Installing new plumbing requires skills that can be learned in just an hour or two.

CHAPTER PREVIEW

Working with copper pipe
page 98

Installing plastic drainpipe
page 100

Working with CPVC and plastic supplies
page 102

Working with PEX tubing
page 104

PVC and copper pipe are relatively inexpensive so buy more than you think you'll need to allow for mistakes.

Advanced plumbing projects call for special preparations. Clear away furniture and lay down a thick, absorbent drop cloth. A drop cloth will protect the floor from dropped tools and fittings. In addition it will soak up any residual water and catch any spilled primer, putty, and debris.

Installing steel pipe
page 106

Working with cast-iron drainpipe
page 108

Running pipes through walls and floors
page 110

Connecting new to old
page 112

WORKING WITH COPPER PIPE

A properly soldered (or "sweated") joint on copper pipe is as strong as the pipe itself. However, a poorly soldered joint will leak the next day, or in a year or two.

The trick is to work systematically because each step depends on the previous one: The pipe must be cut straight and all burrs removed. The inside of the fitting and the outside of the pipe must be brushed or sanded to a shine. Flux must be applied for the solder to adhere. The solder must be fully drawn into the joint. Even wiping is essential: a droplet of solder can weaken a joint.

Keep it round

Pipe ends and fittings must be perfectly round. If either is dented or even slightly flattened, it is all but impossible to restore the original roundness. Cut the pipe again or buy a new fitting.

Cutting with a tubing cutter ensures roundness. If space is tight and you must cut with a hacksaw, do it slowly and gently. If you must bend a pipe to move it away from a wall, work carefully.

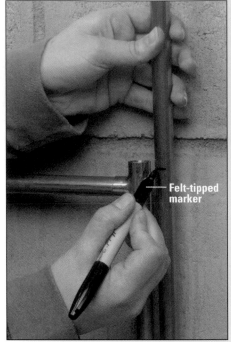

Felt-tipped marker

1 Hold a pipe in place to measure for a cut or use a tape measure. Take into account the distance the pipe will travel into the fitting. Mark with a felt-tipped marker or a pencil.

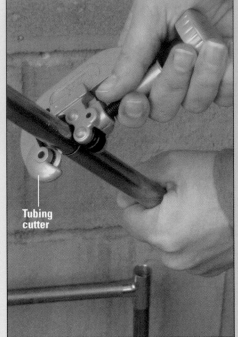

Tubing cutter

2 Use a large tubing cutter or a small one if space is tight. Align the cutting wheel with the cut mark. Twist the knob until the wheel starts to bite into the pipe. Rotate the cutter once, tighten a half turn or so, and repeat until the pipe is cut. Assemble all the parts of a joint in a dry run.

PRESTART CHECKLIST

☐ **TIME**
About 15 minutes to cut a pipe and join a fitting

☐ **TOOLS**
Tubing cutter or hacksaw, multiuse wire brush, propane torch (preferably with a trigger igniter), flux brush, groove-joint pliers, flame guard

☐ **SKILLS**
Cutting pipe, soldering

☐ **PREP**
Protect any flammable surfaces with a fiber shield or a cookie sheet

☐ **MATERIALS**
Copper pipe and fittings, flux, solder (95 percent tin for drinking water supply), damp rag

REFRESHER COURSE
Sweating a brass valve

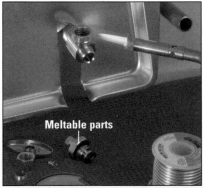

Meltable parts

If a valve has any plastic parts—as is the case with most stop valves—disassemble the valve and remove all the meltable parts. Heat the brass valve body as you would a fitting. It may take a bit longer to heat than a fitting. After sweating, wait for the valve to cool before replacing the plastic parts.

STANLEY PRO TIP

Protect walls and framing from the torch flame

While caught up in the sweating process you may not notice that the flame is charring a joist or wall surface. Protect flammable surfaces with a fiber shield *(page 20)* or use an old cookie sheet or two. **Keep a home fire extinguisher handy.**

If you can't pull a pipe more than a half inch away from a wall or framing member, don't worry about heating all around the fitting. As long as you heat two opposite sides, the solder will draw evenly around the joint.

Avoid MAPP gas, an alternative to propane fuel. It produces an extremely hot flame and is not recommended for most residential work.

After the job is complete, **check the area an hour later to be sure no flammable surfaces are smoldering.**

Multiuse wire brush

Flux brush

3 Using a wire brush made for the size of the fitting, ream out every inside opening until it is shiny. Oil from your hand may weaken the joint. If you accidentally touch a brushed opening, ream it again.

4 Brush or sand the outside of the pipe to be joined until it shines by inserting the pipe end in the multiuse brush and spinning the brush a few times. Re-brush or re-sand if you touch the shiny area.

5 Using the flux brush (it often comes with the can of flux), apply flux to all the inside openings of the fitting and to the outside of the pipe. Take care to keep the flux brush away from any debris; clean it if any particles stick to it.

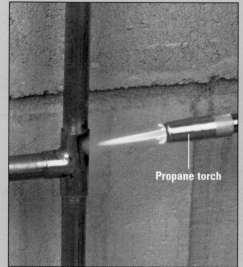

Propane torch

Solder

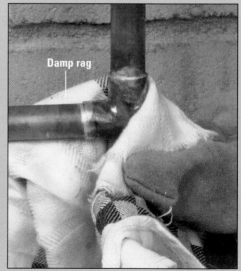

Damp rag

6 Ignite a propane torch and point the flame at the fitting near the joint—not at the pipe and not at the joint. The tip of the blue portion of the flame should just touch the fitting. Move the flame back and forth so you heat two opposite sides of the fitting.

7 When the fitting starts to smoke, remove the flame and touch the tip of the solder to the joint. If it does not melt, heat again. Once the fitting is hot enough, the solder will be drawn into the joint. Move the solder around so the entire joint is soldered.

8 Immediately repeat the process for any other joints in the fitting. This will go quickly because the fitting is already hot. Once all the joints are soldered, quickly wipe all the joints with a damp rag. Avoid bumping the fitting for 10 to 15 minutes.

INSTALLING PLASTIC DRAINPIPE

Plastic PVC pipe and fittings are inexpensive and easy to install. However, do not take this work lightly. Once glued together, a joint is rock-hard and cannot be adjusted. If you make a mistake, you'll have to cut out the section and start all over again.

Making a dry run
To prevent a mistake, cut and assemble the pipes in a dry run: Cut and temporarily join five or six pipes and fittings together and make sure that the last pipe in the run is facing the right direction. Use a felt-tipped pen to make alignment marks on all the joints where the fitting must face correctly. Disassemble, keeping careful track of the order of installation. Apply primer to each pipe end and each fitting. Apply cement and join each pipe in order.

PRESTART CHECKLIST

☐ **TIME**
About an hour to cut and assemble five or six pipes and fittings

☐ **TOOLS**
PVC saw or backsaw and miter box or power miter saw, deburring tool, felt-tipped marker

☐ **SKILLS**
Sawing, measuring, working methodically

☐ **PREP**
Make a drawing of the drain/vent assembly; clear a path for the pipes

☐ **MATERIALS**
Primer and cement for your type and size of pipe (see opposite)

Plastic-pipe saw Miter box

Deburring tool

1 When measuring, allow for the distance the pipe will travel inside the fitting. Use a felt-tipped marker to mark the pipe. You can use a hacksaw or backsaw to cut PVC, but a plastic pipe saw is easier to use. A power miter saw with a fine-cutting blade is easiest of all. Cut it square.

2 Remove all the burrs from the cut pipe end. You can do this by scraping with a knife, but a deburring tool does a better job and is easier to use. Assemble cut pipes and fittings in a dry run (see below).

DRY RUN FOR DRAINPIPE

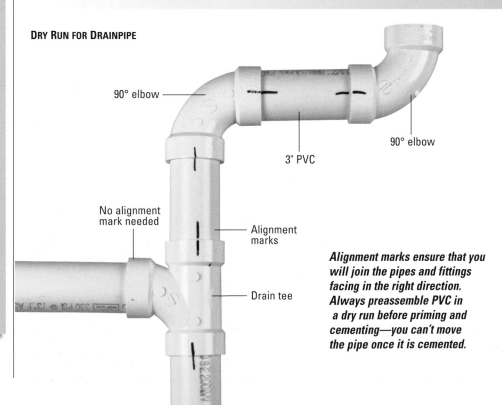

90° elbow

90° elbow

3" PVC

No alignment mark needed

Alignment marks

Drain tee

Alignment marks ensure that you will join the pipes and fittings facing in the right direction. Always preassemble PVC in a dry run before priming and cementing—you can't move the pipe once it is cemented.

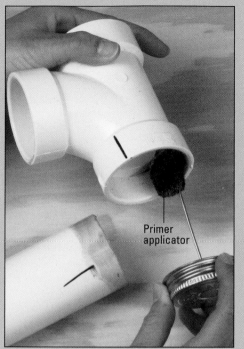

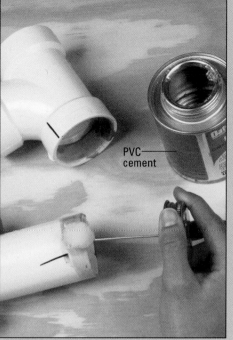

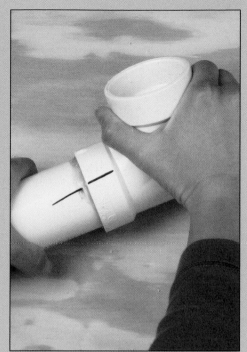

3 Apply primer to the inside of the fitting openings and to the pipe ends. The applicator should be wet enough to produce a fairly dark line, but not so wet that the primer drips. Place the pieces where they will not get dirty. If debris sticks to the primer, it will be difficult to join the pipes.

4 Apply cement to the inside of one fitting opening and to the end of one pipe. Work quickly—the cement starts to set up in a few seconds.

5 Push the pipe into the fitting, and twist so the alignment marks line up. Hold for a few seconds, then wipe with a damp cloth. In a minute, the joint will be strong enough so you can assemble the next piece. After 15 minutes, you can run unpressurized wastewater through the pipes.

WHAT IF...
You are connecting ABS pipe?

Most codes require PVC for drain lines, but if you already have black ABS pipe in your home, local codes may allow you to add to your system using the same material instead of making a transition to PVC.

Cut and assemble the black ABS pipe in much the same way as you would PVC pipe. Use a plastic-cutting saw or backsaw with a miter box, remove the burrs, and put pipe and fittings together in a dry run. Use a sharpened, light-colored crayon to make alignment marks.

Instead of primer, apply ABS cleaner to pipe ends and fitting openings. Use special ABS cement to glue the pieces together. Push the pieces together and twist.

To connect PVC pipe to existing ABS pipe, use a no-hub fitting *(page 112)*.

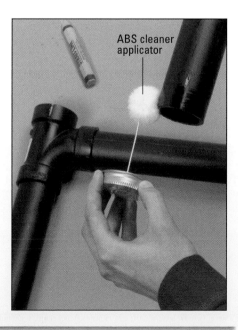

Use the right products

Check the label on a can of primer or cement to make sure it's made for your type of pipe. Local inspectors may or may not approve of "all-purpose" cement. The larger the pipe's diameter, the bigger the applicator should be so you won't have to dip it twice. As a general rule, an applicator should be about half the diameter of the pipe to be joined.

WORKING WITH CPVC AND PLASTIC SUPPLIES

Check local codes before installing any type of plastic supply pipe; many building departments do not permit it for interior installations.

However, CPVC and other types of extra-strong plastic pipe are often used for irrigation systems and other outdoor installations. Because plastic pipe can be cracked when bumped (say, by a lawn mower), some codes allow it only for underground installations and require metal pipe aboveground.

Often rigid plastic supply pipe is used with flexible tubing such as PEX, both for outdoor and interior installations. In a typical irrigation system, rigid pipe is used for long runs, and flexible tubing is used for shorter runs leading to sprinkler heads or bubblers.

PRESTART CHECKLIST

☐ **TIME**
About an hour to cut and join five or six pieces of pipe and fittings

☐ **TOOLS**
Scissors-type plastic pipe cutter or plastic-pipe saw and miter box, deburring tool, plastic tubing cutter, adjustable wrench, groove-joint pliers

☐ **SKILLS**
Cutting, measuring, cementing

☐ **PREP**
Cut holes behind walls or under floors to clear a path for the supply pipes

☐ **MATERIALS**
Plastic supply pipe approved by local codes, appropriate primer and cement, damp rag, flexible pipe, compression fittings

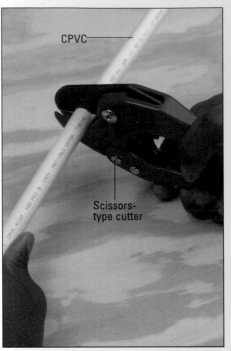

CPVC

Scissors-type cutter

1 Measure for the desired length and mark the pipe with a felt-tipped marker. Cut small-diameter plastic pipe with a scissors-type cutter (shown) or use a saw and miter box.

Deburring tool

2 Scissor cutters cut cleanly; but if you use a saw or there are any burrs, use a deburring tool to smooth the inside and outside of the cut end. Dry-fit the pipes and make alignment marks.

PLASTIC PIPE SYSTEM

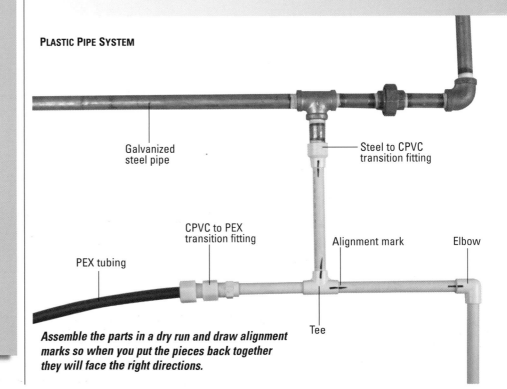

Galvanized steel pipe

Steel to CPVC transition fitting

CPVC to PEX transition fitting

PEX tubing

Alignment mark

Elbow

Tee

Assemble the parts in a dry run and draw alignment marks so when you put the pieces back together they will face the right directions.

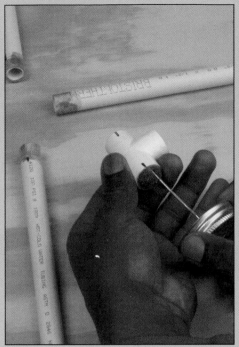

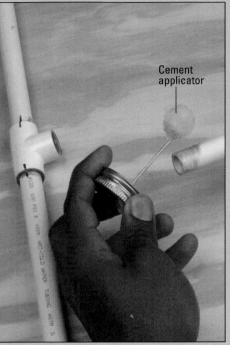

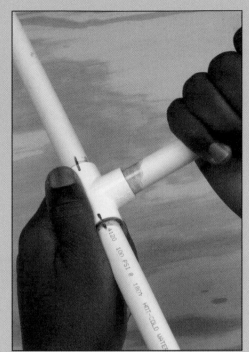

3 Using a small can with a small applicator brush, apply purple primer to the inside of the fitting and to the pipe end. Place the pieces on a surface where they will not get dirty.

4 One pipe and fitting at a time, apply cement to the inside of the fitting and to the pipe end.

5 Quickly insert the pipe into the joint and twist. Where there are alignment marks, make sure they meet. Hold for a few seconds and then wipe the joint with a damp rag.

Breaking into plastic pipe with a compression tee

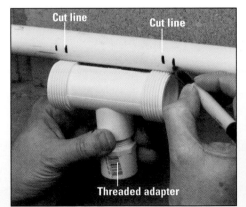

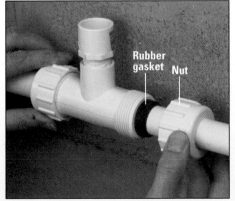

1 Plastic compression tees are ideal for breaking into an existing line where it is difficult to glue a standard tee. Note the distance that the pipe should be inserted into each end of the compression tee—usually ¼-inch. Mark the length of the tee and the insertion points (your cut lines).

2 **Turn off the water and drain the system.** Use a plastic-pipe saw or other fine-toothed saw to cut the pipe. Deburr the pipe (see Step **2, opposite**). Slip the nut and rubber gasket onto each end of the pipe. Bend the pipe out slightly to slip the tee into place.

3 Tighten the nuts with a groove-joint pliers. **Do not overtighten.** Add the extension to the line, following the steps above for cementing plastic pipe. Turn on the water to test the extension.

WORKING WITH PEX TUBING

The supply pipe of the future may already be here. Older PE (polyethylene) tubing has long been used for irrigation systems, but it must be buried for protection and it can carry only cold water. Cross-linked polyethylene (PEX) is stronger and can handle hot as well as cold water. It is approved for use in many areas of the country—especially the South—and is gaining acceptance elsewhere.

PEX is an installer's dream. It is easily cut, and it is flexible enough to make gentle bends around corners. To join compression fittings, no special tools or materials are required—just a pair of pliers or an adjustable wrench. More permanent fittings require a special crimping tool (see Steps 2 and 3). Where approved by local codes, PEX is an ideal material if you want to replace old galvanized pipes because it can be snaked through walls.

Another advantage of PEX is that it offers a manifold fitting (Step 2), which allows you to pull one water supply line to a location and then add branch lines to various fixtures.

PRESTART CHECKLIST

☐ **TIME**
To run and install about 50 feet of pipe with 5 fittings, about an hour

☐ **TOOLS**
Plastic tubing cutter or plastic pipe cutter, crimping tool, groove-joint pliers, adjustable wrench, reaming tool, drill

☐ **SKILLS**
Understanding of supply pipes

☐ **PREP**
Bore holes for running pipe through joists or studs

☐ **MATERIALS**
PEX tubing, compression fittings, crimp rings

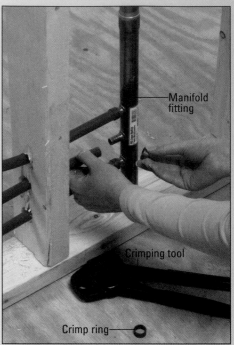

Manifold fitting

Crimping tool

Crimp ring

Flexible tubing cutter

1 Holes for PEX tubing need not be carefully laid out in a straight line. PEX can be bent around corners, but don't make too sharp a bend, or the tubing may kink. In most cases, you can run the pipe through the holes and then cut it in place. Drill 1-inch holes for ½-inch tubing.

2 Make sure the tube end is cut straight and that the cut end is free of burrs. To make a crimped connection, slide the crimp ring onto the tube, and then slip the tube onto the fitting.

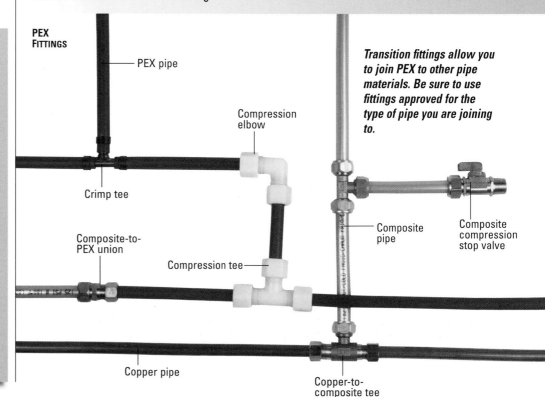

PEX FITTINGS

PEX pipe

Crimp tee

Composite-to-PEX union

Compression elbow

Compression tee

Copper pipe

Copper-to-composite tee

Transition fittings allow you to join PEX to other pipe materials. Be sure to use fittings approved for the type of pipe you are joining to.

Composite pipe

Composite compression stop valve

3 Grasp the ring with the crimping tool, and squeeze until you feel the ring compress. Tug on the connection to make sure it is rock-solid.

4 To install a stub-out, temporarily screw the drop-ear elbows, mark the tubing for cutting, and cut with a tubing cutter.

5 Remove the elbow, attach it to the tubing using the crimping tool, and reattach the elbow. To ensure against rattling noises when water is turned on and off, clamp the pipe firmly every couple of feet. Where pipe runs through a hole, tap in a wooden shim.

Installing composite pipe

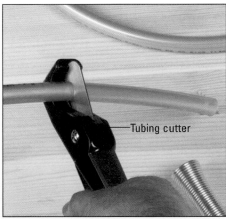

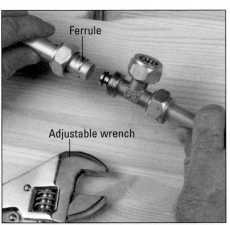

In addition to straight polyethylene pipe, composite pipe, with an aluminum core sheathed in plastic, is approved in some areas both for water supply and for gas lines. Cut it with a tubing cutter.

Use a reaming tool to true the tubing into round and to clean out the inside of the cut end. Insert the tool and give it a couple of twists. Make sure no scrapings are left inside the tube.

Slip a nut and a ferrule onto the tube end, then slip the tube onto the fitting. Finger-tighten, taking care not to cross-thread. Then tighten the nut with one full turn (no more), using an adjustable wrench or pliers.

INSTALLING STEEL PIPE

New water supply lines are usually copper or plastic; but if your home has galvanized pipe and you need to replace a leaky section of pipe or add a short run, it makes sense to use the same material.

Almost all gas lines are black threaded pipe, which is installed the same way as galvanized pipe (see opposite).

Buying materials

Don't try to cut and thread steel pipe yourself. Measure carefully, keeping in mind that ½- and ¾-inch pipe goes about ½ inch into each fitting. Then have a home center or hardware store cut and thread pieces to these exact measurements.

A more flexible strategy is to estimate your pipe and fitting needs. Then you can buy long pipes as well as a variety of "nipples"—short lengths of threaded pipe ranging from 1 to 12 inches. Also buy extra couplings. When you come close to the end of a run, you can probably create the correct length simply by combining nipples and couplings.

PRESTART CHECKLIST

☐ **TIME**
About an hour to cut into a line and install several fittings and pipes

☐ **TOOLS**
Two pipe wrenches (14-inch wrenches are a good choice), groove-joint pliers, hacksaw or reciprocating saw

☐ **SKILLS**
Careful measuring and planning, firm tightening using a pipe wrench

☐ **PREP**
Shut off water to the pipe you will break into. If you can find a nearby union fitting, you may be able to avoid cutting a pipe.

☐ **MATERIALS**
Threaded pipe lengths and nipples, pipe-thread tape or pipe joint compound

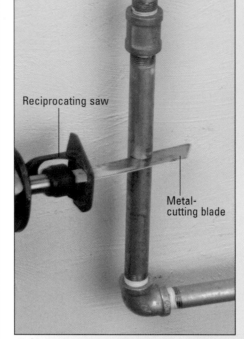

1 **Shut off water to the line.** To tap into the middle of a line when there is no nearby union fitting, cut through a pipe with a reciprocating saw equipped with a metal-cutting blade or with a hacksaw. Unscrew the pipe on both sides of the cut.

2 Before threading a pipe into a fitting, wrap the threads with several windings of pipe-thread tape. With the pipe end facing you, wrap clockwise. Or, brush pipe joint compound onto the threads of both the pipe end and the inside of the fitting.

GALVANIZED PIPE SYSTEM

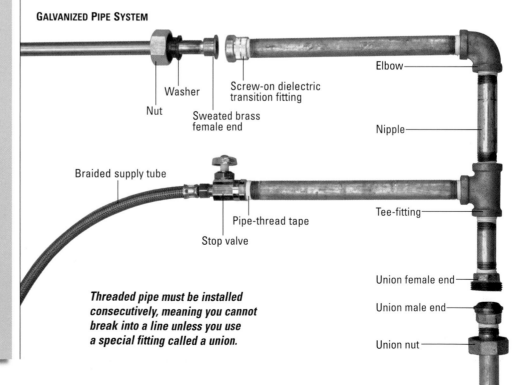

Threaded pipe must be installed consecutively, meaning you cannot break into a line unless you use a special fitting called a union.

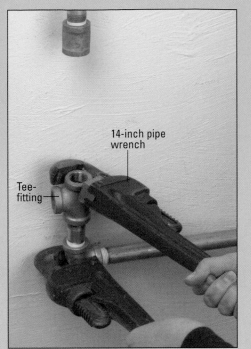

14-inch pipe wrench

Tee-fitting

3 Twist on a pipe or fitting by hand. If it does not turn easily, the joint is not straight and the threads are crossed. Back up and try again. Then firmly tighten each pipe or fitting in turn, using a 14-inch pipe wrench. You may need a second wrench to hold the adjacent piece steady.

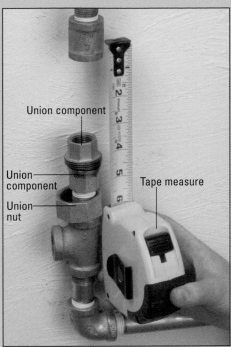

Union component

Union component

Union nut

Tape measure

4 Once the tee-fitting for the new line is installed, add a nipple and slip on the nut for the union, checking that the threads are toward the joint. Apply tape and install half of the union. Set the second half of the union in place and measure for the final section of pipe.

5 Attach the second half of the union to the final piece and install. The union halves should line up so they can seat against each other. Slip the union nut up and hand-tighten. Then fully tighten the nut with a pipe wrench to complete the union.

Dielectric fitting for transition to copper

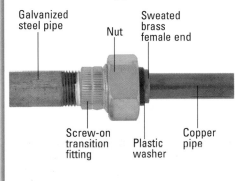

Galvanized steel pipe

Nut

Sweated brass female end

Screw-on transition fitting

Plastic washer

Copper pipe

To install a dielectric union, screw the threaded part onto the steel pipe. Before sweating the brass fitting of the copper pipe, slip on the nut and sleeve then push them well away from the heat of the torch. Once the fitting is sweated and cools, join the two parts. Use only groove-joint pliers to tighten the nut.

STANLEY PRO TIP: **Safely joining black gas pipe**

1 Before working with black threaded gas pipe, **shut off the gas** and ventilate the room. Follow the steps shown above, but use black pipe and fittings instead of galvanized. Wrap threaded ends with special yellow pipe-thread tape, made for use with gas pipe.

2 After installation, turn the gas back on and test for leaks. Spray gas-joint testing fluid, or brush liquid soap (shown) or soapy water on a joint. If you see bubbles, there is a leak. Tightening the nipple or valve will likely stop the leak. Retest.

WORKING WITH CAST-IRON DRAINPIPE

If a section of cast-iron pipe needs replacing, or if you want to tap into a cast-iron pipe with a new drain line, don't install more cast-iron pipe. Instead, make the transition to PVC drainpipe.

Several types of no-hub fittings are available; check local codes to see which are accepted. A no-hub fitting has a neoprene sleeve and clamps that are tightened around the cast-iron pipe and the plastic replacement piece to hold them in place and make a watertight joint. Such fittings are considered a permanent joint.

Cast-iron pipe is extremely heavy, so work carefully and use a helper. Never move or cut a piece until you are sure it is adequately supported with clamps and perhaps with framing as well. Add clamps above and below the new joint or leave the frame permanently in place.

PRESTART CHECKLIST

☐ **TIME**
A full day to support, cut, and install a replacement piece with two banded couplings; an hour or two to install a saddle-tee fitting (opposite)

☐ **TOOLS**
Carpentry tools, cast-iron snap cutter or circular saw with metal-cutting blade, hex screwdriver or torque wrench, tools for installing plastic drainpipe (page 100)

☐ **SKILLS**
Good carpentry skills, measuring, attaching with bolts

☐ **PREP**
Examine how the existing pipe is clamped; determine how best to hold it firmly as you work

☐ **MATERIALS**
Plastic pipe or fitting matching cast-iron pipe, banded couplings, riser clamps

Cast-iron drain
Riser clamp
2×4 frame

1 **Secure the pipe above and below the point that will be cut** so that neither end can fall or move sideways while you work. To be safe, build a frame like the one shown here and attach the pipe to it with riser clamps.

Circular saw with metal-cutting blade

2 Next to a snap cutter (below), the quickest way to cut cast iron is with a circular saw equipped with a metal-cutting blade. **Wear eye and ear protection.** If a circular saw will not reach all the way around, cut all or part with a reciprocating saw equipped with a metal-cutting blade.

STANLEY PRO TIP: **Make a quick, clean break with a snap cutter**

Another way to cut cast-iron pipe is with a snap cutter, which can be rented. After supporting the pipe above and below, wrap the cutter's chains around the pipe. Each chain link has a little wheel cutter. Follow manufacturer's instructions. Typically a handle sets the ratchet for loosening or tightening. Set it for tightening; pump the lever slowly until the chain is tight. Continue ratcheting until the cutting wheels crack through the pipe. Cut both sides and, wearing gloves, remove the scrap piece of pipe.

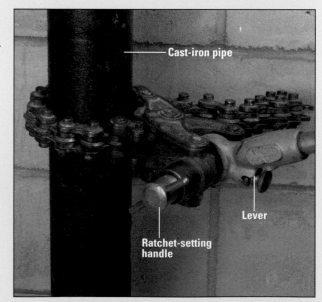

Cast-iron pipe
Lever
Ratchet-setting handle

No-hub fitting

Y-fitting with short pieces of pipe installed

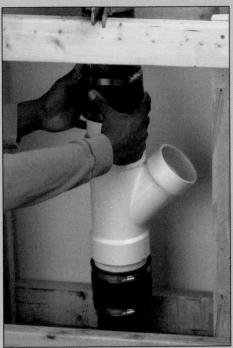

Hex screwdriver

3 To install a tee or Y, glue two short pieces of pipe to each end of the fitting *(pages 100–101),* making sure the resulting component will fit snugly between the pipes. Slip the no-hub fitting onto each of the cast-iron pipe ends.

4 Position the fitting or replacement piece between the two cut cast-iron ends and pull the neoprene sleeve over the plastic.

5 At each joint slide the neoprene sleeve of the no-hub fitting so it's centered on the joint. Tighten the band nuts using a hex screwdriver. Some codes may require the use of a torque wrench, which will stop tightening when you reach the proper band tightness.

Installing a saddle-tee drain fitting

Grinder with metal-cutting blade

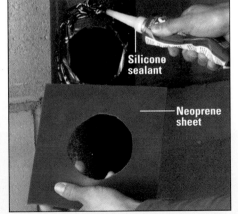

Silicone sealant

Neoprene sheet

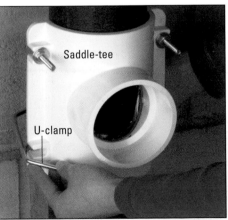

Saddle-tee

U-clamp

1 If it's approved by your local inspector, a saddle fitting is easier and quicker to install. Cut a roughly circular hole in the cast-iron pipe using a grinder equipped with a metal-cutting blade (shown). The hole should be slightly larger than the opening in the fitting.

2 Hold a neoprene sheet for the fitting against the hole and trace the outline of the hole. Cut a hole in the sheet that's slightly larger than the hole in the pipe. Squeeze silicone sealant around the hole.

3 Position the sheet over the hole and press the plastic fitting over it. Slip a U-clamp over the back of the pipe and slide its threaded ends through the plastic fitting. Screw on the two nuts finger-tight. Attach the other clamp the same way, then tighten all four nuts.

RUNNING PIPES THROUGH WALLS AND FLOORS

O nce you've drawn a plan for new plumbing service and have had it approved, develop a strategy for running those pipes. If you are lucky enough to work in a new building or addition where all the framing is exposed, this is fairly easy. If you are remodeling, be prepared for a few surprises and slight changes in plan once you've removed some of the wall surface and flooring.

Removing wall and floor surfaces prior to plumbing takes about half a day of hard work. But replacing finished surfaces after plumbing (especially patching walls) usually takes several days. A large wall patch—even replacing an entire wall—takes little more time than a small patch, so open up plenty of space for working.

Once you've opened up the vent and drain lines, running the supplies—which usually run alongside DWV (Drain-Waste-Vent) lines—will be relatively easy.

PRESTART CHECKLIST

☐ **TIME**
For a modest bathroom, two or three days to cut into walls and flooring and run pipes through framing

☐ **TOOLS**
Demolition tools, drill with various bits and hole saws, reciprocating saw, level, tools for installing pipe

☐ **SKILLS**
Carpentry, knowledge of your home's structure, installing pipe

☐ **PREP**
Have your plan approved by the local building department

☐ **MATERIALS**
Pipes, fittings, clamps, and assembly materials listed on your plan

1 If you need to run a new stack (see *pages 14–15*), assess your framing. An installation with a toilet must have a 3-inch drain, which can be installed only if the stud wall is made of 2×6s or larger. (2-inch pipe can be run through a 2×4 wall.) Remove the wall surface up to the ceiling.

Cutout for new stack

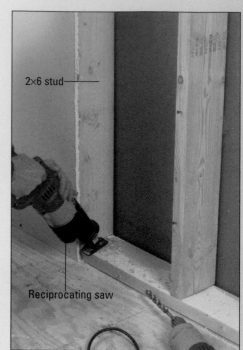

2 Cut a hole with some wiggle room for the new pipe. For a 3-inch pipe, use a drill and reciprocating saw to cut a hole about 4¼ inches by 10 inches through both the bottom plate of the room you are working in and the top plate of the room below. Cut away a 10-inch by 2-foot section of flooring.

2×6 stud

Reciprocating saw

Stabilizing and protecting pipes

Shim

Whenever possible, run pipes through holes in the center of framing members. To keep pipes from rattling, line the holes with felt or use wood shims. Slip a shim under the pipe and tap in until it is firmly in

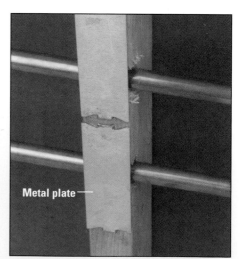

Metal plate

place, but not tight, to allow for expansion.

If notches are needed, make them as small as possible; they weaken the framing member. Protect pipes from nails by attaching metal plates.

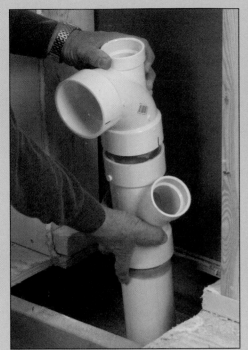

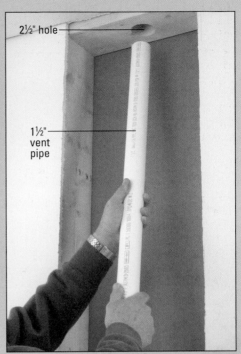

Right-angle drill

Hole-cutting saw

2½" hole

1½" vent pipe

3 Assemble the approved fittings onto the top of the drainpipe. Take special care that they face the right direction. The drainpipe should be longer than needed—you can cut it to size from below later. Slip the pipe down through the hole.

4 You may need to cut a hole in the wall of the room above or below to guide the vent pipe up or the drainpipe down. In the attic, you may be able to run the vent over to tie into an existing vent. If not, drill a hole in the attic ceiling and have a roofer install a roof jack for the vent pipe.

5 Anchor the drainpipe with straps. Cut a smaller opening in the ceiling for the vent pipe. For a 1½-inch vent pipe, a 2½-inch hole is sufficient. Guide the vent pipe up through the hole and into the attic or room above and slip its lower end into the fitting at the floor.

Running pipe through a floor

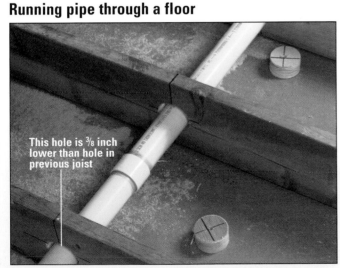

This hole is ⅜ inch lower than hole in previous joist

Running drainpipe through joists calls for meticulous work. The holes must follow a straight line across the floor and must ascend or descend so the pipe will be sloped ¼ inch per foot. (If joists are 16 inches on center and pipes run across them at a right angle, holes should differ in height by about ⅜ inch.)

Running pipe through walls

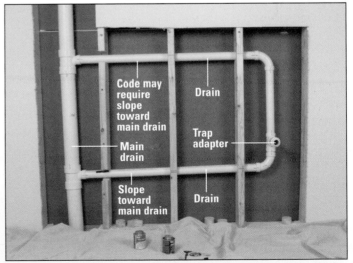

Code may require slope toward main drain

Drain

Main drain

Trap adapter

Slope toward main drain

Drain

Vent pipes may run level, though some codes may call for a slight slope toward the main drain. All drain lines must be sloped. For a precise slope, strike a level line on the studs and measure down ¼ inch per running foot. Codes may call for fireproof caulking in walls.

CONNECTING NEW TO OLD

Whether installing a new drain, vent, or supply line, the most common way to tie into an existing line is to cut the old line and install a tee fitting. If you happen to find a pipe that is capped at its end, simply install an elbow or coupling there instead.

Shut off water to existing supply pipes and drain the lines. Flush all toilets and caution others not to use drains. After opening a drain line, make sure no one uses a sink or faucet that drains into it. Seal any open drain lines with a large rag to protect against fumes.

If joining pipes of different materials, make sure the transition fitting conforms to local code.

Typically it doesn't matter exactly where you join to an existing pipe, but the new service must be precisely located. So it's usually easier to start pipe runs at the new location and travel toward the existing pipes rather than vice versa.

PRESTART CHECKLIST

☐ **TIME**
Once pipes are run, usually less than two hours to connect new to old

☐ **TOOLS**
Cutting and fitting tools for any type of pipe you will be working with, carpentry tools, reciprocating saw, hex-head driver

☐ **SKILLS**
Cutting and joining the type of pipe used in the project

☐ **PREP**
Run new pipes from the new service location to the existing pipe. Install the last pipe a little longer than it needs to be so you can cut it to length when you make the connection to the old pipe.

☐ **MATERIALS**
Joining materials for the type of pipe you will work on, transition fittings

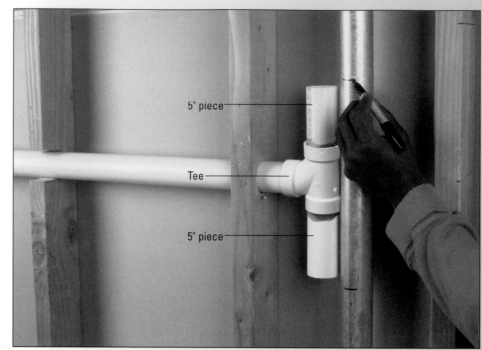

1 To join a new plastic drainpipe to an old steel pipe, run new pipe into the room. Prime and glue two 5-inch pieces of pipe to a tee fitting. Temporarily run pipe— longer than it needs to be—so it comes near the old pipe. (When running pipe across a stud wall, you may need to notch- cut some of the holes, using a reciprocating saw.) Dry-fit the tee assembly onto the new pipe and hold it next to the existing pipe. Mark the existing pipe for cutting. You may need to cut the opening larger than the tee assembly to accommodate the neoprene sleeves on the banded couplings.

WHAT IF...
You need to connect new PVC to old ABS?

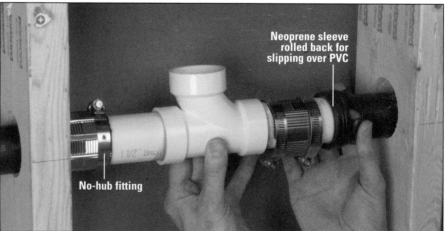

Even though there are specialty primers and cements intended for joining PVC pipe to an old ABS line, local codes may not permit connecting in this manner. Instead use a no-hub fitting, which has a neoprene sleeve and metal clamps, to hold it firm. Some municipalities may require that the fitting be accessible for future repairs.

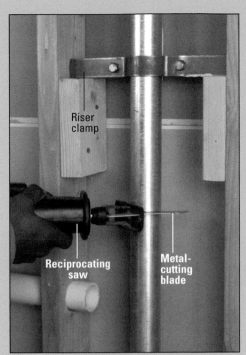

2 Support the pipe above and below with riser clamps so it cannot drop or sway as you work, and so the PVC fitting will not have to bear the weight of the drain. You will probably need to install a new stud or two as well as blocking for the upper clamp.

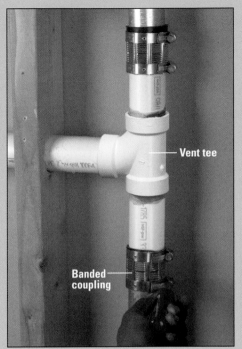

3 Slide a no-hub fitting onto each end of the old pipe, slide back the banded coupling, and fold up the neoprene sleeves. Position the tee assembly. Fold the neoprene sleeves over the assembly and slide the metal bands over the sleeves. Tighten the nuts with a hex-head driver.

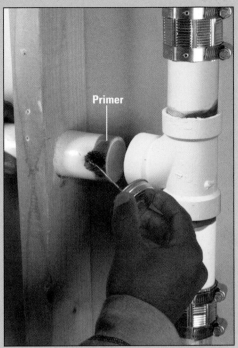

4 Cut the new pipe to exact length and test that it fits into the tee fitting; you may need to loosen the nuts and rotate the fitting slightly. Prime and glue the pipe to the fitting *(page 101)*.

Tapping into supply lines

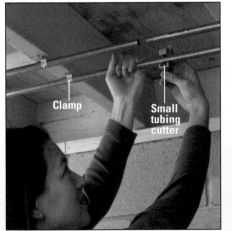

To tap into existing copper lines, shut off the water. With a tubing cutter, cut an opening in each pipe that is about an inch shorter than a tee fitting. Dry-fit the tees. If the pipes are rigidly installed, remove a clamp or two so you can pull the pieces apart slightly.

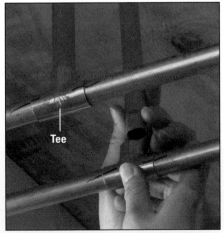

Dry-fit the pipes that will be inserted into the tees and draw alignment marks. Disassemble, wire-brush the fittings and pipe ends, brush on flux, and sweat the joints (see *pages 98–99*).

Joining copper to existing galvanized pipe

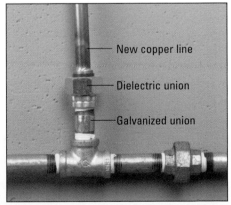

To tie a new copper line into an old galvanized line, follow the steps on *pages 106–107* for installing a new galvanized tee fitting. Screw a galvanized nipple into the tee and connect the copper line to the nipple using a dielectric union *(page 107)*.

PIPE REPAIRS

If a pipe suddenly springs a leak, you may be able to make a temporary repair by wrapping it tightly with electrician's tape. But a more permanent repair must be made as soon as possible.

If a pipe clamp *(page 115)* does not solve the problem, you'll need to remove and replace sections of pipe, and possibly fittings as well. This chapter shows how to cut, assemble, and join copper, steel, and plastic pipe, as well as how to make repairs to cast-iron pipe. In addition, it shows how to repair and replace valves, quiet noisy pipes, and thaw frozen pipes.

Pipe repair can be time-consuming, especially if the pipes are hard to reach. You may spend more time cutting into and patching walls than working on the plumbing.

Running new lines

You can use the techniques in this chapter to make a pipe repair, or to add a new line for additional service. Usually, simply installing a tee fitting allows you to run a new supply line. Armed with this knowledge, you can tackle a simple project like a laundry room *(pages 222–223)* as long as the drain line does not have to travel more than about 5 feet.

To install new service, on the other hand, is usually a complicated matter. Drain lines in particular must follow strict guidelines and must be properly vented *(pages 14–15)*. Contact a professional plumber for any project more complicated than a simple laundry room hookup.

STANLEY PRO TIP

Buy plenty of parts

Many people find the bulk of time spent on a home plumbing repair is actually used for shopping rather than doing the plumbing. Minimize trips with careful planning. List and buy everything that you may possibly need. Don't be afraid of buying too much; you can always return items you don't use.

Pipe repairs call for learning special skills. With a little practice, you can handle most jobs.

CHAPTER PREVIEW

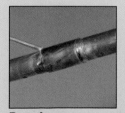

Repairs to copper pipe
page 116

Silencing pipe noises
page 118

Repairs to cast-iron pipe
page 119

Repairs to plastic pipe
page 120

If a galvanized or copper supply pipe gets punctured, a pipe clamp makes a permanent repair, as long as the pipe is exposed. If the pipe is hidden inside a wall, codes require that the pipe be replaced. To install a clamp, shut off water to the pipe and sand smooth the area around the damage. Center the rubber gasket over the puncture and tighten the nuts on the clamp.

Adjustable wrench

Galvanized-steel pipe

Pipe clamp

Leaks at stop valves and supply tubes
page 122

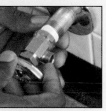

Installing a stop valve on copper pipe
page 124

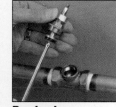

Installing a stop valve on steel pipe
page 125

Replacing a valve
page 126

Thawing pipes and winterizing
page 128

While a properly applied clamp makes a permanent repair, you may prefer to splice in a replacement with like material. To make repairs to copper pipe, see pages 116–117; plastic, pages 120–121; cast-iron, page 119; steel, pages 106–107, 125, 127.

REPAIRS TO COPPER PIPE

Because of its durability, copper is the preferred material for most water supply lines. However, copper pipe can leak when dented, punctured, or weakened from corrosion.

Even if you have galvanized or plastic supply pipe in your house, you may want to use a transition fitting and switch to copper when making a repair or extending a line. When joining copper pipe to steel pipe, be sure to use a dielectric fitting *(page 107)* to avoid corrosion.

Type M copper pipe is fine for most residential work. Buy lead-free solder and flux paste.

For more detail on how to sweat copper pipe see *pages 98–99*.

Sweating a large copper drain line calls for a large propane torch; you're probably better off hiring a pro for such work.

Compression fittings *(page 117)* require no special skills to install, but they are expensive. Use them only where they will be exposed; any joints hidden in a wall must be sweated.

PRESTART CHECKLIST

☐ **TIME**
An hour or two to make most repairs

☐ **TOOLS**
Groove-joint pliers, tubing cutter, hacksaw, propane torch, multiuse wire brush, flux brush

☐ **SKILLS**
Using a pipe cutter, handling a propane torch

☐ **PREP**
Shut off the water; drain the line; position a cookie sheet or protective shield to protect flammable surfaces

☐ **MATERIALS**
Copper pipe and fittings, flux, solder

1 Shut off the water. Use a tubing cutter to cut each side of the damaged area. Screw the cutter tight, rotate it a full turn, tighten, and rotate again until the cut is complete. If there is not enough room, cut with a hacksaw. Exert gentle pressure to avoid flattening the pipe. File off burrs.

2 If either of the existing pipes is moveable, you can use standard couplings *(page 26)*. If not, use slip couplings (Step 3). Measure the replacement piece by holding it in place. It should be the same length. Cut the new piece with a tubing cutter.

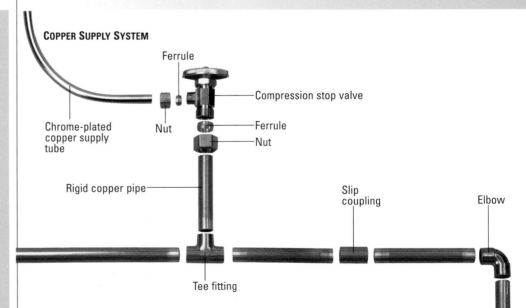

COPPER SUPPLY SYSTEM

Rigid copper joints are soldered together. The resulting joints, if made correctly, are actually stronger than the pipe itself. To add a new supply line, install a tee fitting. Use a compression fitting (opposite) only if it will remain exposed.

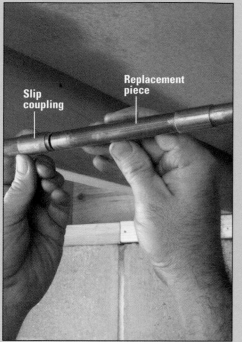

3 Ream and polish the pipe and couplings using a multiuse brush (see *page 99*). Brush on flux, and slide a coupling on each side, position the replacement piece, and slide the couplings back halfway. (To install a standard coupling or elbow, give it a slight twist as you push it all the way into place.)

4 Protect framing and nearby walls with a cookie sheet or fiber shield *(page 20)*. Aim the torch so the tip of the blue flame touches the middle of the fitting. When the flux sizzles after five seconds or so, move the flame to the opposite side and heat it briefly. Touch solder to the joints.

5 Once solder has been sucked into the joint all around, wipe the joint with a rag to smooth the solder and eliminate any drips. **Fold the rag several times and/or wear leather gloves.** Repeat for the other side of the fitting. **Check the work area an hour later to be sure nothing is smoldering.**

Patch a pipe with a tape kit

While not as fail-safe as a sweated patch, fiberglass patch tape can provide a quick, long-lasting cure for a leaky pipe. The kit includes tape impregnated with resin, gloves, and a lubricant that helps you squeeze out voids and bubbles.

STANLEY PRO TIP

Bread trick for wet pipe

If a pipe keeps dripping after you have shut off the water, jam a wad of soft white bread (not whole grain or crusts) into the pipe. Sweat the joint quickly, before the wad becomes saturated. Once the repair is made and the water turned on, open a nearby faucet. The bread will dissolve and flush out. (Or check your home center for gel beads that work the same way.)

Compression fittings

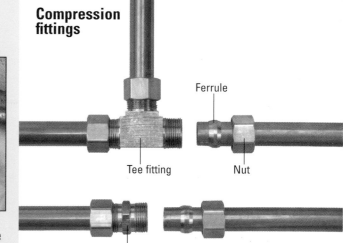

Compression fittings often make sense in tight places where it is difficult to solder. To install one, slide the nut, then the ferrule, onto the pipe. Slip the fitting onto the pipe, slide the ferrule into the fitting, and tighten the nut. No thread tape or pipe compound is necessary.

SILENCING PIPE NOISES

Pipes that rattle and hammer are not only annoying, they also may eventually come apart at the joints. Take steps to stop the noise and prevent possible leaks.

The most common noise is water hammer, a rattle that occurs when water is turned on or off by a faucet or an appliance, such as a dishwasher or clothes washer. The solution is to install a shock absorber, also called an air chamber, which provides a cushion to dampen the water's movement.

The following instructions show how to install a shock absorber using threaded fittings. You can also fabricate one for plastic pipe using a piece of pipe and a cap fitting; see *pages 120–121* for instructions on gluing.

After a few years, the air chamber may fill with water and lose its ability to soften water hammer. Draining and refilling the line will replenish the chamber with a cushion of air.

PRESTART CHECKLIST

☐ **TIME**
An hour or so to install a pipe shock absorber

☐ **TOOLS**
Tools for working with copper *(page 98)*, with plastic pipe *(page 100)*, or with steel pipe *(page 106)*

☐ **SKILLS**
Cutting and joining copper, plastic, or steel pipe

☐ **PREP**
Shut off the water and drain the line

☐ **MATERIALS**
Shock absorber for your type and size pipe, materials for joining the pipe

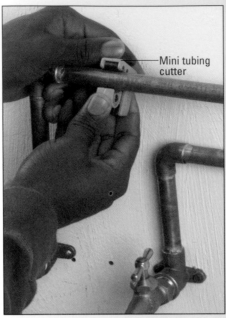

Mini tubing cutter

1 **Shut off water** and drain the line. Measure the shock absorber to determine how much pipe must be cut out; remember that pipe will be inserted into the absorber at each end. Cut the pipe with a tubing cutter, if possible; otherwise saw carefully with a hacksaw.

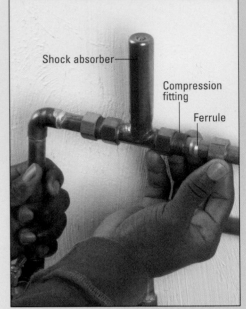

Shock absorber

Compression fitting

Ferrule

2 On each side of the absorber location, slip a compression nut on the pipe, threaded side toward the absorber, then slip on a ferrule. On each side of the shock absorber, push the nut over the ferrule and finger-tighten the joint. Use an adjustable wrench to complete the installation.

Adding pipe insulation

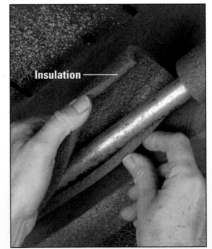

Insulation

A pipe may vibrate when water runs through it, causing it to rattle against a nearby framing member. Cushion the pipe by slipping on foam insulation pieces. Firm up loose pipes with pipe clamps or hanger brackets.

WHAT IF...
There is no access to pipes?

This type of shock absorber is made for use in a laundry room. Simply detach each washer hose from its hose bib, screw on the shock absorber, and attach each hose.

REPAIRS TO CAST-IRON PIPE

Old cast-iron drainpipe can behave unpredictably. Sometimes a small section of a pipe starts to crumble or a joint begins to leak even though most of the pipe is sound.

If a cast-iron pipe is failing at several points, the most economical solution is to replace it with PVC pipe. This is a job for a professional.

Older cast-iron joints were sealed with molten lead, but this is not a danger to your health, since only wastewater passes through the pipes.

PRESTART CHECKLIST

☐ **TIME**
An hour or two to install a clamp around a damaged area

☐ **TOOLS**
Screwdriver, adjustable wrench, wire brush, hammer, cold chisel, putty knife

☐ **SKILLS**
Assembling a clamp and tightening screws

☐ **PREP**
Make sure that the pipe is well supported.

☐ **MATERIALS**
Repair paste or plumber's epoxy

SAFETY FIRST
Support cast-iron pipe

Cast-iron pipe is very heavy and must be held in place with special clamps attached to framing members. Never disturb these clamps; if one weakens, a long section of pipe could come crashing down.

Cold chisel

1 If water or a bad smell comes from an old leaded joint, use a cold chisel and hammer to gently tap the lead back into the joint. Use a wire brush and rag to clean away the corrosion.

2 Fill the resulting void with cast-iron pipe repair paste. Use a putty knife to apply the paste.

WHAT IF...
A cast-iron pipe has a hole?

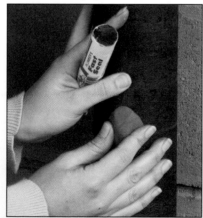

If a pipe rusts through or is punctured, clean the opening with a wire brush and fill the hole with two-part plumber's epoxy. Check the manufacturer's instructions for drying time. Don't use the pipe until the patch has completely set.

 **STANLEY** PRO TIP

Replacing a section of cast-iron pipe

If more than a small area is damaged, this is a job for a professional. Hire a plumber to cut out a section of the pipe and replace it with PVC pipe (see *pages 108–109*).

First, the pipe must be supported both below and above the area to be removed. At least one new pipe clamp must be installed. It may be necessary to build a wooden frame and attach the clamp to it.

Once the pipe is cut, a section of PVC pipe is attached at both ends to the cast-iron pipe using neoprene sleeves. After the installation is complete, you may or may not be able to remove the new clamp, depending on the situation.

REPAIRS TO PLASTIC PIPE

White PVC pipe is the current material of choice for most drain lines. Existing black ABS pipe can be replaced with PVC. If you use a transition fitting, you can connect PVC to galvanized drainpipe. Special fittings also allow you to attach PVC to cast-iron pipe.

Using PVC for supply lines is not allowed by many building codes; check with your local building inspector before using it. CPVC is approved for many outdoor uses, such as lawn sprinkler systems.

Plastic pipe is easy to assemble, but take care to do it right. Joints must be primed and glued completely or they may leak. If you install a fitting that makes a turn, such as a tee or an elbow, use alignment marks to ensure the fitting faces the right way. There is no correcting mistakes—if a glued joint points in the wrong direction, you must cut out the error and start over. PVC pipe is inexpensive, so before you tackle the real thing, practice cutting and gluing pieces until you feel proficient.

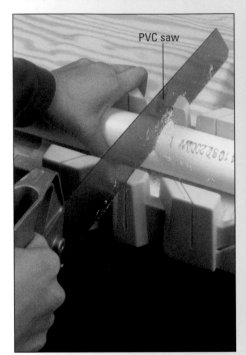

1 Cut PVC pipe using a PVC saw, a hacksaw, or most any saw with fine teeth. A miter box helps hold the pipe to make perpendicular cuts.

2 Scrape the inside and outside of the sawed edge with a utility knife to remove burrs.

PRESTART CHECKLIST

☐ **TIME**
About an hour to make a simple repair

☐ **TOOLS**
PVC saw and miter box, utility knife, tape measure, felt-tipped pen

☐ **SKILLS**
Measuring, cutting PVC

☐ **PREP**
Spread a drop cloth to catch any spilled primer and glue

☐ **MATERIALS**
PVC pipe and fittings, primer, cement

SAFETY FIRST
Beware of fumes

PVC primer and cement are flammable and give off unpleasant and dangerous fumes. Keep flames and sparks away and open a window to provide ventilation. Cap the cans when they are not in use. Tighten the caps firmly when done.

Also be sure to use the correct primer and cement for your type of plastic pipe. PVC and CPVC use different products. The wrong primer and cement can ruin the installation.

WHAT IF...
Flexible plastic is used for a repair?

Compression/threaded coupling

Compression coupling

Flexible PEX supply pipe is approved in some areas. The pipe's flexibility makes it easy to turn corners. Fittings attach with compression joints, so no gluing is needed and mistakes can be easily corrected. However these fittings cannot be hidden behind a wall surface.

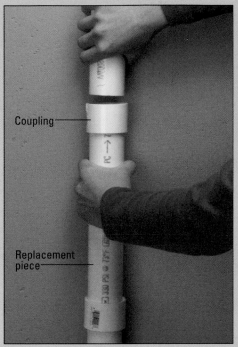

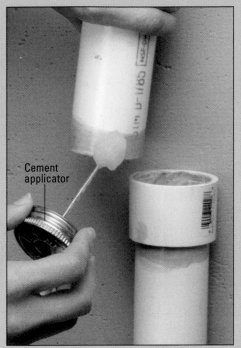

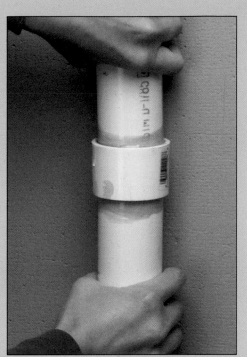

3 Assemble the pieces in a dry run to make sure everything fits. Disassemble the pieces, keeping track of the order in which they will be reassembled.

4 Apply primer to the pipe ends and to the insides of the fittings. The strip of primer on the pipe should be wide enough so that some can still be seen after the fitting is attached. Apply cement to the outside of the pipe, then to the inside of the coupling.

5 Immediately insert the pipe into the fitting and give it a slight twist. Some cement should ooze around the joint. Hold the joint for about 20 seconds, then wipe away any excess cement. Wait at least 30 minutes before running drain water through the pipes.

STANLEY PRO TIP: **Repair to a supply pipe**

Cut PVC or CPVC supply pipe with the scissors-like PVC pipe cutter. Deburr, make a dry run, apply primer, and glue pieces together just as you would for drainpipe (Steps 2 to 5 above).

Because water pressure is greater in a supply pipe than a drainpipe, wait several hours for the cement to fully cure before you run water through the pipes.

A similar tool can be used to neatly cut flexible pipe and tubing.

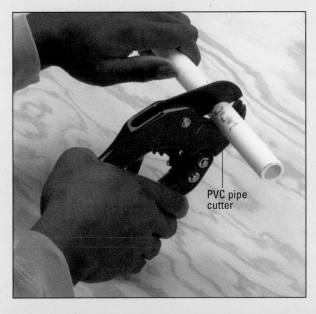

PVC pipe cutter

Adding a tee fitting for a new line

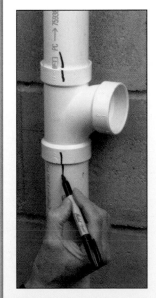

To add a new drain line, cut the pipe and install a tee fitting. Use alignment marks to make sure the tee is facing the right way. Once the tee is installed, assemble the lengths of pipe and fittings needed to reach the new location.

LEAKS AT STOP VALVES AND SUPPLY TUBES

If water is dripping onto the floor of a cabinet below a sink, leaky supply pipes may be the cause. More likely, however, a stop valve or supply-tube connection is the culprit.

To find the source of a leak, shine a bright flashlight into the cabinet and feel the pipes and tubes, stopping to dry your hand every so often. You can also dry the area, place dry newspaper under the suspect plumbing, and watch for spots of water.

A solid chrome-plated copper supply tube looks and feels more stable than a flexible braided tube. But the solid tube is actually more likely to develop a leak because it is inflexible. When bumped, a braided tube is less likely to be damaged. Still, many people prefer the appearance of a solid tube.

PRESTART CHECKLIST

☐ **TIME**
Less than an hour to tighten nuts or install a new supply tube

☐ **TOOLS**
Adjustable wrench, groove-joint pliers, basin wrench, tubing cutter, tubing bender

☐ **SKILLS**
Measuring and cutting a tube, connecting a compression fitting

☐ **PREP**
Place a bucket or towel below the leaking plumbing; make the area comfortable for working

☐ **MATERIALS**
Solid or braided supply tube

Tightening stop valve connections

Adjustable wrench

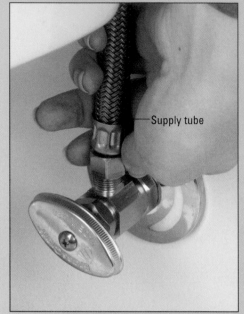

Supply tube

1 If water leaks at the stop-valve spout, use an adjustable wrench to tighten the nut that connects the supply tube to the valve. (If the valve moves, brace it with another wrench.) If water leaks from where the supply tube enters the faucet, tighten the nut with a basin wrench.

2 If that doesn't solve the problem, **shut off the water** at the stop valve. Unscrew the nuts at either end and remove the supply tube. Replace with a flexible braided tube or install a new solid supply tube *(page 123)*.

Stop-valve quality

An inexpensive stop valve (bottom) has plastic inner parts, making it more likely to break down. Its inner parts must be removed before sweating. The more substantial unit (top) has all-metal inner parts that are long-lasting and don't need to be removed before sweating.

A stop valve has a stem much like that in a compression faucet. The packing washer and stem washer can be replaced, but it's easier to simply replace the entire valve.

Replacing a solid supply tube

1 Bend a chrome-plated copper or plain copper supply tube carefully by hand or use a tubing bender *(page 20)*.

2 Insert one end of the tube into the faucet inlet above, hold the other end near the stop valve, and mark it for a cut. Make the cut with a tubing cutter. (See *page 116* for how to use a tubing cutter).

3 At the upper end, slip on the mounting nut and a ferrule. Poke the tube into the faucet inlet, slide the ferrule up to the inlet, and tighten the nut. Slip a nut and ferrule onto the lower end of the tube and attach to the stop valve in the same way.

STANLEY PRO TIP

Buy the right supply tube

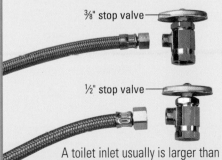

A toilet inlet usually is larger than a faucet inlet. When buying a braided tube, check whether it is made for a toilet or for a faucet.

Stop valves have spouts that are either ½ inch or ⅜ inch in diameter. Be sure to buy a tube made to fit your valve.

A common mistake is to buy a supply tube that is too short. Play it safe and buy a tube that's longer than you think you need.

WHAT IF...
You use a plastic supply tube?

A plastic supply tube seals using a ball-shaped end held firmly by a nylon nut. Some have a rubber ferrule as well.

Kink-proof solid supply tubes

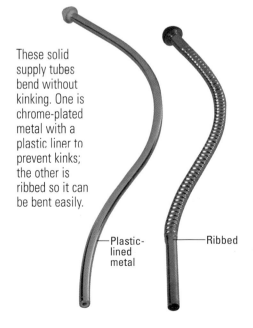

These solid supply tubes bend without kinking. One is chrome-plated metal with a plastic liner to prevent kinks; the other is ribbed so it can be bent easily.

INSTALLING A STOP VALVE ON COPPER PIPE

Every faucet and toilet in a home should have its own stop valve so you can easily make repairs. Installing one is usually not difficult, though you may find yourself working in cramped quarters.

Take care to buy the correct valve. Its inlet must accommodate the size of pipe coming from the wall (usually ½-inch but sometimes ¾- or ⅜-inch). Its threaded spout must match the size of the supply tube—either ½- or ⅜-inch. You can install either a compression or a sweatable valve.

If the pipes are plastic, simply cut with a close-work hacksaw and cement the valve in place (pages 120–121).

To shut off the water where there is no existing stop valve, see page 8. Some water will remain in the pipes and tubes after water has stopped flowing out the faucet, so place a bucket and towel underneath.

PRESTART CHECKLIST

☐ TIME
One or two hours to install a new stop valve in copper pipe

☐ TOOLS
Close-work hacksaw, two adjustable wrenches, propane torch

☐ SKILLS
Cutting and joining copper pipe

☐ PREP
Shut off the water; drain the line; place a bucket or towel below the pipe to be cut to catch debris

☐ MATERIALS
New compression or sweatable stop valve, flux, solder, possibly a new supply tube

Close-work hacksaw

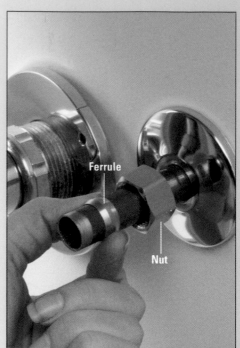

Ferrule

Nut

1 **Shut off the water** to the line and drain the line by turning on a faucet at a lower location. If there is room, cut the copper pipe using a tubing cutter. Otherwise cut slowly and gently with a close-work hacksaw, as shown.

2 Sand the outside of the cut pipe with a combination wire brush, emery cloth, or sandpaper until it is shiny. Slide a nut and ferrule onto the pipe.

STANLEY PRO TIP

Use two wrenches

Adjustable wrench

Slide the stop valve all the way onto the pipe. Hold the valve with one adjustable wrench while you tighten the nut with the other.

STANLEY PRO TIP

Remove stem before soldering

Valve stem

A shutoff valve may have rubber washers and O-rings, or other parts that can be damaged by heat. Before sweating a valve, remove all the inner parts.

It will take more time to heat up a brass valve than it takes to heat a copper fitting, so have patience. Apply solder as you would for a fitting (pages 98–99).

Allow the fitting to cool before replacing the inner parts.

INSTALLING A STOP VALVE ON STEEL PIPE

If an old galvanized pipe comes out from the wall, installing a shutoff valve is usually a straightforward job; simply screw a threaded stop valve onto the pipe.

If possible, unscrew the supply tube at the bottom only, so it remains attached to the faucet or toilet above. If this is not possible, you may have to cut through the supply tube with a hacksaw and replace the tube after installing the valve.

Unscrew the parts up to the nipple that sticks out of the wall. Look into the pipe with a flashlight. If it is partially filled with mineral deposits, replacing it will increase the faucet's (or toilet's) water pressure.

To shut off the water where there is no existing stop valve, see *page 8*. Some water will remain in the pipes and tubes after water has stopped flowing out the faucet, so you might want to place a bucket or a thick towel underneath.

PRESTART CHECKLIST

☐ **TIME**
One or two hours to install a new stop valve in galvanized-steel pipe

☐ **TOOLS**
Two pipe wrenches, adjustable wrench, or groove-joint pliers

☐ **SKILLS**
Cutting and joining steel pipe

☐ **PREP**
Shut off the water; drain the line; place a bucket or towel below the pipe to be cut to catch debris

☐ **MATERIALS**
New threaded stop valve for your size of pipe, pipe-thread tape, possibly a pipe nipple

1 **Shut off the water** and drain the line by turning on a faucet at a lower location. Hold the steel pipe still with one pipe wrench while you remove the elbow with another wrench. If you can't budge the elbow, slip a length of 1¼-inch steel pipe on the wrench handle for more leverage.

Pipe wrench

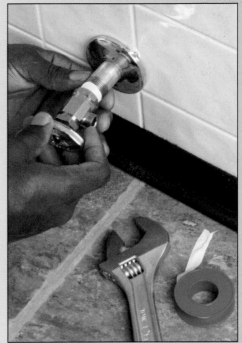

2 Clean the pipe threads and wrap pipe-thread tape clockwise around the threads several times. Screw the stop valve onto the pipe and tighten with an adjustable wrench. (Don't crank hard with a pipe wrench or the valve might crack.)

REFRESHER COURSE
Working with steel pipe

Measure to find the pipe lengths you need; be sure to take into account the distance the pipes will travel inside fittings and valves.

Wrap each pipe end with several windings of pipe-thread tape and use a pipe wrench to firmly tighten each pipe and fitting in order. Tighten with a tool no smaller than a 14-inch pipe wrench; a smaller tool may not have enough power.

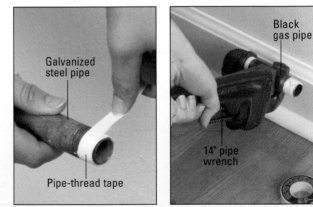

Galvanized steel pipe

Pipe-thread tape

Black gas pipe

14" pipe wrench

Match supply tubes with stop valves.
Stop valves have spouts that are either ½-inch or ⅜-inch diameter. Buy supply tubes to fit the valves and faucet connection.

REPLACING A VALVE

A plumbing system should have a main shutoff valve that controls water to the whole house and intermediate shutoff valves that control water for various areas of the house. There also should be shutoff valves on the incoming cold supply line for a water heater and stop valves (also called fixture shutoffs) that control water leading to individual faucets and appliances.

If an old shutoff valve—usually a gate or globe type—leaks at the packing nut, make sure it's all the way open or closed. If it still leaks, try tightening the packing nut with pliers or an adjustable wrench. (Don't crank down too hard, or you could crack the nut.) If it still leaks, or if it fails to completely shut water off, follow the steps at right to repair or replace it.

Stop valves are often cheaply made and may fail to shut water off completely or may leak from the packing nut. Replace a faulty stop valve with a ball-type model, which costs a little more but is very reliable.

A globe valve inhibits water flow even if it is in good working order. Replacing it with a ball valve may increase water pressure.

PRESTART CHECKLIST

☐ **TIME**
An hour or two to repair or replace a shutoff valve

☐ **TOOLS**
Groove-joint pliers, pipe wrenches, screwdriver, torch, wire brush

☐ **SKILLS**
Working with supply pipe

☐ **PREP**
Shut off water upstream from the valve

☐ **MATERIALS**
Repair parts or a new valve, pipe-thread tape, flux and solder

Servicing an old valve

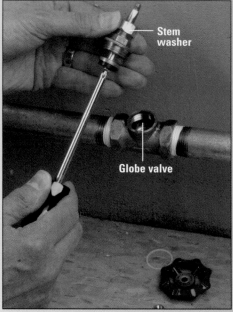

If water leaks from the packing nut of a gate valve, replace the packing washer or the string packing. If the valve does not shut water off completely, try removing the gate and cleaning out any debris in the valve body. If that does not solve the problem, replace the valve.

If water leaks out the packing nut of a globe valve, replace the packing washer or string packing. If the valve fails to shut off water completely, replace the stem washer with an exact replacement. If that does not solve the problem, replace the valve.

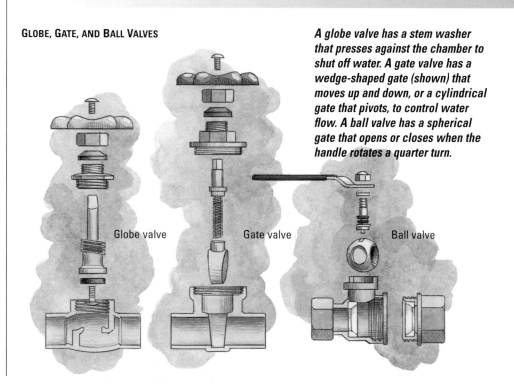

GLOBE, GATE, AND BALL VALVES

A globe valve has a stem washer that presses against the chamber to shut off water. A gate valve has a wedge-shaped gate (shown) that moves up and down, or a cylindrical gate that pivots, to control water flow. A ball valve has a spherical gate that opens or closes when the handle rotates a quarter turn.

Globe valve   Gate valve   Ball valve

Installing a new valve

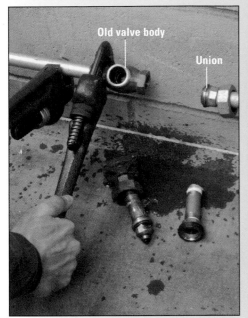

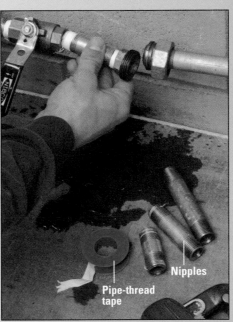

1 If possible, open a nearby union and disassemble a few pipes to get to the existing valve. If not, follow the steps on *pages 106-107* for breaking into steel pipe. If the supply pipes are copper, see *pages 98-99*.

2 The new valve will be about the same size as the old one, so you shouldn't have to change any pipe lengths. (Otherwise have on hand a selection of nipples.) Wrap all threaded pipe ends with several windings of pipe-thread tape and assemble the parts.

3 Tighten the pipes and fittings as you go using two 14-inch pipe wrenches. Finish by assembling and tightening a union. Test for leaks.

Installing a gas shutoff valve

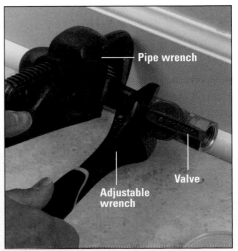

1 A house shutoff is usually located on the gas meter. To shut off gas to the entire house, turn the valve slowly a quarter-turn with a pipe wrench. To make sure no one turns the gas back on, padlock the valve.

2 **Open a window to vent any residual gas. Ignite no flames.** Using two pipe wrenches (Step 3, **above**) to avoid straining any of the pipe joints, remove the cap or old valve. Apply gas-rated pipe-thread tape clockwise.

3 Screw the valve onto the pipe. Gripping the gas pipe with a pipe wrench, use an adjustable wrench to tighten the valve in place. Turn the gas on at the house shutoff. Test your work using liquid soap or test fluid *(page 107)*.

THAWING PIPES AND WINTERIZING

Pipes that are not sufficiently insulated may freeze during cold weather. The result could be a minor inconvenience—the pipes may be undamaged and the water will flow again when they thaw out. Or it could be a major catastrophe in the form of a burst pipe. Take steps now rather than later to protect them.

Exposed pipes are easily insulated or heated. If the pipes are inside a wall, the job may be difficult. If the exterior wall is the inside wall of an attached garage, consider attaching solid foam insulation on the garage side of the entire wall. Otherwise you'll have to remove the exterior or interior wall covering (whichever is easier), insulate the pipes, and then reinstall the wall covering.

If the weather forecast calls for extreme cold and you fear that a pipe may freeze, open a faucet or two on the line just a crack, so water comes out in a little more than a drip. Moving water freezes more slowly than still water.

PRESTART CHECKLIST

☐ **TIME**
An hour or two to protect exposed pipes; much more time to protect pipes behind walls

☐ **TOOLS**
Portable heater, hair dryer, or heat gun; carpentry tools if you need to get at hidden pipes; caulking gun

☐ **SKILLS**
Identifying and locating the pipes that need to be protected

☐ **PREP**
Check the history of freezing pipes in your home; locate the vulnerable ones

☐ **MATERIALS**
Insulation (various types), caulk, electric pipe-heating tape

Insulate vulnerable pipes: Wrap exposed pipes with sections of foam insulation *(page 118)* or fill the surrounding area with fiberglass batts, loose-fill cellulose, or spray foam (shown). Leave part of the pipe exposed to warm, interior air.

Install heat tape: Newer types of electric pipe-heating tape are easy to install and turn themselves on only when needed. Wrap the tape around the pipe and plug the unit into a reliable electrical receptacle. Follow the manufacturer's instructions. Never overlap electric heat tape.

WHAT IF...
Your pipes freeze?

When water stops flowing during cold weather, you know that at least one pipe has frozen. (If only the hot water flows, you know the cold-water pipe has frozen.) A frozen pipe may or may not crack; you'll find out only after the water thaws. Just in case, watch the pipes continually and **be prepared to** **shut off the water.** Have pipe repair materials on hand. If a pipe is exposed, thaw it by pointing a hair dryer or heat gun at it (left). (Don't get too close with the heat gun, and watch carefully for any drip or spray of water.) If the pipe is hidden in a wall, aim a portable heater at the area (right).

WINTERIZING A CABIN

If a cabin will be left unheated during the winter, take steps to prevent pipe damage due to freezing water. In addition to the steps shown, turn off the main shutoff valve and open a pipe nearby to let water drain out. Drain all water-using appliances, such as the dishwasher and clothes washer. If the cabin has hot-water heat, drain the heating system. Some cabins have small drain valves on the pipes; open them.

At the electrical service panel, shut off power to an electric water heater.

If the water heater is gas, shut off the gas that runs to it.

Even after draining the system, water will remain in traps. Pour about 3 cups of full-strength antifreeze into every toilet bowl.

Pour about a cup of antifreeze into each sink.

After shutting off power or gas, drain the water heater.

Drain hose bib

Pour about 2 cups of antifreeze into every shower and floor drain trap.

Drain each accessible trap before adding antifreeze.

Drain each stop valve.

Drain well pump.

Protect your outdoor hose bib with an indoor shutoff valve

PVC saw

1 Using a PVC saw or scissors-type PVC cutters *(page 121),* cut out a section of pipe. Take into account the fact that the pipes will slide into the valves at each side. Remove burrs from the pipes *(page 120).*

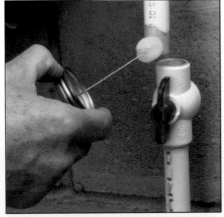

2 Make sure the valve fits. Apply primer outside the pipe and inside the valve. Cement one pipe and one side of the valve. Immediately slip the valve onto the pipe. Give it a slight twist and hold it for 30 seconds. Glue the other side.

Hose bib insulator

When cold weather approaches, disconnect and drain all outdoor hoses. Protect the outdoor faucet (called a hose bib or sill cock) by shutting off the water that runs to it and opening it. To protect it further, strap on a foam insulator like this one. For a long term solution, install an extended sill cock whose valve is indoors, protected from freezing conditions.

SYSTEM REPAIRS & UPGRADES

Home plumbing systems periodically need maintenance and appliance upgrades. These chores are moderately difficult—more involved than "easy installs" but not as complicated as a bathroom or kitchen renovation. Some projects may call for running short lengths of new supply pipe or gas pipe but no elaborate drain-waste-vent installations.

Some building inspectors will want you to obtain a permit for any installation, no matter how small. Others don't want to conduct inspections unless an installation requires running new pipes. To be safe consult with your local building department before tackling any of the projects described in this chapter.

An inspector may provide valuable advice for some of the more complicated connections, such as connecting water, gas, or electric lines to a water heater *(pages 132–135)* or solving water pressure problems *(pages 140–141)*.

Other sources of advice and help

If you have a gas water heater, call the gas company to check for gas leaks and carbon monoxide (which can build up dangerously if the flue is not installed correctly). They may perform these checks for free.

If your main drain line is clogged, have the city inspect its portion of the drain line; again, this should be free.

If you have an old home or if your plumbing is too complicated for you to understand, do not hesitate to call a plumber. Their hourly rates may be expensive, but pros can perform some tasks so quickly that it may be well worth the money to hire them.

These maintenance and upgrade projects are straightforward and can be done in a weekend.

CHAPTER PREVIEW

Repairing a gas water heater
page 132

Repairing an electric water heater
page 134

Replacing a water heater
page 136

Increasing water pressure
page 140

Shut off water before draining

Pressure-relief valve

SAFETY FIRST
Shut down water heater before draining

Always turn off the water heater before draining. With an electric water heater (shown), shut off electric power at the service panel *(page 134)*. With a gas unit, shut off gas at the burner control unit *(page 132)*.

If water in your area is mineral-laden, draining the water heater once a year will prolong its life. Shut off the water and the gas or electricity before draining. Once the water has drained, close the drain valve, turn on the water, and wait for the unit to fill before restoring gas or electric power.

Use a hose to run water to a floor drain or use a bucket, shutting off the drain valve with each filling.

Drain valve

Installing a water filter
page 142

Installing an on-demand water heater
page 144

Repairs to old radiators
page 146

Installing convectors
page 148

REPAIRING A GAS WATER HEATER

Most repairs to a gas water heater are made at the burner control. If your heater leaks, the tank is rusted through and the entire unit must be replaced *(pages 136–138)*. Here's a quick troubleshooting guide to gas water heater problems:

■ If the unit suddenly stops heating water, try relighting the pilot. If it does not stay lit, the thermocouple probably needs to be replaced (right). If that does not solve the problem, you may need to clean the burner.

■ If the flame is mostly yellow rather than mostly blue, clean the burner.

■ If water isn't heating sufficiently even though the thermostat is turned up and the flames are blue, drain the tank and refill it *(page 131)*.

■ If you have hard water, unscrew and remove the anode rod once a year. Look for a 1-inch nut in the top of the heater. Loosen the nut; the anode rod will be attached. If it's encrusted with minerals, replace it to get more efficient operation.

PRESTART CHECKLIST

□ **TIME**
About an hour to replace a thermocouple; two to three hours to service a burner

□ **TOOLS**
Long matches or a barbecue lighter, screwdriver, adjustable wrench, groove-joint pliers, thin wire, soft metal brush

□ **SKILLS**
No special skills are needed.

□ **PREP**
Clear the area; you may need to shut off the gas

□ **MATERIALS**
New thermocouple of the correct length, new pressure-relief valve

A. Replacing a thermocouple

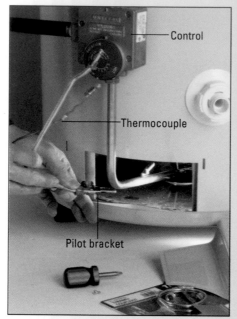

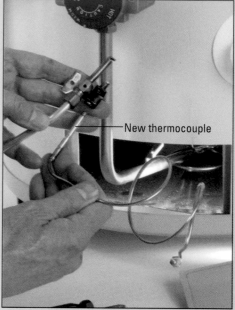

1 If a pilot light won't stay lit after you've followed the lighting directions, **turn the gas-control knob to OFF.** It's often easiest to detach the thermocouple and pilot supply tube at the control and, using a stubby screwdriver, disconnect them from the burner. Pull out the thermocouple.

2 Purchase a thermocouple the same length as the old one. Unroll it carefully to avoid kinking. Insert the tip into the pilot bracket so the pilot flame will heat it. Reinstall the thermocouple and the supply tube and attach them at the control. Turn the gas back on and light the pilot.

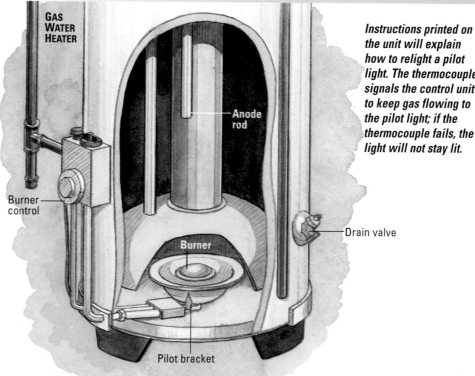

Instructions printed on the unit will explain how to relight a pilot light. The thermocouple signals the control unit to keep gas flowing to the pilot light; if the thermocouple fails, the light will not stay lit.

B. Servicing a burner

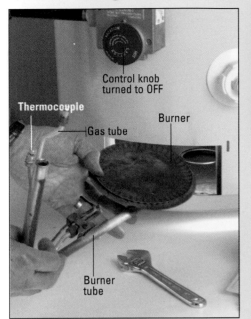

Control knob
turned to OFF

Thermocouple

Gas tube

Burner

Burner
tube

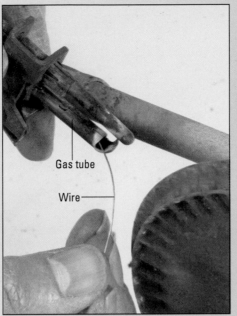

Gas tube

Wire

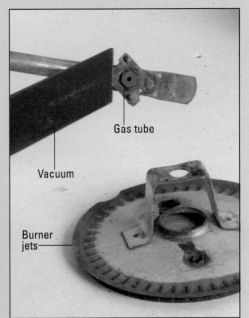

Gas tube

Vacuum

Burner
jets

1 If flames are yellow or erratic, remove and clean the burner. **Turn the gas control knob to OFF.** Unscrew and pull the gas tube, burner tube, and thermocouple from the control. Reach inside the chamber and pull the burner unit out or down until it unclips. Carefully pull the unit out.

2 Unscrew the burner unit from the gas tube. Clean the pilot gas tube with a soft wire brush or poke a thin wire down into its hole.

3 Turn the burner upside down and shake out any debris. Vacuum the jets to remove all dust. Use a thin wire to make sure the opening in the gas tube is clear and vacuum out any debris. Reassemble, reinstall, and relight. If the burner still malfunctions, call for service.

SAFETY FIRST
Check the flue

The flue on a gas water heater should pull all fumes up and send them out of the house. To check that a flue is working, light a match, blow it out, and hold it near the flue. Smoke should be sucked up into the flue. If it isn't, check that all the connections are tight. Have the gas company inspect to be sure.

Maintaining a gas water heater

Keep your heater alive longer by following these tips:

■ In areas with hard water, a gas water heater will last no more than 10 years. If you drain the unit once a year (see *page 131)*, you will not only lengthen the unit's life but also increase its efficiency.

■ The higher a thermostat is set, the shorter the life of the water heater. Set the temperature to just as hot as you want and no higher.

■ A damaged or incorrectly installed flue will lead to elevated levels of carbon-monoxide. Install a carbon-monoxide detector near (or directly above) the water heater to warn of this dangerous gas.

■ New water heaters are well insulated, but an older unit will benefit from a slip-over insulation blanket made specifically for water heaters.

Pressure-relief valve

A temperature-and-pressure-relief valve is a safety device that provides an outlet for water in case the unit overheats. To test that it's working, pull up on the little lever; water should flow out. If not, or if water drips from the valve, install a replacement.

REPAIRING AN ELECTRIC WATER HEATER

Most repairs to an electric water heater are made at the two elements, each of which has a thermostat. If water leaks onto the floor, the tank is rusted through, and the entire unit must be replaced *(pages 136–139).*

■ If water is not hot enough, try turning up the thermostat settings for both elements.

■ If the unit suddenly stops heating water, press the reset button, usually located on the high-limit cutoff. If you hear a click, the unit is reset and the problem may be solved. Also check that power is reaching the unit; call in an electrician if you are not sure.

■ If water gets warm but not hot, replace the upper element and/or thermostat.

■ If water gets hot, but the hot water runs out quicker than it used to, replace the lower element and/or thermostat.

■ If the unit is noisy, drain the tank and refill it. If that does not solve the problem, remove and clean the elements.

■ If water is too hot even with the thermostats turned down, replace either the thermostat or the high-limit cutoff.

PRESTART CHECKLIST

☐ **TIME**
An hour or two for most repairs

☐ **TOOLS**
Voltage tester, groove-joint pliers, screwdriver

☐ **SKILLS**
Testing for electrical power, unscrewing and replacing devices

☐ **PREP**
Prepare the household for doing without hot water for a few hours; arrange for a work light while the power is off

☐ **MATERIALS**
New element, thermostat, or high-limit cutoff for your make and model of water heater

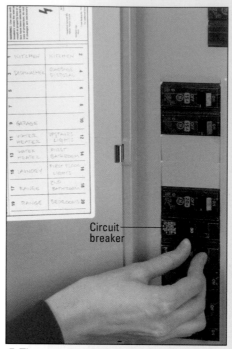

Circuit breaker

1 The amount of power an electric water heater uses is dangerous. Check with an electrician if you are unsure about shutting off power. At the service panel, **shut off the breaker or unscrew the fuse controlling the water heater. Be sure no one will turn power on while you work.**

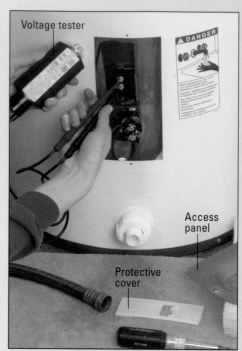

Voltage tester

Access panel

Protective cover

2 Close the water shutoff valve above the tank. Drain the tank *(page 131).* Remove the access panel and the protective cover. Press the two prongs of a voltage tester against the terminal screws that the wires are connected to; test all possible combinations. Be certain that power is off.

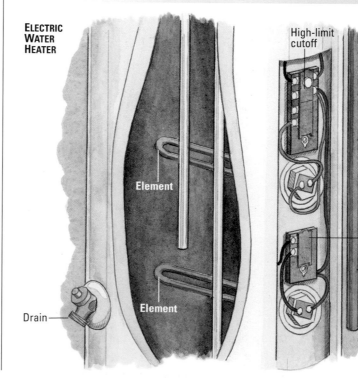

ELECTRIC WATER HEATER

Element

Element

Drain

High-limit cutoff

Thermostat

Pressure-relief tube

Most electric water heaters have two heating elements, each with its own thermostat. The upper element also has a high-limit cutoff to keep water from getting too hot.

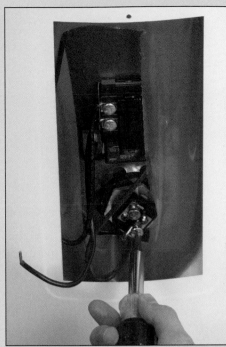

Element

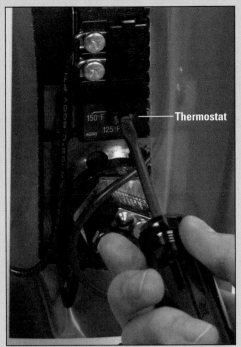

Thermostat

3 Loosen the element's terminal screws and pull the wires away. You don't need to mark the wires—they can be attached to either terminal.

4 Use groove-joint pliers to loosen and unscrew the element. Pull out the element. Have an appliance parts dealer test the element and buy a duplicate if it's defective. If the element is working, try replacing the thermostat.

5 Scrape away any debris from around the opening, then clean it with a rag. Screw in the new element, replace the wires, replace the cover, and refill the tank. Set the thermostat (see below), restore power, and test.

WHAT IF ...
A high-limit cutoff is defective?

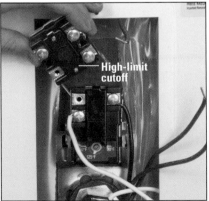

High-limit cutoff

If water overheats or if the unit does not heat water, and other solutions do not solve the problem, remove the high-limit cutoff from the upper element and take it in for testing. Replace it if necessary.

Replacing the thermostat

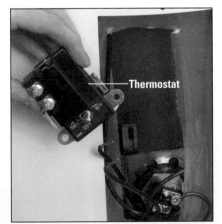

Thermostat

To remove a thermostat, shut off power and test that power is off. Disconnect and tag the wires. Remove any mounting nuts or screws. Pry out the thermostat. Have the thermostat tested; replace it if necessary.

Resetting and adjusting a thermostat

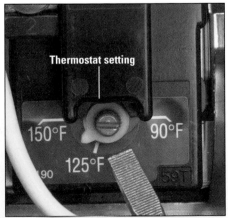

Thermostat setting

150°F 125°F 90°F

A water heater is commonly set to 120°F. If water seems too hot or too cold, adjust the temperature up or down by about 10 degrees. After a day of use, you may want to adjust it another 10 degrees.

REPLACING A WATER HEATER

This job may seem complicated, but it's actually straightforward. If the new unit is the same size as the old one and has connections located in the same places, hooking up the water, the gas, and the flue will be simple. If you need to move any of those lines, the job will take a few more hours to complete.

There should be a shutoff valve for the cold water pipe that enters the water heater (do not add one to the exiting hot water line), and for the gas line as well. If any valves are lacking, install them when you install the new water heater.

If you live in an area that experiences earthquakes, local codes may require that you chain or strap the water heater firmly to a wall.

Arrange for disposal of the old water heater. Your local waste hauler may have special requirements.

PRESTART CHECKLIST

☐ **TIME**
About a day for most installations

☐ **TOOLS**
Groove-joint pliers, screwdriver, pipe wrenches, adjustable wrench, tools for cutting and joining steel and/or copper pipe, two-wheeled cart, torpedo level, hammer

☐ **SKILLS**
Assembling supply pipe and gas pipe, maneuvering and leveling a large appliance, working with a flue

☐ **PREP**
Clear a path for removing the old unit; prepare the household to be without hot water for a day; check local codes

☐ **MATERIALS**
New gas water heater, shims, gas pipe or flexible connector, water pipe and/or flexible connector, heat trap nipples, pipe-thread tape, flue extension (optional), pressure-relief valve

Installing a gas water heater

1 Turn off the gas shutoff valve (so the handle is perpendicular to the pipe). **Shut off water** and allow the tank to cool. Drain the tank *(page 131)*. If there is a gas pipe union, use two pipe wrenches to disconnect it. If there is a flexible connector *(page 138)*, disconnect it.

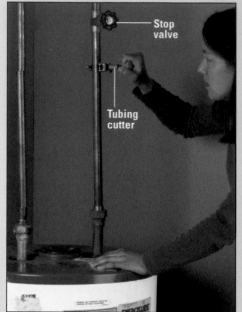

2 Disconnect the water lines. If there is no flexible connector or union to disconnect, you may have to cut through a solid copper pipe. Use a tubing cutter to make a clean cut so you can connect the new line to it.

3 Once the flue has cooled, detach it from the water heater. Tie the flue up to keep it out of the way. With a two-wheeled cart, remove the old unit. Mineral deposits make it heavier than a new unit.

4 Carry or wheel in the new water heater. Position it so the water, gas, and flue connections are as easy to reach as possible. Use a level to check the unit for plumb and shim the legs if necessary.

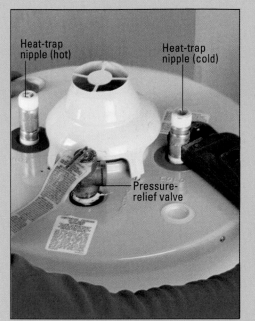

5 Install heat-trap nipples to the water heater inlets. Install the blue nipple, its arrow pointing down, to the cold water inlet. Install the red nipple, its arrow pointing up, to the hot-water inlet. Tighten both with a pipe wrench. Run PVC from the pressure-relief valve to a floor drain *(page 139)*.

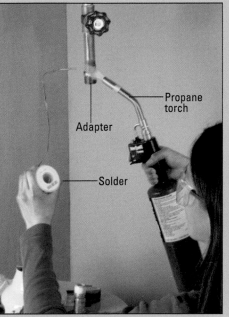

6 Before hooking up the supply lines, you may need to install an adapter. For a copper pipe that has been cut, sweat a male adapter to each pipe.

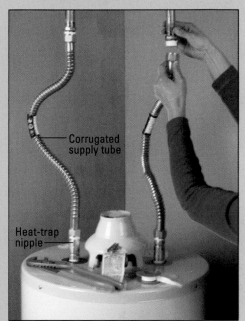

7 Connect the water supply tubes to the heat-trap nipples. Buy connectors approved by local codes, checking that they fit at both ends. If necessary, use reducer fittings to make the transition.

Flexible water connectors

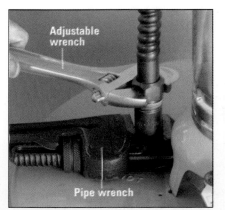

If flexible water lines attach to the old water heater, simply unscrew the nuts with an adjustable wrench to disconnect. Check that the old fittings will work with the new; you may need to buy new lines or a male or female adapter. Check local codes.

Choosing a water heater

Different water heaters serve different needs. When shopping for a new unit consider the following:

■ Check the energy guide sticker on a water heater and choose one that's well insulated. Though it may cost a bit more, it will save money in the long run.

■ If family members complain that water runs out during showers, consider buying a unit with an additional 10 gallons of capacity. It may take more time to install and will use a little more energy.

■ Check the "rate of recovery"—how quickly the unit heats water. A water heater with a quick rate of recovery may solve the problem of running out of hot water.

■ If you have hard water, consider a unit with two anode rods, which attract sediment. Regularly cleaning the rods can add years to the life of a water heater.

Buy connectors approved by local codes

Choosing connectors

Local codes may have specific requirements for the type of pipe or connectors to be used when hooking up a water heater.

Unlike a range, a water heater usually is not moved during its life. However, it may vibrate while in use. Some building departments prefer flexible connectors, while others prefer hard piping—both for the water supplies and for the gas line. Always follow local codes.

If there is no floor drain nearby, you may want to place a drain pan under the water heater to catch water in case of a small leak.

Installing a gas water heater *(continued)*

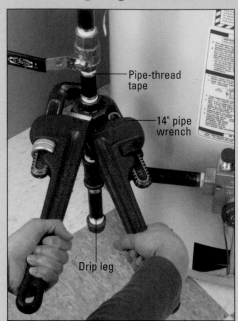

Pipe-thread tape

14" pipe wrench

Drip leg

8 Connect the gas line. A hard-piped gas line should have a drip leg to collect condensation and dirt that can hinder the burner's efficiency. Wrap the pipe threads with yellow pipe-thread tape (made for gas lines). Tighten connections securely using two pipe wrenches (see *page 107).*

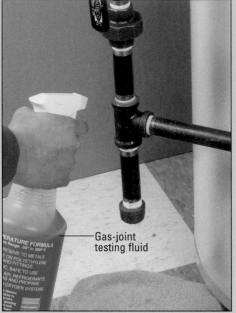

Gas-joint testing fluid

9 Do not light the pilot until you are sure there are no leaks. Turn on the gas. Test for leaks by spraying with gas-joint testing fluid (shown) or by pouring a strong soap-and-water mixture on each joint. Bubbles indicate a leak. Tighten leaky fittings. Recheck, if necessary.

Reset button

10 Follow the manufacturer's instructions for lighting the pilot. Usually this involves lighting the pilot while holding down the reset button and continuing to hold it for a full minute before releasing and turning on the burner.

CONNECT THE GAS LINE
Use a flexible connector

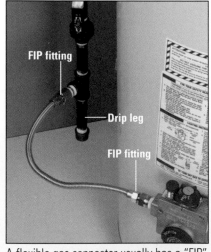

FIP fitting

Drip leg

FIP fitting

A flexible gas connector usually has a "FIP" fitting at each end. For the best burner performance, install a drip leg as shown.

Attaching a flue

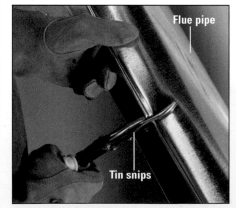

Flue pipe

Tin snips

1 If the new heater is the same height as the old water heater, you can simply hook up the flue in the same way. If you need to add piping, measure and cut pieces to fit with a pair of tin snips.

Sheet-metal screw

2 Connect the pieces by driving three or four sheet-metal screws into each joint. Test to make sure the flue draws *(page 133)* and install a carbon-monoxide detector in the room. If you have any doubts about the flue, have the gas company or a plumbing and heating contractor inspect it.

Installing an electric water heater

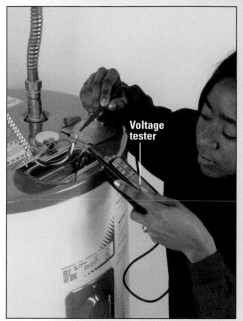

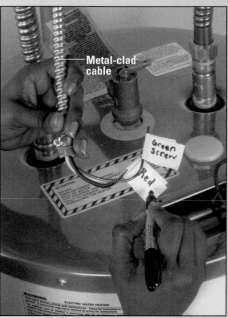

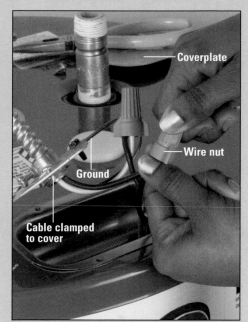

1 To replace an electric water heater, **shut off power** (see *page 134*). Test to make sure power is off. Remove the electrical coverplate and carefully pull out the wires; remove the wire nuts and touch the bare wires with the probes of a voltage tester to make sure there is no power.

2 Once you are sure power is off, loosen the cable clamp screw and pull out the cable, which might be metal-clad (shown), non-metallic cable, or wires running through conduit. Mark the wires for reattaching. Follow steps on *page 136* to disconnect the water lines and remove the old unit.

3 Position the new unit, level it, and shim if needed. Run the electrical cable through the clamp and tighten it. Connect the ground wire to the ground screw. Splice the other wires and screw on wire nuts. Push the wires carefully into the cavity and replace the coverplate.

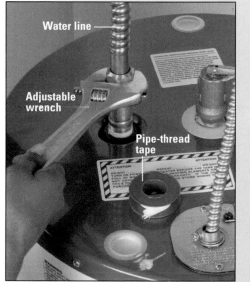

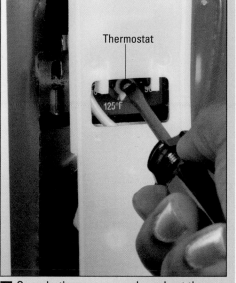

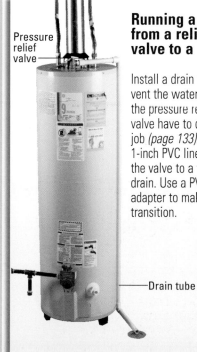

4 Install the water lines (see *page 137*). Open the water shutoff valves and allow the tank to fill. Do not restore power yet.

5 Open both access panels and set the thermostats to the desired settings. Press the reset buttons until they click. Restore power.

Running a line from a relief valve to a drain

Install a drain tube to vent the water should the pressure relief valve have to do its job *(page 133)*. Run a 1-inch PVC line from the valve to a floor drain. Use a PVC adapter to make the transition.

INCREASING WATER PRESSURE

If you have low water pressure, first check that water arrives to your home at 40–100 pounds per square inch (psi). If the incoming pressure is within that range but you have galvanized-steel pipes, sediment or mineral buildup may be the problem. Hot-water pipes are more prone to clogs than cold-water pipes. Horizontal pipes collect more sediment than vertical pipes. However, any galvanized pipe can clog.

The ultimate solution is to replace old plumbing with copper pipes—a time-consuming and expensive job. Here are several simple solutions that are more easily accomplished. The method shown at right is a proven way to clear pipes but can also reveal corroded joints where built-up sediment alone was keeping leaks from happening. **Use compressed air gently.** Clear pipes between a faucet and the water heater, then use the same method to clear pipes from the water heater to the main shutoff. Avoid blasting compressed air through a water heater—you could damage its lining.

PRESTART CHECKLIST

☐ **TIME**
Several hours to assemble the parts and to force out sediment with an air compressor

☐ **TOOLS**
Pipe wrenches, groove-joint pliers, air compressor, hand-crank auger, wire cutters, electrician's fish tape

☐ **SKILLS**
Dismantling and assembling galvanized-steel pipe

☐ **PREP**
Determine which pipes are clogged; map where the pipes run (see *pages 30–31*)

☐ **MATERIALS**
Parts to connect an air compressor to a pipe, pipe-thread tape, pan or bucket

Forcing out sediment with an air compressor

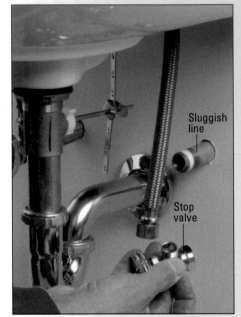

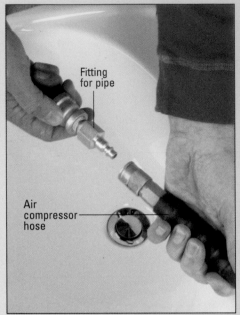

1 Shut off the clogged supply line at a convenient spot on the street side of a union (see Step 3). At the other end of the pipe run to be cleared, disconnect pipes or remove a stop valve.

2 Attach the hose of an air compressor (a model that has a holding tank) to the pipe end. Making this connection requires several fittings; consult with a home center salesperson to assemble them properly.

Clearing aerators and screens

If water flows slowly at one faucet or appliance only, chances are that an aerator or a screen is clogged. At a washing machine, shut off the hose valve and disconnect the hoses from the back of the machine. Pry out the screens located either in the machine's inlets or in the hose ends and clean them.

Use pliers to unscrew an aerator from the end of a faucet spout and clean all the little parts. Replace the aerator if it is damaged.

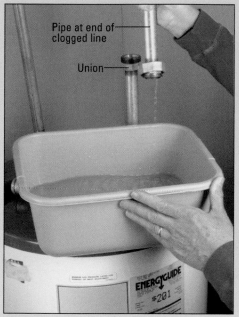

Pipe at end of clogged line

Union

3 While you are at the compressor, have a helper disconnect the union on the house side of the shutoff valve, such as a union near a water heater (shown). Place a pan or bucket under the union. Water contained in the pipes will flow out.

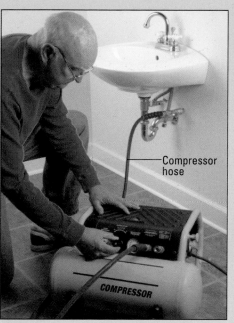

Compressor hose

4 As soon as the union is disconnected, turn on the compressor. Water—along with a good deal of gunk—will gush out the pipe at the other end. Repeat this process once or twice to force out lingering sediment from the pipe.

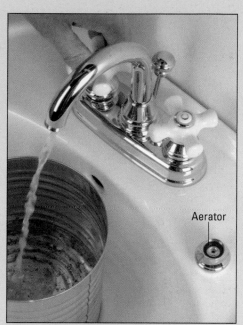

Aerator

5 Reattach the union and the pipe or stop valve to the other end and turn on the water. Remove the aerators from all affected faucets and run water for a minute or two to flush out more sediment.

Augering supply pipes

Wire cutters

1 To ream out a pipe, buy an inexpensive hand-crank auger and cut off its tip with a pair of wire cutters so it can fit into a clogged pipe. The resulting tool will run through straight sections of pipe only. **Shut off the water** and drain the line.

Hand-cranked auger

2 Disassemble the pipe at both ends. Push the auger through, turning the crank if necessary. Pull the auger out and flush the pipe with running water.

STANLEY Pro Tip

Replacing pipes

If water runs slowly throughout the house, replacing a few of the first pipes that enter the house may help substantially. If these pipes are exposed in a basement or crawlspace, replacing them will not be difficult.

Start as near to the street as possible and remove all the pipes—both horizontals and verticals—that you can easily reach. Before installing the new pipes, use a hose to run water backward through the pipes that you did not remove. If you will install copper pipe, connect it to a galvanized pipe with a dielectric union *(page 107)*.

If a single faucet is sluggish, you may be able to remove and replace the short pipe (usually horizontal) to which the stop valve is attached. Often this pipe is clogged, and you'll see significant improvement when you replace it.

Installing a Water Filter

Water from a public utility must meet strict health requirements. If you have reason to think that your water is unsafe (for instance, if it's from a private well), have it tested by a local health department, the utility company, or an extension office of a state university.

Even the safest water may be distasteful and even smelly, and it may produce stains. A filter could be the solution.

If chlorine is the cause of bad taste, a temporary solution is to run water into a pitcher and let it sit in the refrigerator overnight. By morning much of the chlorine will have leached out, often making the water palatable.

When to add a water softener

Hard water—water laden with minerals—can hinder the lathering action of detergent, making it difficult to clean clothes. Hard water may also stain fixtures and ceramic tiles and clog pipes. A water softener uses an ionization process to solve these problems. It also can remove rust from water.

Prestart Checklist

☐ **Time**
An hour or two to install a whole-house filter

☐ **Tools**
Tools for working with copper or galvanized pipe, groove-joint pliers, canister wrench

☐ **Skills**
Working with copper or galvanized supply pipe

☐ **Prep**
Find a convenient location to install the filter so that you can change cartridges easily

☐ **Materials**
Water filter, pipe adapters, shutoff valve, perhaps a jumper wire with clamps

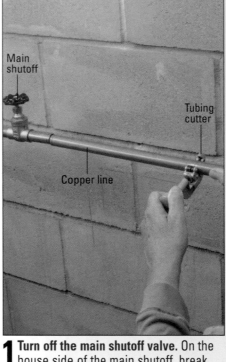

1 **Turn off the main shutoff valve.** On the house side of the main shutoff, break into the supply line. If the pipes are galvanized, find a union or cut with a hacksaw and install a union *(pages 106–107)*. Cut into a copper line using a tubing cutter.

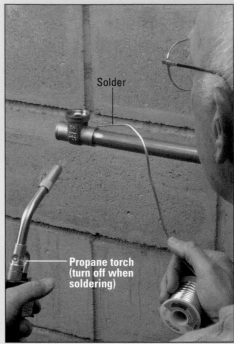

2 Install a ball or gate shutoff valve on the house side of the water filter. Remove the insides of the valve before sweating the valve body in place. (Some plumbers like to install a bypass loop with additional stop valves so water can be rerouted should the entire filter unit need replacing.)

Problem-Solving Filters

A plumbing inspector or local contractor should know which type of filter works best for the water in your area. Here are some qualities of the most popular filter types.

Problem	Solution
Soap does not lather well; soap scum residue on clothes and fixtures	Water softener
Rust stains	Water softener or charcoal filter
Rotten-egg smell due to high sulphur content	Oxidizing filter or a chlorinization feeder system
Chlorine odor and taste	Carbon filter
Water appears cloudy or dirty	Particle filter
Harmful bacteria or chemicals suspected	Reverse-osmosis filter

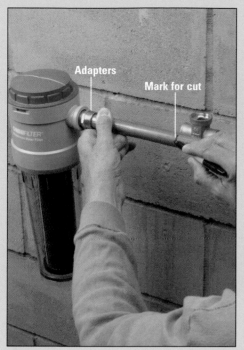

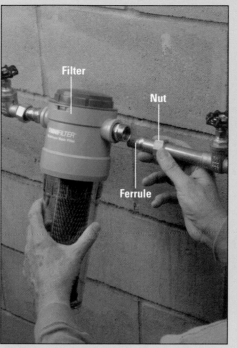

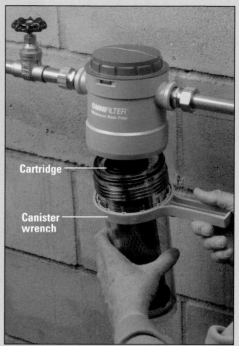

3 Purchase the adapters you need to connect the filter to your size and type of pipe. (These parts may come in a kit, but be sure they fit your pipes.) Install the adapters on either side of the filter. Hold the filter in place and measure for cutting the pipe that emerges from the new shutoff valve.

4 Slide nuts and ferrules onto the pipes on either side. Slip the filter onto the pipes, slide the ferrules and nuts over to the filter, and tighten the nuts.

5 Place a filter cartridge in the canister and twist the canister onto the filter unit. Tighten with a special canister wrench.

SAFETY FIRST
Jumper wire for grounding

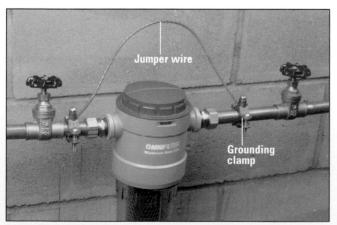

If the electrical system is grounded via the cold-water pipe, adding a water filter will interrupt the path to the ground, leaving all your electricity ungrounded. Install a jumper wire using approved grounding clamps.

Undersink filters

If your main concern is the quality of your drinking water, there's no need to filter all the water entering the house. Install a small filter under the kitchen sink and hook it to the cold water. A unit like this can be installed simply by connecting tubes to the stop valve and to the faucet.

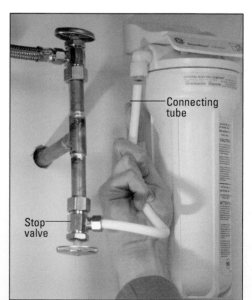

Installing an On-Demand Water Heater

Long popular in Europe, on-demand (or tankless) water heaters are growing in popularity in this country. When a hot-water faucet is opened, the unit fires up, and heats water in seconds.

An on-demand unit is compact, so it can be tucked into a cabinet or closet. It costs more than a standard water heater, but conserves energy, so it typically pays for itself in five years or so. It can usually last twice as long as a standard water heater.

A limitation is that it heats only 3 to 5 gallons per minute, which is plenty for a dishwasher run or a shower, but may not be enough for both at the same time.

This is a major project that calls for running gas lines and supply lines and installing a vent, so you may need to hire a pro. These pages give general installation instructions; manufacturer's literature will present more specific directions. A gas unit is shown; electric units are also available.

Prestart Checklist

☐ **Time**
At least a day to run a gas line, install a vent, and connect plumbing for an on-demand water heater

☐ **Tools**
Drill, screwdriver, groove-joint pliers, tools for running water supply and gas lines, tin snips

☐ **Skills**
Working with supply and gas pipe

☐ **Prep**
Go over your plans with an inspector to make sure the installation will be safe

☐ **Materials**
On-demand water heater, gas pipe and fittings, supply pipe and fittings, vent pipe and fittings

How an On-Demand Water Heater Works

Flue pipe

Flue

Hot water

Heat exchanger

Cold water

Main burner

Draft diverter

Pressure-relief valve

Temperature adjustment

Pressure relief tube

Gas

Hot water

Cold water

Water passes through the heat exchanger, where it is instantly heated by the main burner. Valves automatically turn on and off as needed.

Mounting hook

1 Install the water heater in a code-approved location. Manufacturers' specifications determine acceptable distances between the unit and vent pipes and combustible surfaces. Make sure the room is well ventilated. Mount it using the hardware provided.

Pressure regulator

Gas-rated pipe-thread tape

Union

Drip leg

2 Attach the pressure regulator, which ensures safe flow of gas to the unit. Run an approved gas line *(page 25)*. Use ¾-inch pipe for any runs more than 10 feet; ½-inch pipe can be used for shorter runs. Connect the line to the regulator, turn on the gas, and test for leaks.

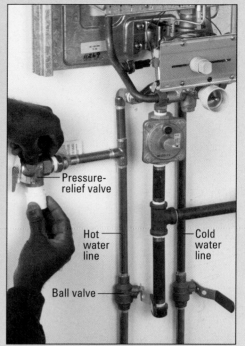

Pressure-relief valve

Hot water line

Cold water line

Ball valve

3 Copper is recommended for the water supply pipe, at least for 3 feet before and after the water heater. Install a pressure-relief valve (some manufacturers provide it) before the ball valve on the outgoing hot water line.

Setting water temperature

When you first use the unit, turn the gas valve switch off and wait for five minutes to clear out any gas (check the manufacturer's specific instructions). If you smell gas, test for leaks. Once you are sure there are no leaks, turn the switch on, and turn on the hot water of a nearby faucet. An automatic spark will light the pilot light, which will fire the burner. After 10 to 30 seconds, the pilot will go off while the burner remains on.

Turn on the faucet's hot water to maximum flow; wait a minute for the water to reach maximum heat. Turn the temperature dial counterclockwise to lower the heat and clockwise to increase the heat. If incoming water becomes colder in the winter, you may need to turn the dial up to achieve the desired temperature.

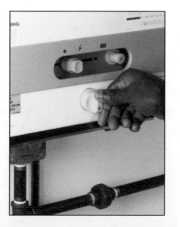

Installing vent piping

The water heater must be vented to the outside of the house in a code-approved manner, using flue pipes at least 5 inches in diameter (follow manufacturer's instructions). For the flue to draw efficiently, maximize the vertical rise—it should be at least 6 feet—and use as few elbows as possible. Test the flue before using to make sure it draws *(page 133)*.

Flue pipe

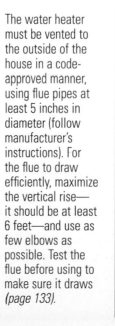

PAIRS TO OLD RADIATORS

Many older homes are heated with radiators that use either steam or hot water. Newer homes are typically heated with convectors (*pages 148–149*). A do-it-yourselfer can perform minor repairs to radiators; problems with a boiler or main supply and return pipes require the attention of a heating professional.

Steam or hot-water?

A steam radiator has a small chrome air vent near the top that emits small bursts of steam when the radiator heats up. Steam radiators cycle between getting very hot and then cooling down. Most are connected to only one pipe at the floor, but some have two. You can dismantle and service a steam radiator valve if the boiler is not firing. It can be difficult to work on, however, because the high heat tends to seize up the pipe joints.

Hot-water radiators are connected to two pipes at the floor. They maintain a constant warmth, rather than cycling between hot and cold. Before you dismantle a hot-water radiator valve, you must drain the system.

PRESTART CHECKLIST

☐ **TIME**
To replace a radiator valve, about two hours, plus time for finding the parts

☐ **TOOLS**
Pipe wrenches, groove-joint pliers, screwdriver, longnose pliers, level, prybar

☐ **SKILLS**
To drain a hot-water system, be sure you are familiar with your system

☐ **PREP**
Turn down the thermostat so the boiler will not come on while you work

☐ **MATERIALS**
Radiator valve replacement parts, or a new valve; pipe-thread tape

Installing a new valve

1 If water leaks from beneath the handle, turn down the thermostat and wait for the radiator to cool. Tighten the packing nut (just under the handle) using groove-joint pliers, and tighten the larger union nut using a pipe wrench. If this does not solve the problem, move on to the next step.

2 With a hot-water system, water must be drained from the radiator. First turn the thermostat down. Attach a hose to the boiler's drain valve; open the valve to drain the system into a nearby floor drain. Open the bleeder valves (see opposite, below) of all radiators, starting at the top floor.

IDENTIFYING HOT-WATER AND STEAM RADIATORS

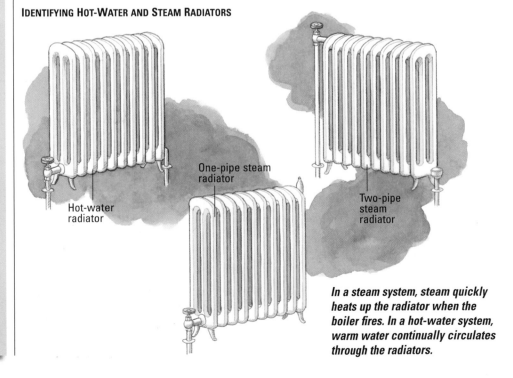

In a steam system, steam quickly heats up the radiator when the boiler fires. In a hot-water system, warm water continually circulates through the radiators.

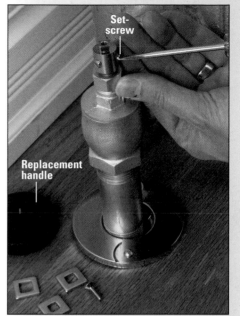

Installing a new handle

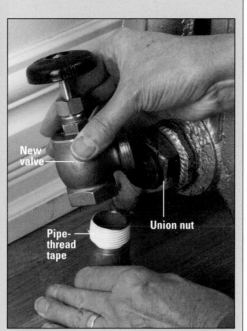

3 Unscrew the packing nut and remove the stem, first by unscrewing and then by pulling it out. If the leak originates just under the handle, wrap the stem with strand packing and reinstall. If the leak is lower down, or if this does not solve the problem, replace the valve (Step 4).

4 Unscrew the union nut that attaches the valve to the radiator, then unscrew the valve from the pipe. Take the old valve to a plumbing and heating supply store for an exact replacement; look carefully to be sure it will fit. You may also need to replace the short pipe that emerges from the radiator.

If a handle is cracked or loose, remove the top screw and pull the old handle off. If the stem's threads are in good shape, buy a replacement handle that has the same size screw. If the stem is damaged, buy a "fits-all" handle, which clamps onto the stem with a setscrew.

Repairs to radiators

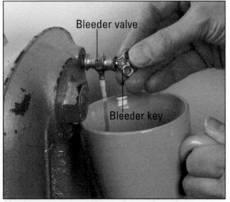

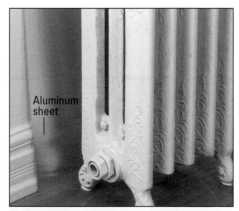

A steam radiator valve must be turned either all the way on or all the way off. An adjustable air vent makes it possible to turn the heat up or down. Turn the thermostat down and use pliers to unscrew the old air vent. Buy a compatible adjustable unit. Wrap the threads with pipe-thread tape and screw the new unit in place.

If a hot-water radiator is not heating enough, air may be trapped inside. Turn the thermostat up and wait for the radiator to get warm. Hold a cup under the bleeder valve, and open it with a bleeder key, longnose pliers, or screwdriver. Spluttering water or hissing air may come out. Once water flows in a steady stream, tighten the valve.

To improve a radiator's performance, move furniture and other obstructions out of the way. Air should flow freely under and above the radiator. A sheet of aluminum or reflective insulation placed behind the radiator directs more heat into the room.

INSTALLING CONVECTORS

An older radiator can be unattractive and take up a lot of space. Buying a radiator cover will improve appearances. Check the yellow pages or ask a plumbing and heating store for companies that custom-make metal units to fit all sizes of radiators. However, if you want more space in a room and you have a hot-water (not steam) system, you may be able to replace your radiator with a convector.

The steps shown at right can be used to add a convector to an existing convector system. Consult with a heating contractor to be sure you install a unit of the right size.

A convector is surprisingly simple and lightweight. The system usually has a copper pipe surrounded by thin aluminum fins. When the boiler heats the water running through the pipe, the fins direct the heat away from the pipe.

A convector's cover may appear to be merely decorative, but it is actually precisely sized to produce convection; cool air enters below the fins, and warm air comes out the top. Keep obstructions at least a foot away from a convector.

PRESTART CHECKLIST

☐ **TIME**
A day to remove a radiator and install a new convector; half a day to add a convector to a convector system

☐ **TOOLS**
Pipe wrenches, groove-joint pliers, screwdriver, drill, carpentry tools, propane torch

☐ **SKILLS**
Connecting copper to steel pipe, basic carpentry skills

☐ **PREP**
Consult with a heating expert to determine the convector size needed

☐ **MATERIALS**
New convector, copper pipe, dielectric unions, valves as needed

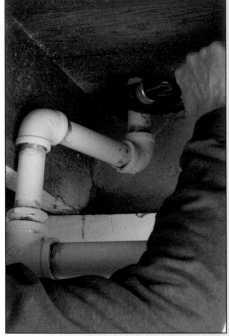

1 Drain the system (*page 146*, Step 2). Unscrew the union nuts at each end of the old radiator and remove the radiator. From below, remove the plumbing leading from the old radiator to the heat pipe. These old pipes may be difficult to detach.

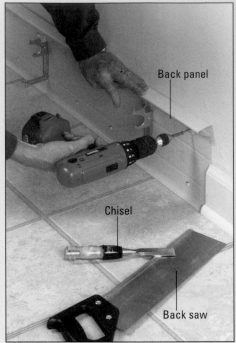

Back panel

Chisel

Back saw

2 Using a fine-tooth saw like a back saw (shown) and a chisel, cut the baseboard molding to accommodate the convector's back panel. Attach the back panel to the wall with screws driven into studs.

THREE TYPES OF CONVECTOR SYSTEMS

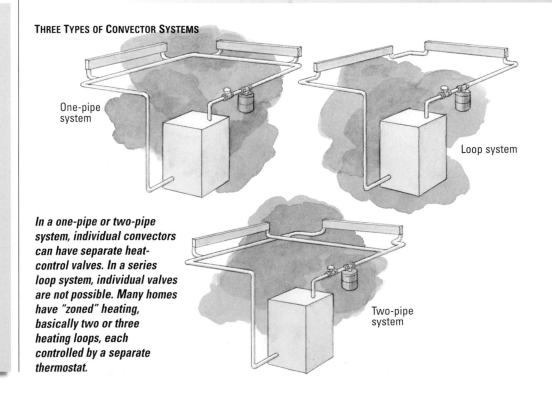

One-pipe system

Loop system

Two-pipe system

In a one-pipe or two-pipe system, individual convectors can have separate heat-control valves. In a series loop system, individual valves are not possible. Many homes have "zoned" heating, basically two or three heating loops, each controlled by a separate thermostat.

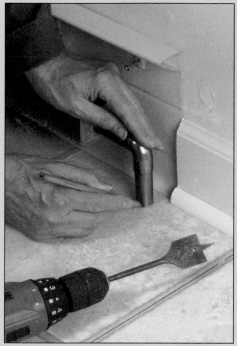

3 Temporarily mount the convector onto the back panel and mark the location of the floor holes. Drill holes wide enough so that the pipes will be at least ½ inch from any wood surfaces.

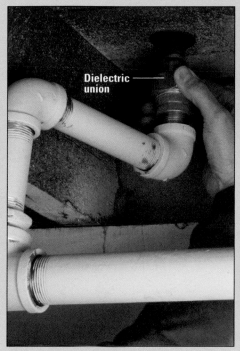

4 From below, install plumbing to reach the convectors. Use a dielectric union to make the transition from steel to copper. If needed, a flexible connector easily makes complicated turns.

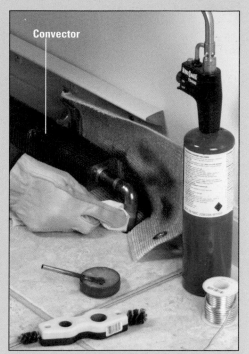

5 Mount the convector onto the back plate, and sweat the joints (for how to sweat copper pipe, see *pages 98–99)* at each end. Install the end caps and the front panel of the convector unit.

Maintaining convectors

If a convector has a bleed valve, bleed air from it using the method shown on *page 147.* A balance or heat-control valve may have a handle, or you may need a screwdriver to open and close it. When the slot is parallel to the pipe, the valve is wide open; when it is perpendicular, the valve is closed.

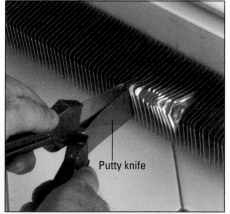

If fins are bent, the convector will radiate air less efficiently into the room. Straighten the fins using two putty knives, a pair of broad pliers, or a fin comb.

If a convector makes a humming or grating sound, the fins may be rubbing against the support bracket. Slip a piece of plastic between the fins and the bracket to dampen the sound.

REMOVING AND REPLACING A BATHTUB

Bathtubs and showers sustain heavy use and are frequently scoured, so it's not surprising they eventually need to be replaced. This chapter shows how to remove an old tub and install a new one, as well as how to spruce up a tub or shower enclosure. If you need to install a new tub or shower with new plumbing, see the chapter "Installing a New Bathroom" *(pages 160-189).*

Some inspectors don't require an inspection for fixture replacements. As long as no new drain or supply pipes are to be installed, no permit will be required.

But check with your building department; this is a major job. It's to your benefit to have an inspector sign off on it. If you are running new lines for a shower *(pages 180–181),* be sure to schedule inspections.

Plan the whole job
Replacing a tub or installing a shower is a remodeling project, involving not only plumbing but also carpentry, wall repair, and perhaps tiling. Count the cost and prepare for all aspects of the job. Allow yourself plenty of time. Just patching and painting a wall can take several days.

Leaks below a bathroom
If water drips from the ceiling below a bathroom, incompletely sealed walls and floors or cracked tiles are usually the cause—not necessarily the plumbing. Even a small gap in caulking or grout can provide a pathway for stray shower and bath water. By the time you notice a leak, there may be serious damage to walls, ceilings, and framing members. Every few months, inspect the grout and caulk. Encourage family members to dry off in the tub or to use an absorbent rug so that water does not puddle on the floor.

Replacing a tub or installing a shower is a major project that can take more than a week.

CHAPTER PREVIEW

Removing a tub
page 152

Replacing a tub
page 155

Installing a prefab tub surround
page 158

Cavity cut out for
tub installation

Cement
board

When replacing a tub, allow plenty of
time for wall repair. Removing an old tub
requires removing the wall material at
least 8 inches above the rim of the tub.
For a tiled tub surround like this, you
must fill in the cavity with cement board.

REMOVING A TUB

If your tub is chipped, difficult to keep clean, or just plain ugly, consider refinishing rather than replacing. You'll probably find several companies in the phone book that use various methods. Check out samples of their work and read their guarantees carefully. Note that no refinishing method can produce a finish that is as hard and durable as a new tub.

Plan and prepare

If you decide to remove and preserve your old tub, measure it and make sure you will be able to get it past other fixtures and out the door. Remove the sink or the toilet if they will be in the way.

A dropcloth is probably not enough protection for the floor. Cut and tape pieces of plywood to the floor and cover with a dropcloth.

Sometimes old tiles can be removed and reused. However, at least some will probably break. Either find tiles to match or plan to retile the walls. Or install a solid-surface tub surround *(pages 158–159).*

PRESTART CHECKLIST

☐ **TIME**
A full day to remove a bathtub

☐ **TOOLS**
Groove-joint pliers, flat pry bar, crowbar, hammer, drill, screwdriver, utility knife

☐ **SKILLS**
Basic carpentry skills, dismantling a trap

☐ **PREP**
Locate access to the tub plumbing in the basement below or in an adjacent room; if necessary, install an access panel (opposite page)

☐ **MATERIALS**
Plywood and dropcloth to protect the floor

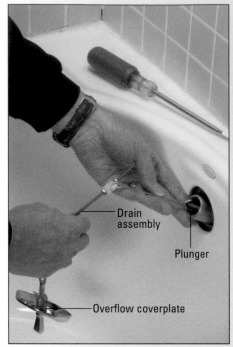

Drain assembly

Plunger

Overflow coverplate

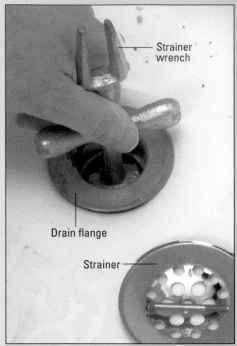

Strainer wrench

Drain flange

Strainer

1 From inside the tub, unscrew and remove the overflow coverplate. If a drain assembly is attached to it, pull it out. (A drain assembly with a plunger is shown.) If there is one, unscrew and remove the mounting bracket.

2 To disconnect the drain, you may need to remove a screw or two and remove the strainer. Or you may need to lift out a stopper and a rocker assembly (see *page 156).* Use a strainer wrench to remove the drain flange.

WASTE-AND-OVERFLOW INSTALLATIONS

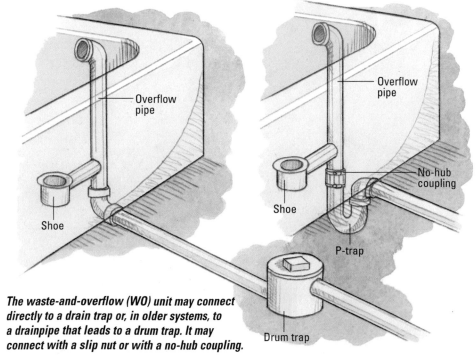

Overflow pipe

Shoe

Overflow pipe

Shoe

No-hub coupling

P-trap

Drum trap

The waste-and-overflow (WO) unit may connect directly to a drain trap or, in older systems, to a drainpipe that leads to a drum trap. It may connect with a slip nut or with a no-hub coupling.

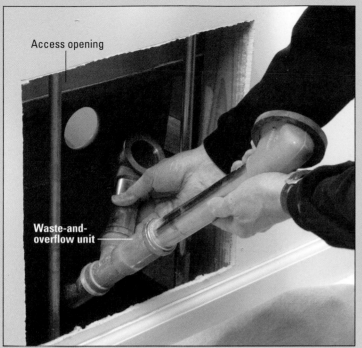

3 From an access panel behind the tub or from below, disconnect the waste-and-overflow (WO) unit from the drain line. Depending on the installation, you may need to unscrew a slip nut or loosen the screws on a no-hub coupling (see *page 155* for alternatives). If the parts are cemented plastic, you'll have to cut through a pipe. Remove the WO unit from the tub. (You may not need to remove the old WO unit if it will fit exactly on the new tub. Measure carefully.)

4 Remove the tub spout and remove the wall surface all around the tub to a height of about 8 inches. (If there are tub faucet handles, leave them in place if they are at least 8 inches above the tub.) Use a flat pry bar or putty knife to pry off tiles. Cut through drywall with a drywall saw. If the wall is plaster, use a reciprocating saw, taking care not to cut into the studs. Pry off or unscrew nails and screws.

WHAT IF...
You need to install an access panel?

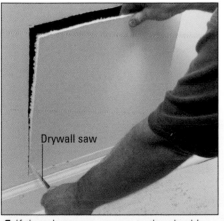

1 If there is no easy access to the plumbing behind the tub, install an access panel in the adjacent room. Use a drywall saw to cut a hole in the wall surface, spanning from stud to stud.

2 Screw 2×2 cleats to either side of the opening. Cut a piece of plywood 2 or 3 inches larger than the opening. Paint it to match the wall and attach it with screws.

REFRESHER COURSE
Add a ready-made panel

Purchase a ready-made plumbing-access panel for a quicker installation and a neater appearance. Follow manufacturer's instructions for cutting the hole and installation.

Removing a tub (continued)

Crowbar

Tub flange

5 Pry out or unscrew any nails or screws anchoring the tub flange to studs. Where the tub rests on the floor, use a utility knife to cut through a bead of caulk, if there is one. Use a crowbar to pry the tub an inch or so away from the back wall.

6 Unless the tub is an old-fashioned clawfoot or other type of stand-alone, it will fit fairly tightly between studs on either side. That means you probably can't slide it outward unless you cut away the wall surface on both sides. The best way is usually to lift the tub up on one end. Pry up one end of the tub first with a crowbar, then with 2×4s. Working with a helper, stand the tub upright.

STANLEY PRO TIP

Removing a cast iron tub

A cast-iron tub weighs 300 to 400 pounds—a bear to remove. If you plan to discard it anyway, break it into manageable pieces. Wear eye protection and gloves. Cover it with an old drop cloth (to prevent pieces from flying) and hit it repeatedly with a sledge hammer.

Choosing a tub

Acrylic or fiberglass tubs are inexpensive, light, and easy to install. Some have finishes that are fairly durable, but they may become dull in time. An enameled steel tub has a sturdier finish but lacks insulating properties; bath water will cool quickly. Enameled cast iron is the most expensive and heaviest material but may be worth the cost because it retains a gleaming finish for decades, fills quietly, and keeps water warm the longest.

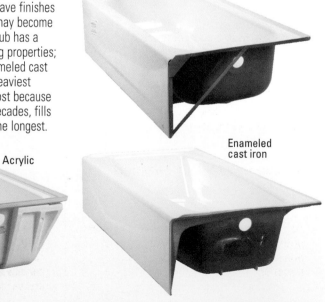

Enameled steel

Acrylic

Enameled cast iron

REPLACING A TUB

An inexpensive tub may be narrow and may not cover the the same floor space as the old tub. Many people find a narrow tub uncomfortable. Purchase a tub with ample width.

Home centers carry spa (or whirlpool) tubs that can fit in a standard tub opening. Installing one of these models is not much more work than installing a standard tub; the difference is that a spa or whirlpool needs to plug into a GFCI (Ground Fault Circuit Interrupter) electrical receptacle. For a more elaborate spa installation, see *pages 182–185*.

Preparing the floor and the walls

If the bead of caulk at the base of a tub has even a small gap, water that puddles on the bathroom floor will seep underneath the tub, quickly damaging any bare wood. To be safe, install protective flooring on the entire floor, including the area the tub will cover.

Most tubs fit into a 60-inch opening, but some older ones may be longer. Measure to make sure your replacement tub will fit.

PRESTART CHECKLIST

☐ **TIME**
About a day to install a replacement tub where there is an existing drain

☐ **TOOLS**
Groove-joint pliers, pry bar, level, drill, screwdriver, strainer wrench, putty knife, drill

☐ **SKILLS**
Making drain connections in a tight spot, basic carpentry skills

☐ **PREP**
Clear the area; cover the floor with plywood and a drop cloth

☐ **MATERIALS**
Tub, waste-and-overflow unit, plumber's putty, pipe-thread tape, caulk, cement board and tiles, or other wall-finishing material

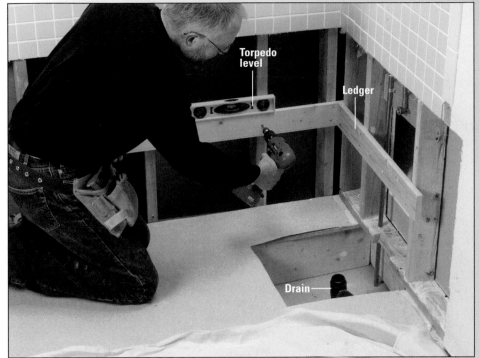

1 Check the drain and replace any damaged parts. Consult the manufacturer's literature and measure to make sure the drain is in the correct location. Purchase a waste-and-overflow unit *(page 156)* and determine how you will connect it to the drain line (see below). Screw ledger boards to the studs at the height recommended by the manufacturer.

Ideally, the finish flooring material should run under the tub.

DRAIN CONNECTIONS

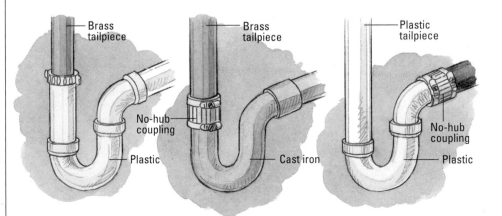

Waste-and-overflow (WO) units have been attached to drain lines in a various ways over the years. Here are some of the most common methods. A rubber no-hub coupling (sometimes called a mission coupling) may be used to connect to a cast-iron or a plastic drain line.

Usually the WO tailpiece connects to the drain via a slip nut. Whichever method you use, plan ahead so that you won't have a nasty surprise after the tub has been wrestled into position.

Replacing a tub (continued)

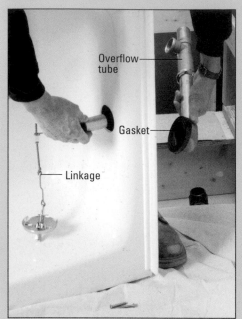

Overflow tube

Gasket

Linkage

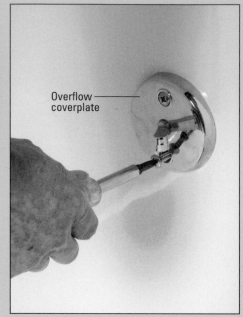

Overflow coverplate

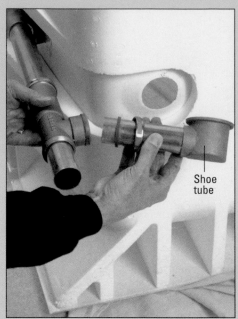

Shoe tube

2 Working with the tub turned on its side, dry-fit the overflow tube and the shoe. Make any necessary cuts, then make permanent connections. Place the gasket on the overflow flange, position it behind the overflow hole, and insert the linkage.

3 Inside the tub, slip the screws into the overflow trim. Hold the overflow flange in place and hand-tighten one of the screws. Start the second screw and tighten both with a screwdriver.

4 Insert the shoe tube into the opening in the overflow tube, and slip the other end up into the drain hole.

WHAT IF...
You have an extra-deep tub?

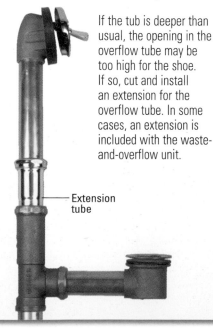

Extension tube

If the tub is deeper than usual, the opening in the overflow tube may be too high for the shoe. If so, cut and install an extension for the overflow tube. In some cases, an extension is included with the waste-and-overflow unit.

BATHTUB WASTE-AND-OVERFLOW ASSEMBLIES

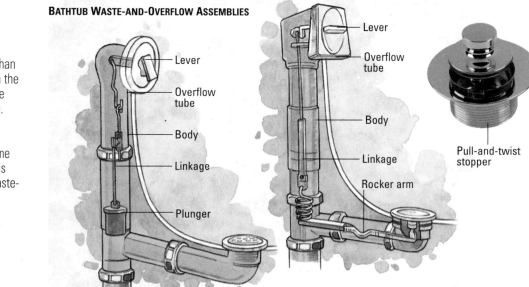

Lever

Overflow tube

Body

Linkage

Plunger

Lever

Overflow tube

Body

Linkage

Rocker arm

Pull-and-twist stopper

A plunger design has a brass cylinder (or plunger) that slides up and down through the overflow pipe to open or close the drain. A brass pop-up drain has a rocker arm that pivots to raise or lower the stopper.

Many plastic units have no interior mechanism; instead, the stopper itself (above right) is raised and lowered by the bather's toe. This method drains more slowly than the other two methods.

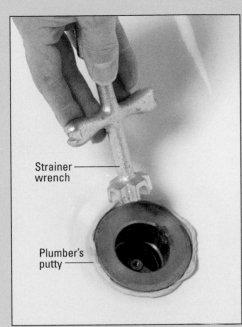

Strainer
wrench

Plumber's
putty

5 Inside the tube, place a rope of plumber's putty under the strainer or drain flange. Hold the shoe with one hand while you screw in the flange. Finish tightening with a strainer wrench. Clean away the squeezed-out putty with a plastic putty knife.

6 Before tilting and moving the tub, plan the move so you avoid damaging the waste-and-overflow unit, which protrudes below the tub. It may work best to rest the tub on 2×4s part of the time. With a helper move the tub into position. You may have to tilt the tub as shown. Slide it into the

opening and gently lower the tub in place. You might want a helper to guide the overflow tube into the drain line (see Step 8) while you do this. Slide the drop cloth or any other protective material out from under the tub. Protect the interior of the tub.

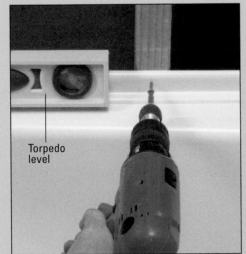

Torpedo
level

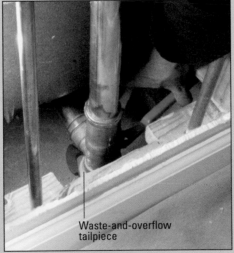

Waste-and-overflow
tailpiece

Backer board

7 Check the tub for level; an out-of-level tub may not drain completely. Attach the tub to the studs according to manufacturer's directions. You will probably nail or screw through an acrylic tub flange (shown). For a metal tub, drive nails just above the flange.

8 Working from behind or below, connect the waste-and-overflow tailpiece to the drain line, using one of the methods shown on *page 155*. To test for leaks, close the stopper and fill the tub. Open the stopper; watch and feel for any sign of wetness.

9 To fill in the gap above the tub, cut and install strips of cement backerboard, which is more moisture-resistant than green drywall. Install tiles to fit, allow the adhesive to set for a day, and apply grout. Apply silicone or "tub and tile" caulk where the tiles meet the tub.

INSTALLING A PREFAB TUB SURROUND

A prefab surround is a quick way to give a tub and shower area a fresh start. High-quality units have colorful, durable finishes, as well as convenient niches and towel bars.

Make sure the unit you buy has panels with flanges that overlap each other so you don't have to cut the panels to fit precisely. With a standard 60-inch-wide opening, you probably won't have to cut at all, other than making holes for the spout and the faucet control or handles.

Preparing the wall surface

The walls should be smooth and even. Scrape away any peeling paint and patch any cracks or weak spots. Apply primer paint to the walls to ensure a strong bond with the adhesive. It's possible to install over tile, but the panels will have gaps at the front edges, which must be covered with tile or acrylic.

PRESTART CHECKLIST

☐ **TIME**
Several hours to install a solid-surface tub surround

☐ **TOOLS**
Level, drill, caulk gun (or tube), notched trowel, tape measure, utility knife

☐ **SKILLS**
Measuring and drilling holes

☐ **PREP**
Clean and prime the walls, close the drain and place a drop cloth in the tub; remove the spout and the faucet control or handles

☐ **MATERIALS**
Shower surround kit, manufacturer's recommended adhesive, masking tape, cardboard for a template

Notched trowel

Center panel

1 Press a corner piece into position and mark the sides and top with a pencil. Using a notched trowel or a caulk gun (depending on the manufacturer), apply adhesive to the area inside the pencil lines. Apply evenly so the panel will not be wavy.

2 Press the center panel in place and smooth it with your palm. Install other pieces in the same way, following the manufacturer's installation procedures.

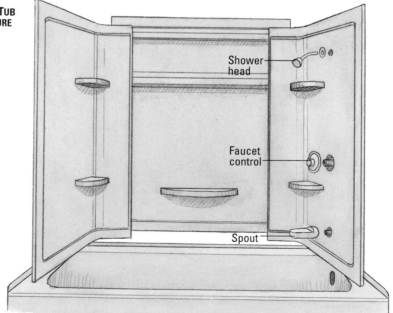

PREFAB TUB ENCLOSURE

Shower head

Faucet control

Spout

Available acrylic or polystyrene tub surrounds may have a modern, decorative, or retro look and come in various colors. While these units are less permanent than tile, they install quickly, are relatively inexpensive, and will last for many years.

Utility knife

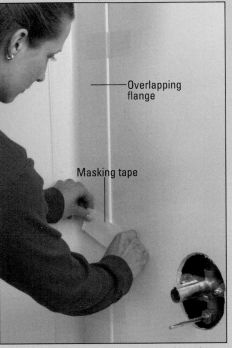

Overlapping flange

Masking tape

Tub-and-tile caulk

3 Place the piece that will cover the plumbing wall on a scrap piece of plywood. Make a template and cut holes using a utility knife or drill bits and hole saws of the correct size. Install the end pieces in the same way as the back pieces.

4 The panels can be adjusted before the adhesive hardens, which usually occurs about a half hour after application. Apply pieces of masking tape to ensure that their top edges form a straight line. (The bottom edges will be caulked, so they can be slightly uneven.)

5 Apply caulk to the space between the strips and a bead where the panels meet the tub. Practice applying even pressure to the tube while drawing smoothly along the joint. After applying the caulk, smooth it with your finger. Clean up any mistakes with a damp sponge.

Make a template

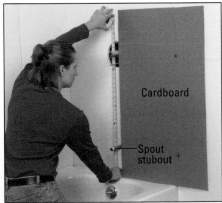

Cardboard

Spout stubout

To prevent mistakes in cutting holes, cut a piece of cardboard the same width as the panel to be installed. For each hole, measure up from the tub and over from the corner panel and mark the center of each hole. (If the panel will overlap the corner panel, take that into account.) Cut holes with a utility knife.

Hold the template up against the wall as a trial run. Once you are certain the holes are correct, place the template over the panel and mark it for drilling the holes.

WHAT IF...
You're installing a shower faucet?

If you need to replace the shower faucet, remove the wall surface. Follow the plumbing instructions on *pages 180–181*. Cover the wall with cement backerboard or water-resistant drywall (greenboard) .

INSTALLING A NEW BATHROOM

Installing a new bathroom with a toilet, sink, and tub may well be the most challenging do-it-yourself project you'll ever tackle. You'll need a thorough understanding of plumbing systems and techniques, a good helper, and the patience to keep at it until you get everything right.

Getting a handle on the plumbing

The following pages show how to install the three major bathroom plumbing fixtures in a common configuration. You'll find quite a few variations on this basic arrangement. Your situation may call for pipe runs that differ from those shown, so you may need to develop a unique plan that suits your home.

You'll need a good understanding of the basic skills and techniques of plumbing. Study the first chapter of this book, then develop a general plan for hooking the new plumbing to the old. Pay special attention to the drain vents and make sure you use pipe types and sizes that conform to code. If possible, hire a professional plumber to spend an hour or two giving you advice. This modest investment could save time and money later on.

The entire project

Whether you are remodeling an existing bathroom or installing one in a new addition, you will need carpentry skills. Modifying the framing sometimes can make the plumbing work easier. Plan and install the plumbing so it damages joists and studs as little as possible; reinforce any framing members that have been compromised. It's usually best to run any electrical lines after the plumbing has been installed.

A complete bath installation calls for thorough planning, advanced plumbing skills, and patience.

CHAPTER PREVIEW

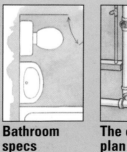

Bathroom specs
page 162

The overall plan
page 163

Preparing the site
page 164

Running drain and vent lines
page 166

Running copper supply lines
page 172

Capping off supply lines allows you to test your work before installing final fittings; cap the lines, turn on the water, and check for leaks. Caps also keep out debris that could later clog faucets and spouts.

Tape off all drain openings or buy ready-made caps or fittings with knockouts.

Roughing in supply, drain, and vent lines is the most demanding part of a plumbing project. Once an inspector has approved the essentials of your project, you can finish the walls and install fixtures, hardware, and trim. In the meantime, seal all drain openings to keep debris from falling into drain lines and sewer gas from entering the house.

Installing a bathroom vanity sink
page 1/4

Connecting a toilet
page 176

Pressure-assist toilet
page 177

Installing a pedestal sink
page 178

Hooking up a shower or tub faucet
page 180

Installing a whirlpool tub
page 182

Building a shower enclosure
page 186

BATHROOM SPECS

Specifications for the placement of plumbing fixtures and the dimensions of pipes are intended to make the bathroom a comfortable room with plenty of capacity for incoming water and outgoing drains and vents. The specs shown here will meet the requirements of most building departments, but check local codes to be sure.

Bathroom layout

Where you place the toilet, sink, and tub may depend partly on the existing plumbing. Most homes have a "wet wall," an interior wall that is thicker than most walls because it contains the main stack. Minimize long horizontal runs of drain and vent pipes by installing fixtures close to the wet wall.

Also plan for a layout that is comfortable and convenient. The following pages show how to install a basic 5×8-foot bathroom—

just enough room for the three major fixtures with adequate space between them.

Most codes require that no fixture be closer than 15 inches from a toilet's centerline. There must be at least 24 inches of space in front of the toilet (it's OK for a door to swing into this space).

Sinks and vanity sink tops range from 20 to 30 inches in width. A standard bathtub is 60 inches by 32 inches. If your plans call for a larger tub, alter the layout to fit it. The tub shown on *pages 182–185* will be 36 inches wide once framing and tiles are installed.

The framing—not the finished wall— must be 60 inches wide to accommodate a standard tub length. If the opening is any smaller, the tub will not fit; if the opening is more than ¼ inch too long, making a tight seal along the wall will be difficult. Framing must be almost perfectly square.

Choosing materials

These plans call for 3-inch PVC pipe for the main drain and the short length leading from the toilet to the drain, and 2-inch PVC for the other drain lines and the vents. Local codes may call for a 4-inch main drain, and some plumbers prefer to run larger vent pipes.

Cast-iron drainpipe is making a comeback in some areas because it's quieter than plastic pipe. However, cast-iron should be installed by a pro. (You can reduce the noise of water draining through PVC by wrapping the pipe with insulation.)

Rigid copper pipe is the most common material for supply lines. However, PEX or other plastic materials may be permitted in your area. Bathrooms are usually supplied with ½-inch pipe. For maximum water pressure, however, run ¾-inch pipe to the bathroom and use ½-inch for short runs only.

MINIMUM CLEARANCES

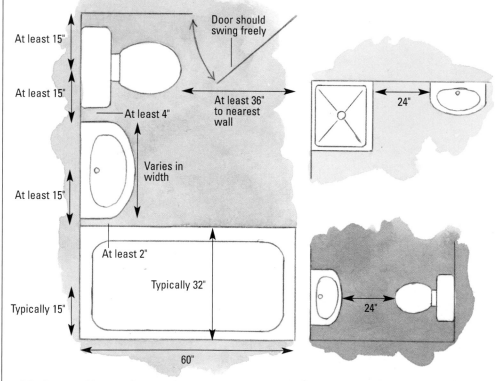

A bathroom with a 5×8-foot interior space allows the minimum clearances that most municipal codes require for fixtures. While

exploring layout options, maintain these clearances in your plan to assure ease of use and installation.

STANLEY PRO TIP

Standard dimensions

Make sure your plans follow these standard specs:

Drain and vent pipes
Toilet: 3–4 inches; 2-inch vent
Sink: 2-inch drain, connecting to 3-inch horizontal run; 2-inch vent
Tub/shower: 2-inch drain, connecting to 3-inch horizontal run; 2-inch vent
Main stack: 3–4 inches
Sink drain: 19 inches above floor
Toilet drain: 12 inches from wall

Supply pipes
Tub/shower: ¾-inch pipe
Sink, toilet: ½-inch pipe
Sink stubout: 19 inches above floor, 8–10 inches apart
Toilet stubout: 8 inches above floor

Tub/shower fittings
Tub control(s): 28 inches from floor
Spout: 6 inches above top edge
Shower head arm: About 76 inches above floor
Shower control: 48 inches above floor

THE OVERALL PLAN

Once you have decided on the basic layout and have a general idea of how the drain and vents will run, make specific plans. Measure the existing room and/or plan for new framing right down to the inch; take into account the thickness of the wall finishing material—usually ½ inch for drywall and perhaps another ⅜ inch for wall tiles. (See *pages 38–39* for tips on producing drawings.)

Vents

Start by figuring the vents; see *pages 14–15*. As a general rule, the drain line for each fixture should connect to a vent within a few feet of the fixture. A true vent never has water running through it, although "wet venting" is permitted in some situations.

This plan calls for running a new vent up through the ceiling and either tying into an existing vent in the attic or running out through the roof. Or you may be able to tie into an existing vent on the same floor.

Consider how new lines will affect existing vents. For instance, if you install an upper-story bathroom and tie into an existing stack, you may end up draining water through a pipe that is now used as a vent.

Drains

In this plan, a new main drain line for the bathroom runs down to the floor below. If the new bathroom is on the first floor, you can probably simply tie into the house's main drain line in the basement or crawlspace below. If the new bathroom is on the second floor, the bathroom's main drain will have to travel through the wall on the first floor and down to the basement or crawlspace. (See *page 165* for how to trace the location of a drainpipe through an intervening story.)

If a drain line is nearby, you may choose to run a new drainpipe across the floor to join to it, rather than running a new line. However, it may be difficult to run a toilet's 3-inch (or 4-inch) drain through a floor, especially if you have to go through joists.

In the room below the installation, the drain lines turn outward at 45-degree angles to avoid running 3- or 4-inch pipe through studs. If the room below is finished, you will need to build a soffit around these pipes *(page 164)* or run the pipes through the studs. This plan calls for a 3-inch horizontal drain; codes may permit 2-inch pipe.

Seal openings where pipes enter attics or crawlspaces to prevent drafts and to act as fire stops.

BATHROOM SUPPLY, DRAIN-WASTE-VENT OVERVIEW

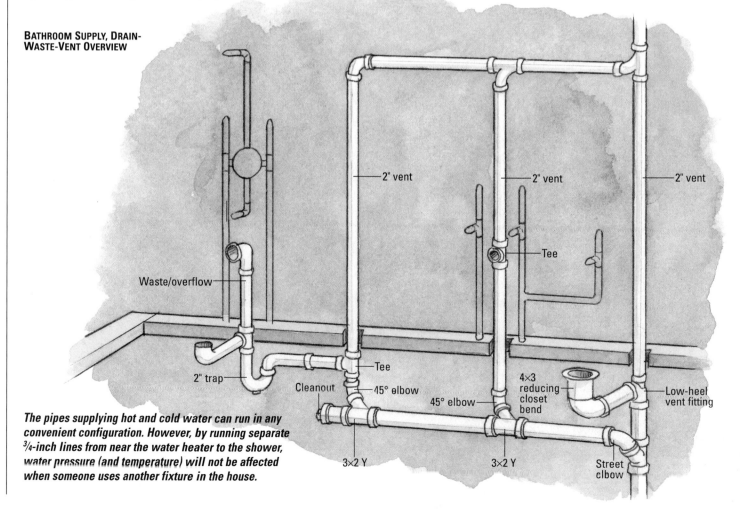

The pipes supplying hot and cold water can run in any convenient configuration. However, by running separate ¾-inch lines from near the water heater to the shower, water pressure (and temperature) will not be affected when someone uses another fixture in the house.

PREPARING THE SITE

An installation like this typically requires an extra-wide "wet wall" built of 2×6s or two side-by-side 2×4 walls. However, since only 2-inch pipe runs through the walls, codes sometimes permit a standard 2×4 wall. Unless you live in an area with a warm climate, avoid running pipes in an exterior wall.

To carve a new bathroom out of existing rooms, you may need to move a wall. (For more information on moving or building walls, see *Stanley Interior Walls.)* Before removing a wall, make sure it's not load-bearing; check with a carpenter or structural engineer if you are not sure.

Whether you are framing a new space or remodeling an existing space, make sure the framing accommodates the tub.

Remove drywall or plaster from the areas where you will run plumbing. Clear out all cabinets, fixtures, and other obstructions.

If wiring is in the path of plumbing, shut off power to the circuit and test to make sure. You may want to remove cables and reinstall them after the plumbing is in place.

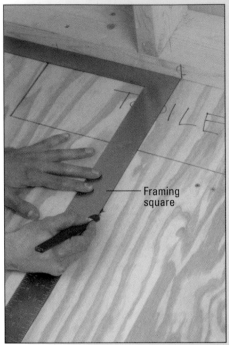

Framing square

1 Determine the exact center of the toilet drain. For most toilets, this is 12 inches from the finished wall surface. If you will install ½-inch drywall, measure 12½ inches out from the framing. (Toilets with drains set 10- and 14-inch from the wall are available, though usually in white only.)

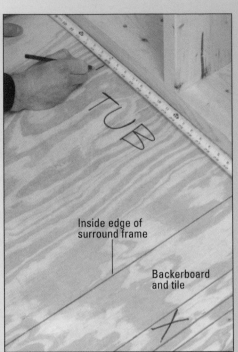

Inside edge of surround frame

Backerboard and tile

2 Study the instructions that come with the tub and the waste-and-overflow assembly to determine exactly where the tub drain needs to be *(pages 152–157)*. Mark the tub outline on the floor. In this case, the framing, backerboard, and tiling for a whirlpool tub must be added.

PRESTART CHECKLIST

☐ **TIME**
A day or more to remove wall coverings; about half a day to mark for positions of fixtures

☐ **TOOLS**
Hammer, pry bar, level, framing square, drill, hole saw, saber saw, circular saw, reciprocating saw

☐ **SKILLS**
Basic carpentry skills, planning for plumbing runs, careful measuring

☐ **PREP**
Have your plumbing plans approved by your building department.

☐ **MATERIALS**
Lumber for any framing that's needed

PLANNING FOR FINISHING THE ROOM BELOW

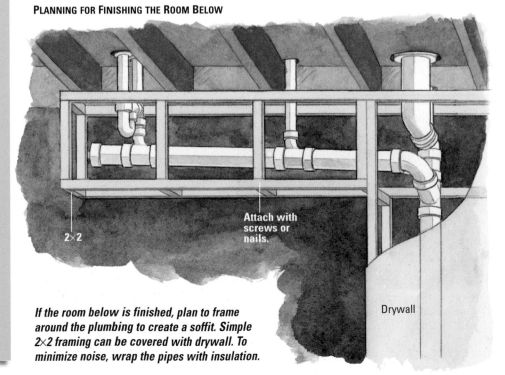

2×2

Attach with screws or nails.

Drywall

If the room below is finished, plan to frame around the plumbing to create a soffit. Simple 2×2 framing can be covered with drywall. To minimize noise, wrap the pipes with insulation.

Tub supply location

Sink drain, marked for cutting with hole saw

Notch marked for drain/vent fitting

Circular saw

Hole for toilet drain

Reciprocating saw

3 Mark the bottom plate for the location of the vent and drainpipes. Position the tub/shower vent so it will not interfere with the installation of the faucet *(pages 180–181)*. You may need to move a stud or two to make room for the tub/shower faucet. Also mark where the supply lines will enter the room. Check all your measurements twice.

4 Use a hole saw or saber saw to cut a hole in the floor for the toilet drain. Use a circular saw and a reciprocating saw to cut a section of flooring large enough to allow you to run the plumbing. Wherever you need to run pipes through joists, give yourself plenty of room to work.

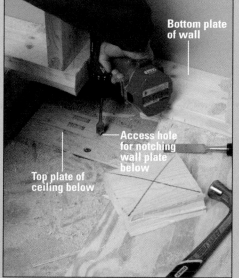

Bottom plate of wall

Access hole for notching wall plate below

Top plate of ceiling below

Hole cutting saw

5 Drill holes or cut notches as needed. To make room for the toilet drain *(page 166)*, a large notch must be cut in the bottom plate of the wall and the top plate of the ceiling below.

6 Using a hole saw, cut 2¼-inch holes for the tub and sink drains. Remove a 12×14-inch section of flooring for the tub/shower drain—cut a larger opening if you don't have access from behind or below.

STANLEY PRO TIP:

Running pipe through an intervening story

Light shining down wall cavity

If the new bathroom is on the second story, you will need to run a drainpipe down the wall of a first-story room. Don't tear into the wall to confirm the drain location. Instead, cut the bathroom drain hole and position a bright light over it. Take measurements and drill a test hole in the basement. If the location is right, you'll see the light.

RUNNING DRAIN AND VENT LINES

Because they are complicated and in some cases must be positioned precisely, drain and vent lines should be installed before the supply pipes. However, sometimes it may be possible to simplify supply runs by moving a vent pipe over a few inches.

If you must run drainpipes across a floor, carefully calculate the altitude—the amount of vertical room available—so you can pitch the drainpipe at 1/8 to 1/4 inch per running foot.

Sometimes it's difficult to visualize just how drainpipes will travel through walls and floors. Once you start assembling the pieces and testing them for fit, you may need to modify your plans.

Some inspectors want horizontal vent pipes to be sloped so moisture caused by condensation can run back to the drainpipes; others don't consider this important. Err on the safe side and slope the vents.

PRESTART CHECKLIST

☐ **TIME**
Working with a helper, about two days to install drain and vent lines for a simple bathroom

☐ **TOOLS**
PVC saw or power saw, level, reciprocating saw, drill, carpentry tools

☐ **SKILLS**
Cutting and joining PVC pipe, running pipes through walls, connecting new pipe to old

☐ **PREP**
Have your plans approved by an inspector; prepare the room *(pages 164–165)*

☐ **MATERIALS**
PVC pipe and fittings to meet codes, fitting to join to existing drainpipe, PVC primer and cement, pipe strap

A. Running the main drain line

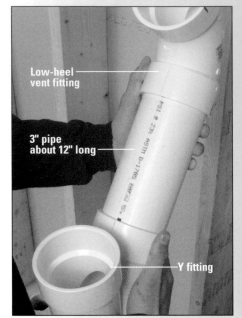

Low-heel vent fitting

3" pipe about 12" long

Y fitting

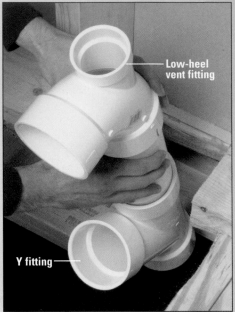

Low-heel vent fitting

Y fitting

1 Start with a length of 3-inch pipe long enough to reach the basement or crawlspace (Step 5, *page 168*). You may be able to cut it to exact length after it has been installed. Dry-fit a Y fitting, a length of pipe, and a low-heel vent fitting as shown, lining them up precisely.

2 Insert the assembly down through the wall plates and temporarily anchor it. Make sure the Y fitting is low enough to allow for installation of the other drain lines (Step 2, *page 169*). Once you are sure of the configuration, pull up the assembly and prime and glue the pieces.

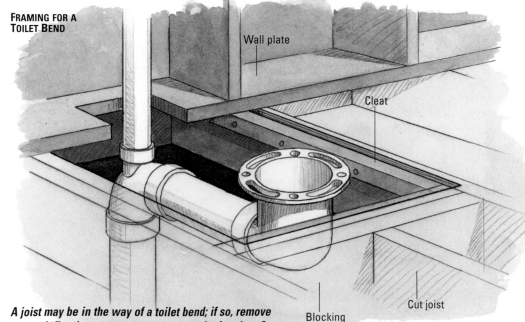

FRAMING FOR A TOILET BEND

Wall plate

Cleat

Blocking

Cut joist

A joist may be in the way of a toilet bend; if so, remove as much flooring as necessary to get at the framing. Cut the joist, install a blocking piece, and attach 2×4 cleats around the opening.

3 Place the assembly back into the hole. Secure the low-heel vent fitting to the framing with pipe strap. Secure the pipe from below as well.

4 Dry-fit a length of 3-inch pipe and a 4×3 reducing closet bend to the low-heel fitting. Check that the center of the closet bend hole is the correct distance from the wall—in most cases 12½ inches from the framing to allow for ½-inch drywall. Check that the pipe slopes ⅛ to ¼ inch down to the fitting. (If necessary you can trim the top of the closet bend after the flooring has been replaced.)

Once you are sure the toilet drain setup is correct, mark the alignment of the fittings and disassemble. Glue the pieces together. Support the closet bend with a strap.

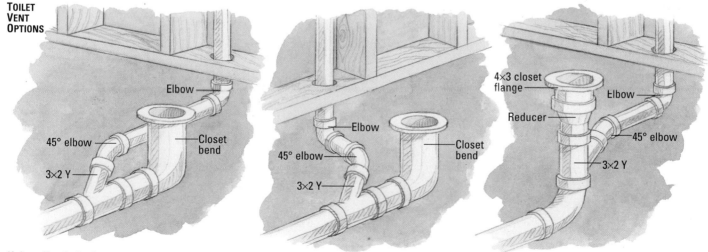

TOILET VENT OPTIONS

If the toilet drain does not connect directly to a vent, you must find another way to vent it. If the drain line runs away from the wall where you want the vent, use a reducing Y and a 45-degree street elbow to point the vent line toward the wall. The horizontal vent pipe runs right next to the closet bend.

If the vent wall is parallel to the drain pipe, install a 45-degree reducing Y and a street elbow to point toward the wall. You may need another elbow (of any degree) to position the vertical vent where you want it.

If the vent wall is opposite the drain line, use a reducing Y and a street elbow. The fittings can be pointed straight at the wall or at an angle, as needed.

Running the main drain line *(continued)*

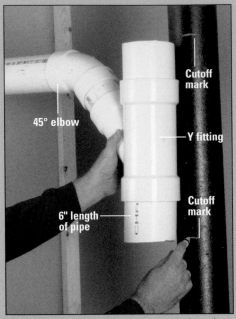

45° elbow
Cutoff mark
Y fitting
6" length of pipe
Cutoff mark

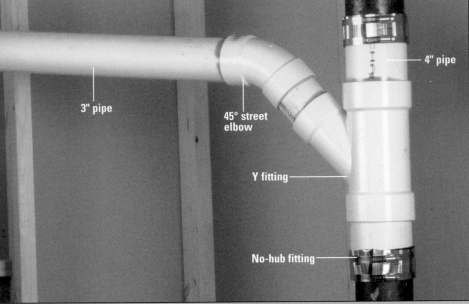

3" pipe
45° street elbow
Y fitting
No-hub fitting
4" pipe

5 Run a horizontal pipe to the existing pipe and assemble the parts needed for tying into it. All fittings should be Ys or drain elbows so wastewater can flow easily. Hold the horizontal pipe so it's sloped at ⅛ to ¼ inch per foot and mark the existing pipe for cutting *(pages 112–113)*.

6 If the existing pipe is cast-iron, take care to support it securely before cutting. In the setup shown, a 4×3 Y connects to the house drain using no-hub fittings (which should be used to connect to either cast iron or ABS). Once you are sure the fittings are correct and the horizontal pipe slopes correctly, make alignment marks. Disassemble the parts, apply primer, and reassemble the pieces in order, starting at the existing drain.

OTHER DRAIN CONFIGURATIONS

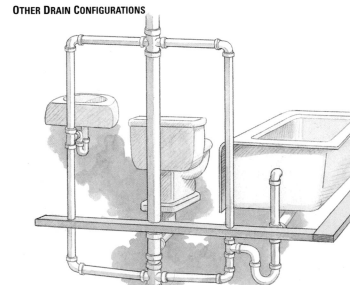

Your situation may call for another drain configuration. This example shows a single-floor home in which all the fixtures tie into horizontal pipes, which in turn run to the stack.

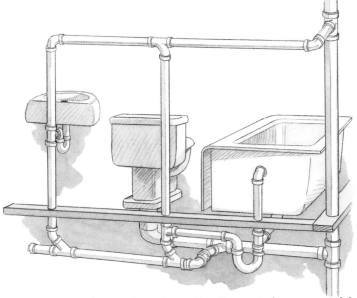

In this example for a two-story home, first-floor vent pipes run up to join the second-floor vents at the top of their runs, so that all the vents tie in at a point well above the second-floor fixtures.

B. Running individual drain lines

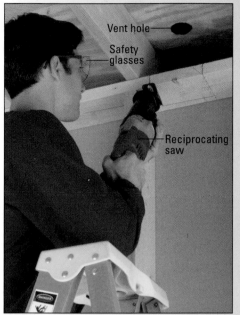

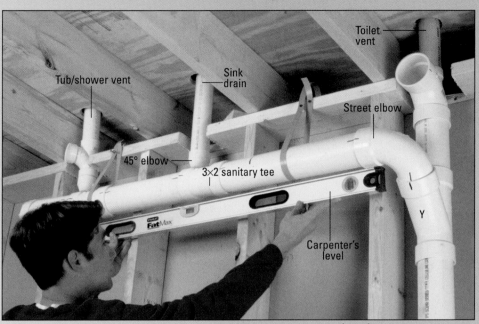

1 Slip lengths of 2-inch pipe down through the holes drilled in the floor plate for the tub and sink vents. Have a helper hold the pipes plumb as you mark the plate below for notching. Cut notches about an inch wider than the pipe to accommodate a fitting.

2 Cut and dry-fit the horizontal drainpipe and the fittings for connecting the tub and the sink drains. (A 3-inch horizontal pipe is shown, but your inspector may permit a 2-inch pipe.) Insert a street elbow into the Y and hold the other pieces in place to mark for cutting. Make sure the horizontal pipe slopes at a rate of ⅛ to ¼ inch per running foot. Install a reducing tee and a 45-degree elbow (or street elbow if you need to save room) for both joints. If the pipe will be accessible, install a cleanout on the fitting for the tub; otherwise, install a drain elbow instead of a tee.

WHAT IF...
You need to run a drain for a shower only?

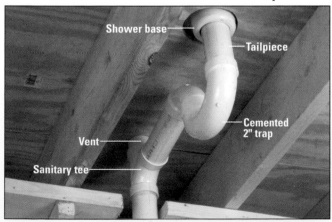

A 1½-inch drain trap is often permitted for a shower, but a 2-inch trap will ensure quick flow of water and will be less likely to clog. A shower has no waste-and-overflow assembly, so the rough plumbing consists of a cemented trap that rises to the correct height for the shower base *(page 186)*.

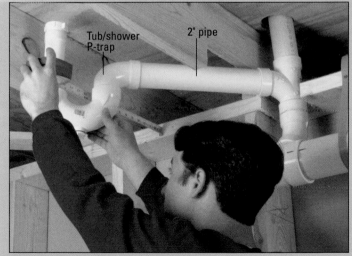

3 To plumb the drain for the tub, dry-fit a 2-inch trap onto a length of 2-inch pipe that is longer than it needs to be. Study the directions for the tub to determine precisely where the trap should be located. Hold the trap-and-pipe assembly in place and mark it for a cut. Dry-fit and check that the horizontal pipe slopes correctly. Once all the parts are accurately assembled, draw alignment marks and prime and glue the pieces together.

C. Installing the vents

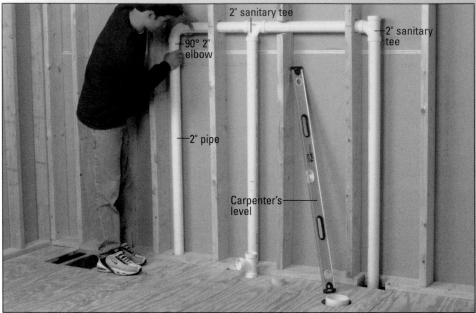

2" sanitary tee

2" sanitary tee

90° 2" elbow

2" pipe

Carpenter's level

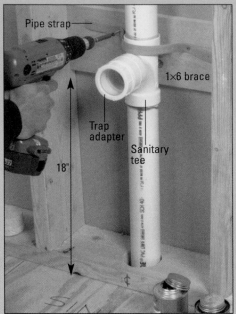

Pipe strap

1×6 brace

Trap adapter

Sanitary tee

18"

1 Your codes may require the horizontal revent lines be as high as 54 inches above the finished floor, or at least 6 inches above the fixture flood level (the point where water will start to spill out). Use a carpenter's level to mark the studs for drilling holes. Run the horizontal vent lines sloped downward toward the fixtures at a rate of ⅛ to ¼ inch per running foot. Drill holes, cut pipes, and connect them in a dry run using drain fittings.

2 Install a sanitary tee facing into the room for the sink trap. The ideal height is usually 18 inches above the finished floor, but check your sink instructions to be sure. Cement a 1¼-inch trap adapter into the tee. Install a piece of 1×6 blocking and anchor the pipe with a strap.

RUNNING A VENT AROUND AN OBSTRUCTION

If a medicine cabinet, window, or other obstruction prevents you from running a vent straight up, you'll have to turn a corner for a short distance, then turn again to head upwards. Horizontal runs should be at least 6 inches above the fixture flood level—the rim of a sink, for example.

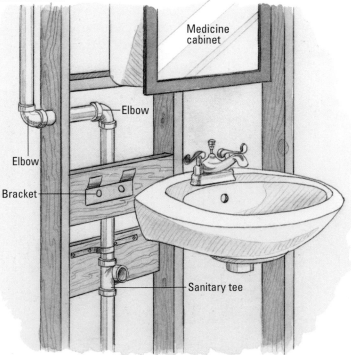

Medicine cabinet

Elbow

Elbow

Bracket

Sanitary tee

Running up through the ceiling

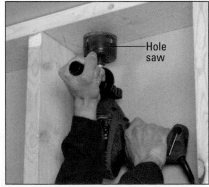

Hole saw

To run a vent pipe through the ceiling, first drill a test hole to make sure you won't bump into any joists in the attic. You may need to move the hole over a few inches. The top plate may be doubled, meaning you have to drill through 3 inches. You may need to drill with a hole saw first from below (shown), then from above.

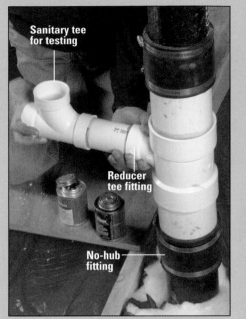

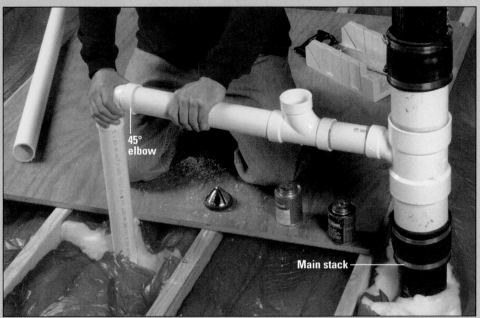

3 In the attic, tap into a conveniently located vent pipe. Following the steps shown on *pages 112–113*, cut the pipe and connect a reducer tee fitting. Use no-hub fittings to connect a PVC fitting to cast-iron or ABS pipe.

4 Run the new vent line over to the tee fitting. The pipes should slope gently down away from the existing vent pipe so water can travel downward.

Your inspector may want you to include a tee fitting to be used for testing: Once the

drain system is assembled and cemented, plug the drain pipe at the lower end. Pour water into it until all the drain and vent pipes are filled with water. Allow the water to sit for a day to make sure there are no leaks.

INSTALLING A ROOF JACK

Check local codes for the correct way to install a roof jack. In most areas you will need to install a 4-inch pipe. Some areas allow for a plastic pipe to extend out the roof (shown); in other areas a metal pipe is required. Purchase a roof jack with a rubber flange that will seal a 4-inch pipe.

Cut the 4-inch pipe to roughly the same angle as the roof slope and hold it plumb, its top touching the attic ceiling. Mark for the hole, which will be oval. Cut the hole using a drill and a reciprocating saw.

You may need to cut some roofing shingles back. Slip the jack under the roof shingles at its upper half; the lower half of the jack rests on top of shingles. Poke the vent pipe up through the rubber flange. To anchor the jack, lift up some shingles and drive roofing nails. If any nails are not covered by shingles, cover the heads with roofing cement.

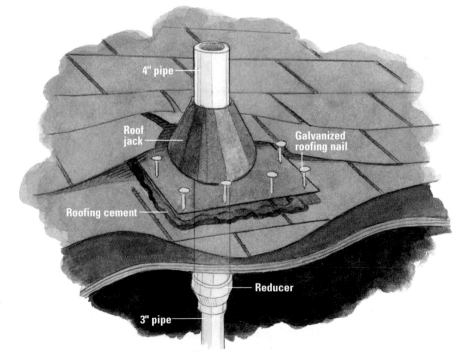

RUNNING COPPER SUPPLY LINES

Rigid copper is the material of choice for supply lines in most locales, although flexible or rigid plastic is permitted in some areas. An hour or two of practice will prepare you to cut copper pipe and sweat joints quickly and securely *(pages 98–99).*

Supply lines can be routed along almost any path, although extending a pipe run and adding bends will lower water pressure slightly. This plan shows running pipes so that they do not cross drainpipes or vents. In most cases, it's easier to make the horizontal runs below the room in the crawlspace or basement. If you need to run pipes horizontally in the room, see the box on *page 173.*

Installing hammer arresters (Step 3) ensures against a banging noise when you turn on or off a faucet.

Copper pipe can last for many decades. However, it is easily punctured or dented. Position it out of harm's way and install nailing plates to the studs to protect pipes against errant nails.

Hot water is always on the left, cold water on the right.

PRESTART CHECKLIST

☐ **TIME**
About half a day to run supply lines for a sink and toilet

☐ **TOOLS**
Drill, bit and bit extender, propane torch, tubing cutter, multiuse wire brush, flame guard, groove-joint pliers, carpentry tools for installing braces

☐ **SKILLS**
Accurate measuring and drilling, working with copper pipe

☐ **PREP**
Install all or most of the drain and vent pipes; determine the supply routes

☐ **MATERIALS**
Copper pipe and fittings, flux, solder, damp rag

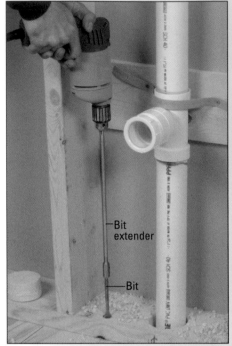

1 Consult the manufacturer's instructions to position pipes for the shower faucet, sink, and toilet. For example, the shower faucet in this plan calls for vertical pipes 10 inches apart. Use a spade bit attached to a bit extender to drill holes in the center of the wall plate, if possible.

Bit extender

Bit

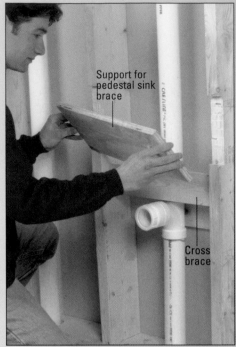

2 Install cross braces so you can anchor the pipes firmly. Cut pieces of 2×4 or 1×4 to fit snugly between studs and attach them by drilling pilot holes and driving screws. If you plan to install a pedestal sink *(page 178–179),* attach a 2×6 or a ¾-inch plywood brace (shown) to support its bracket.

Support for pedestal sink brace

Cross brace

Running and securing supply pipes

A copper supply strap attaches to the face of the studs. Pipes fit into notches or holes, sized and spaced for correct placement. The pipes can be soldered onto the strap using the same techniques as for sweating fittings.

Supply strap

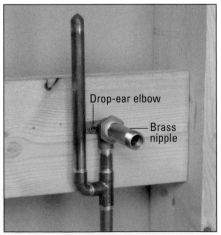

A drop-ear elbow makes the most secure attachment. If you use one, the hammer arrester must be connected to a tee and an elbow just below the drop-ear elbow. Insert a brass threaded nipple into the elbow.

Drop-ear elbow

Brass nipple

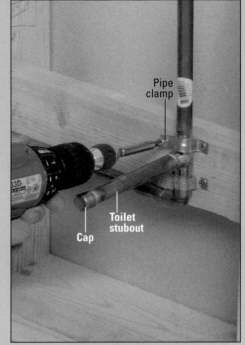

3 Tie into existing supply lines *(page 113)*. The hot and cold stubouts usually should be 8 to 10 inches apart and 19 to 23 inches above the floor; consult the manufacturer's instructions to be sure. A toilet stubout is usually 8 inches above the floor.

Dry-fit a complete assemble for the sink and the toilet. For each stubout, use a tee fitting, a 6-inch length of pipe (which you will cut off later), and a cap to protect the pipe. Install a hammer arrester to each.

4 Sweat all the parts following instructions on *pages 98–99*. Anchor the pipes with at least one—preferably two—clamps at each stubout as shown.

Tap into shower supplies

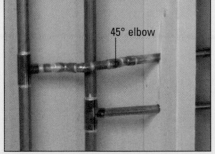

Rather than running sink supply lines from below, you may want to run them horizontally from the shower. If the shower lines are ¾ inch, use reducer tees to tap into the lines. Use 45-degree elbows to snake one line past the other (in this case, the hot past the vertical cold-water line). If the sink is used at the same time as the shower, water temperature will change

WHAT IF...
Supply lines must run past drain or vent pipes?

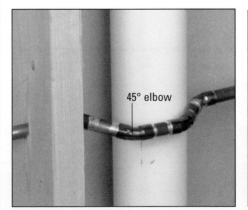

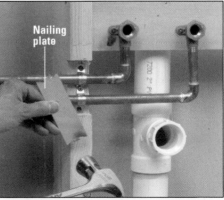

To run supplies around an obstruction such as a drain or vent pipe, use four 45-degree elbows. This arrangement makes for smoother water flow and less loss of water pressure than using 90-degree elbows.

Another option is to cut notches rather than holes and run supply pipes in front of the vent pipes. If you do this, be sure to install protective nailing plates or the pipes could be punctured by a nail when the drywall is installed.

INSTALLING A BATHROOM VANITY SINK

Installing a bathroom sink in a vanity is simplified by the fact that the supply lines and the drain are all hidden within a cabinet. If the cabinet has no back, simply attach it to the wall so it encloses the plumbing. However, if the cabinet has a back, measure and cut three holes for the two supply lines and the drain.

Choosing a cabinet and top

A high-quality vanity cabinet is made of hardwood to resist water damage. A less expensive cabinet made of laminated particleboard will quickly disintegrate if it gets wet.

A vanity top typically is a single piece comprised of the bowl, countertop, and backsplash. Acrylic or plastic vanity tops are inexpensive, but they scratch and stain more easily than other materials.

PRESTART CHECKLIST

☐ **TIME**
Two to three hours to install a basic cabinet and vanity top with faucet

☐ **TOOLS**
Drill, hammer, screwdriver, level, adjustable wrench, groove-joint pliers, basin wrench

☐ **SKILLS**
Installing a faucet, attaching a P trap, connecting supply tubes, simple carpentry

☐ **PREP**
Shut off the water and remove the old sink

☐ **MATERIALS**
Vanity cabinet and top, faucet, P trap, supply tubes that fit the stop valves, plumber's putty, wood shims, screws

Stop valve

Drain

1 The stop valves and drainpipe should be in place and close enough together to be enclosed by the cabinet. If your vanity cabinet has a back (many do not), remove the handles from the stop valves. Then measure and cut holes for the drain and the two supply pipes.

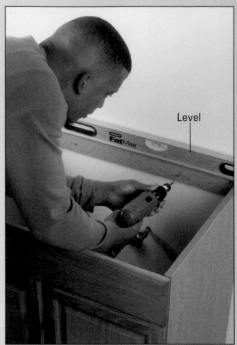

Level

2 Slide the cabinet into place and check it for level in both directions. If necessary, slip shims under the bottom or behind the back of the cabinet. Drive screws through the cabinet framing into wall studs to secure the cabinet.

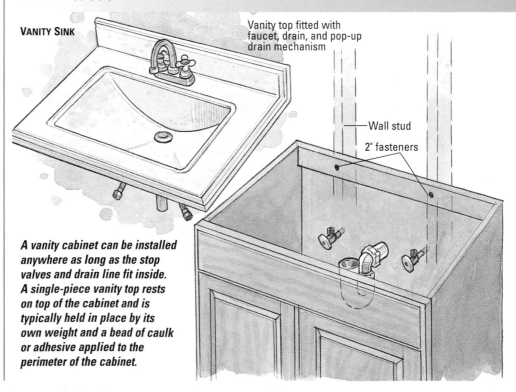

VANITY SINK

Vanity top fitted with faucet, drain, and pop-up drain mechanism

Wall stud

2" fasteners

A vanity cabinet can be installed anywhere as long as the stop valves and drain line fit inside. A single-piece vanity top rests on top of the cabinet and is typically held in place by its own weight and a bead of caulk or adhesive applied to the perimeter of the cabinet.

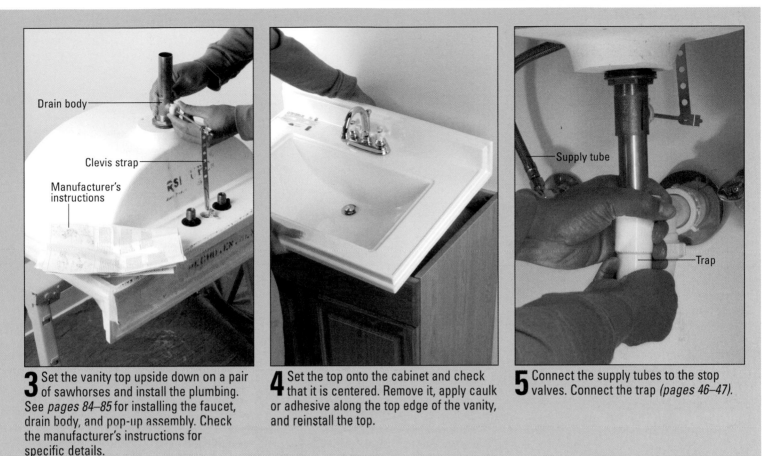

Drain body

Clevis strap

Manufacturer's instructions

Supply tube

Trap

3 Set the vanity top upside down on a pair of sawhorses and install the plumbing. See *pages 84–85* for installing the faucet, drain body, and pop-up assembly. Check the manufacturer's instructions for specific details.

4 Set the top onto the cabinet and check that it is centered. Remove it, apply caulk or adhesive along the top edge of the vanity, and reinstall the top.

5 Connect the supply tubes to the stop valves. Connect the trap *(pages 46–47)*.

Installing a drop-in sink

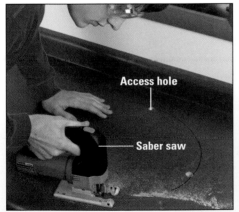

Access hole

Saber saw

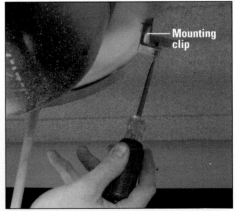

Mounting clip

1 To install a drop-in self-rimming sink, first install a laminate countertop, or for a tile countertop, plywood and concrete backerboard. Use the template if provided, or turn the sink upside down on the counter and trace its outline. Draw a line ¾ inch inside the first line. Cut this second line with a saber saw.

2 Plumb the sink (Step 3 above). Apply a bead of bathtub caulk or a rope of plumber's putty around the hole and set the sink. If the sink doesn't have mounting clips, apply a bead of silicone caulk instead of putty. Set the sink in, wipe away the excess caulk, and wait several hours before attaching the plumbing.

3 If your sink has mounting clips, slip several of them in place and turn them sideways so they grab the underside of the counter. Tighten the screws. Attach the supply lines and the drain trap.

CONNECTING A TOILET

Once the rough plumbing is completed, run electrical lines and install the lights, switches, receptacles, and a ceiling fan. Lay the finish flooring if you haven't already done so. Install cement backerboard on the walls that surround the tub/shower *(pages 188–189)* and moisture-resistant drywall (also called greenboard) on the other walls. Tile or apply prefab sheets to the tub/shower surround. Tape, prime, and paint the walls and the ceiling. You may want to install baseboard and trim, but often it's best to wait until the sink and toilet are installed to avoid bumps and nicks on the trim.

To install a stop valve for the toilet, follow the instructions on *pages 124-125*. Measure the length of the supply tube needed and confirm the connection dimensions.

PRESTART CHECKLIST

☐ **TIME**
Half a day to install a toilet

☐ **TOOLS**
Adjustable wrench, groove-joint pliers, torpedo level, screwdriver, drill

☐ **SKILLS**
Assembling plumbing parts, cementing PVC fittings

☐ **PREP**
Finish all the wiring, carpentry, and wall preparation; remove the drop cloth from the floor

☐ **MATERIALS**
Toilet, wax ring, toilet flange with bolts, supply tubes and decorative flanges toilet, plumber's putty, silicone sealant, caulk, PVC primer and glue

Installing a toilet

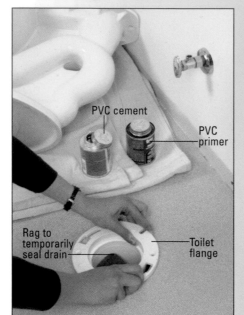

PVC cement
PVC primer
Rag to temporarily seal drain
Toilet flange

1 Install finish flooring to within an inch of the drain hole. The toilet flange can rest on top of the finished floor or on top of the subflooring. Test-fit the flange, then prime and glue it so that you will be able to place the hold-down bolts on either side of the opening (Step 2). Remove the rag.

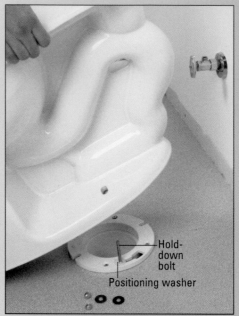

Hold-down bolt
Positioning washer

2 Press a wax ring onto the bottom of the toilet. Place the hold-down bolts in the flange and slip plastic positioning washers over them. Lower the bowl, threading the bolts through the holes in the bowl. Press down to seat the bowl firmly. Slip on washers and nuts and gently tighten.

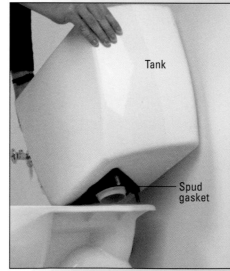

Tank
Spud gasket

3 Assemble the tank and the bowl of a new toilet following the manufacturer's instructions. A large spud gasket seals the opening below the flush-valve seat. Place a rubber washer under the head of each mounting bolt. Don't over-tighten the nuts.

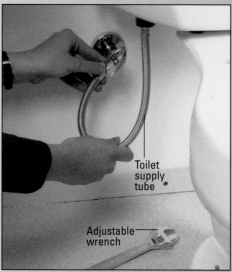

Toilet supply tube
Adjustable wrench

4 Attach a toilet supply tube by hand-tightening the nuts at the underside of the tank and the stop valve. Tighten a half turn or more with a wrench and open the stop valve. You may need to tighten the connection a bit further.

PRESSURE-ASSIST TOILET

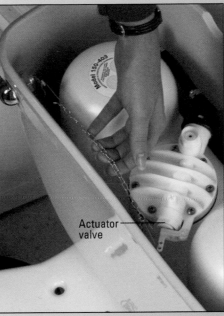

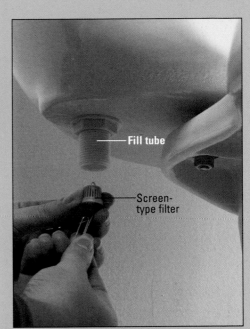

1 Many people want more flushing power than modern 1.6-gallon toilets provide. A pressure-assist toilet delivers a more forceful flush. It installs the same way as a standard toilet *(pages 94–95).*

Tighten nut on flange bolt
Supply tube

2 Some manufacturers use a chain to link the flush handle to the actuator valve. Check that the chain is nearly taut; too loose a chain won't fully open the actuator valve and will interrupt the flush.

Actuator valve

3 A screen-type filter at the base of the fill tube catches bits of rust and minerals. Check it periodically by turning off the supply valve and detaching the supply tube. Pry out the filter with a bent paper clip and flush it with hot water. Reassemble and attach the tube.

Fill tube
Screen-type filter

HOW IT WORKS

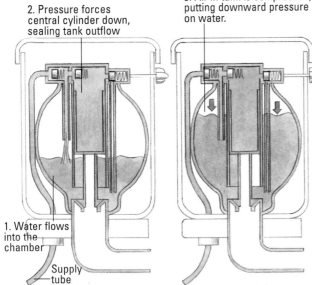

2. Pressure forces central cylinder down, sealing tank outflow

3. Air in tank is compressed, putting downward pressure on water.

4. When lever turned, pressure is relieved above central cylinder. It rises, starting flush.

Lever

1. Water flows into the chamber
Supply tube

5. Forced air pushes water out and into the bowl.

As the chamber is filled, household water pressure compresses air. The chamber holds the compressed air, primed for the next flush. When the flush lever is tripped, the central cylinder rises, releasing a rush of water into the toilet bowl.

How much will you save?

Old toilets use from 3 to 5 gallons per flush. That adds up to serious water usage, so current federal regulations require that toilets use no more than 1.6 gallons per flush.

The first low-use toilets were no different from their older counterparts, except they allowed less water into the tank. As a result, people often had to flush two or more times to clear the bowl, sending water savings down the drain!

Newer 1.6-gallon toilets are better designed, so water flows more smoothly and waste is more effectively flushed away. For maximum efficiency, buy a power-assist toilet such as the one shown on this page.

If you have an older toilet and want to decrease water consumption, put a brick or two into the tank to displace water.

INSTALLING A PEDESTAL SINK

A pedestal sink saves space in a bathroom but requires strong support from the wall, which often means adding extra framing.

Installing the framing and patching the wall will take more time than the plumbing. The project will probably require several days: On the first day, install the framing and patch the wall. On the second day, finish the patching and paint the wall. Install the sink on the third day. (If you have a tiled wall, consider installing the framing by cutting into the wall in the room behind the sink location.)

An inexpensive pedestal sink may actually rest on the pedestal—an arrangement that makes the plumbing installation difficult and future repairs nearly impossible. Buy a sink that mounts on a bracket; the pedestal is for looks only.

If your supply lines are close together, you may be able to hide them behind the pedestal. Otherwise, let the plumbing show.

PRESTART CHECKLIST

☐ **TIME**
About 5 hours of work spread over a period of three days (see above)

☐ **TOOLS**
Drill, hammer, drywall saw, taping knife, sanding block, paintbrush, screwdriver, adjustable wrench, groove-joint pliers

☐ **SKILLS**
Installing a bathroom faucet with pop-up drain, connecting a trap, cutting drywall

☐ **PREP**
Locate studs behind the wall near the plumbing

☐ **MATERIALS**
Pedestal sink, bathroom faucet, supply tubes that fit the stop valves, plumber's putty, 2×6 or 2×8 piece, screws, drywall, joint compound, drywall tape, paint

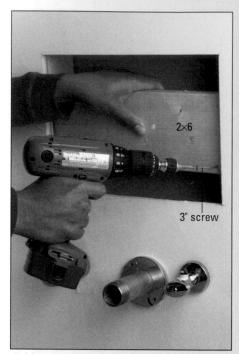

1 Measure and mark the bracket height. To support the bracket, cut a hole in the wall that spans two studs. Cut a piece of 2×6 or 2×8 to fit between the studs and attach it with screws. Drive the screws at an angle through the brace and into the studs.

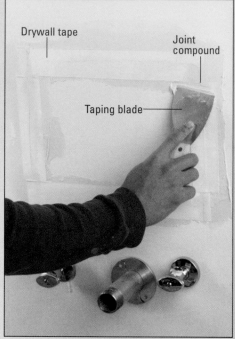

2 Cut a piece of drywall to fit and attach it to the brace with screws. Smooth pieces of drywall tape around the edges. Use a taping blade to cover the tape with joint compound. Allow the compound to dry, then sand until the patch is smooth. Paint the patch.

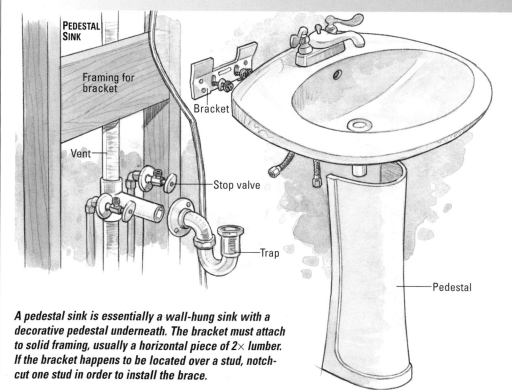

A pedestal sink is essentially a wall-hung sink with a decorative pedestal underneath. The bracket must attach to solid framing, usually a horizontal piece of 2× lumber. If the bracket happens to be located over a stud, notch-cut one stud in order to install the brace.

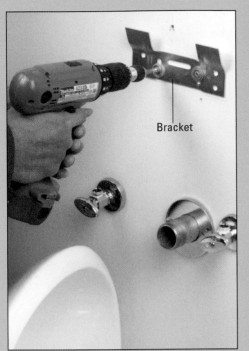

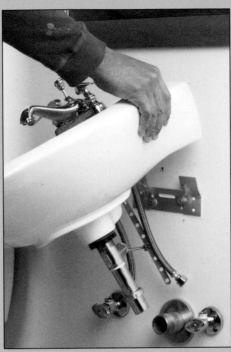

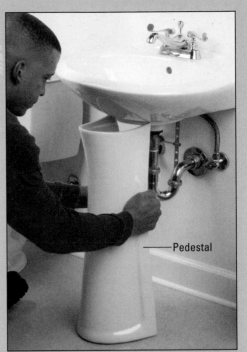

3 Set the sink on top of the pedestal and against the wall. Hold the bracket in place and mark the position of the bracket. Install the bracket by driving screws through the wall into the 2× brace.

4 Install the faucet and the drain body on the sink *(pages 84–85)*. Lower the sink onto the bracket. Slide the pedestal in place to make sure the bracket is at the right height and adjust it, if necessary. Hook the supply tubes to the stop valves and attach the drain.

5 Slide the pedestal under the sink. Stand back to determine if the pedestal looks level and sits squarely on the floor. Adjust it as needed. You may caulk the bottom of the pedestal or leave it uncaulked so it can be removed for cleaning.

WHAT IF...
You want a freestanding bowl sink?

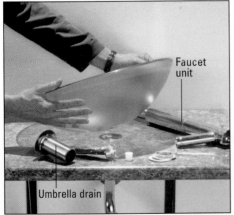

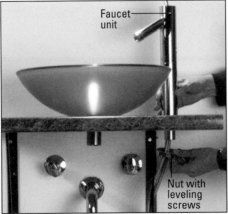

1 Drill two holes in the top, one for the drain and one for the faucet. There is no overflow, so use an umbrella drain (shown) which covers the drain but does not close it. Apply silicone sealant and anchor by tightening the nut from below.

2 The faucet unit comes with flexible supply tubes already attached. Apply silicone sealant to the bottom of the faucet and drop the lines through the hole in the countertop. Anchor the faucet from below by tightening the nut and leveling screws.

3 Wrap the threads of the stop valves with pipe-thread tape and attach the supply tubes. Make a tailpiece from a section of trap and attach it with a rubber washer and trap nut.

HOOKING UP A SHOWER OR TUB FAUCET

This plan calls for separate ¾-inch lines to supply the shower. This ensures good water pressure and protects anyone in the shower from a sudden change of temperature when a faucet is turned on or the toilet tank refills. Tap into the house's cold and hot water lines as near to the water heater as possible.

Choose the tub or shower faucet before you start installing pipes. Read the manufacturer's directions carefully so you know exactly where the pipes should go.

If your faucet does not have integrated shutoff valves (see box, opposite), install reachable shutoff valves on the lines leading to the shower so you can easily turn off the water if repairs are needed.

Assuming an 18-inch-tall tub, position the faucet about 28 inches above the floor for a tub, about 48 inches for a shower. You may want to compromise and position it about 38 inches above the floor.

PRESTART CHECKLIST

☐ **TIME**
About half a day to run supply lines and install a tub/shower faucet

☐ **TOOLS**
Drill, propane torch, tubing cutter, multi-use wire brush, flame guard, damp rag, groove-joint pliers

☐ **SKILLS**
Accurate measuring and drilling, working with copper pipe

☐ **PREP**
Tap into the hot and cold water lines and run ¾-inch pipe up into the room. If needed, move a stud to make room for the plumbing behind the tub.

☐ **MATERIALS**
Tub/shower faucet, copper pipe and fittings, flux, solder, pipe-thread tape

1 Most faucets come with a plastic cover that protects the faucet and serves as a guide for the depth at which it must be set. To determine where to place the braces, consider the total thickness of the finished wall—often ½-inch-thick backerboard plus ¼-inch-thick tiles.

Cross brace

1× scrap stands for ½" backer board plus ¼" tile.

2 Determine how high you want to locate the spout (make sure it will clear the tub), the faucet handles, and the showerhead. Install a 2×6 brace for each. Anchor the braces with screws rather than nails so you can move them more easily if they need adjustment.

2×6 cross brace

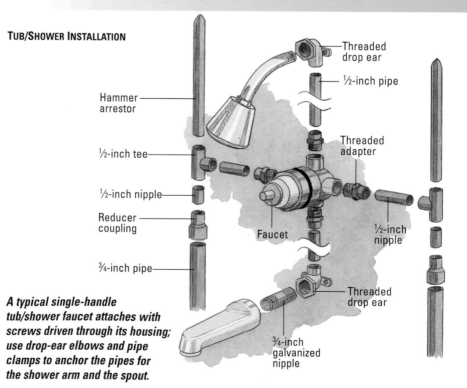

TUB/SHOWER INSTALLATION

Threaded drop ear

½-inch pipe

Hammer arrestor

Threaded adapter

½-inch tee

½-inch nipple

½-inch nipple

Reducer coupling

Faucet

¾-inch pipe

Threaded drop ear

A typical single-handle tub/shower faucet attaches with screws driven through its housing; use drop-ear elbows and pipe clamps to anchor the pipes for the shower arm and the spout.

¾-inch galvanized nipple

3 Assemble all the pipes in a dry run. Install ¾-inch pipe up to the height of the faucet, add reducing couplings or elbows, and run short lengths of ½-inch pipe to the threaded adapters on the faucet. Add hammer arresters. Anchor the faucet according to manufacturer's directions.

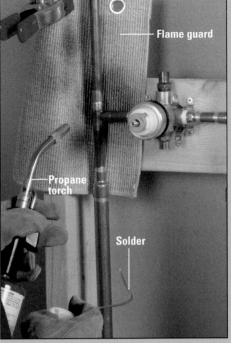

4 Once you are sure of the connections, sweat all the fittings *(pages 98–99)*. Start at the faucet, then move on to the shower arm and spout connections. Run ½-inch pipe up to the shower arm and down to the spout; attach drop-ear elbows at both spots.

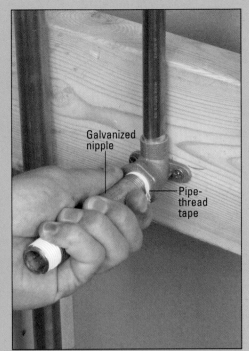

5 Finger-tighten a threaded nipple—either brass or galvanized—into both drop-ear elbows. Once the wall covering is in place, remove them and install the shower arm and the tub spout.

STANLEY PRO TIP

Add reinforcement to shower-arm dropears

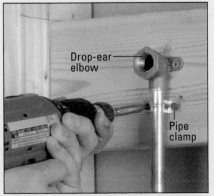

Whacking the showerhead with your elbow can bend or crack a drop-ear elbow. As an extra safeguard, screw a pipe clamp just below the drop ear.

WHAT IF...
You have other faucet setups?

A three-handle faucet may require that supply pipes be spread farther apart than for a single-handle faucet. Threaded adapters screw in for the supplies, spout, or shower arm.

A faucet with integral shutoffs comes with a large escutcheon (coverplate), so you can more easily reach the shutoff valves.

Installing a Whirlpool Tub

Some whirlpool tubs (also called spas) have a finished side or two, so framing for the side panel and tiling are not required. Rectangular models install much like a standard tub *(pages 155–157),* except that a GFCI electrical receptacle is required. Triangular whirlpools fit into a corner.

The drop-in model shown on these pages fits into a frame. No special supply lines are needed; the whirlpool circulates water after it's filled by a standard spout. Some models have heaters to keep the water hot without replenishing. Other models have their own spouts; follow manufacturer's instructions for running supply lines.

Large whirlpools are very heavy when filled with water, so you may need to strengthen the floor by adding joists. Check the whirlpool's instructions and local codes.

Ideally it's best to lay flooring after the tub is framed and installed but before tiling.

Prestart Checklist

☐ **Time**
Two or three days to frame, install, and tile a whirlpool tub

☐ **Tools**
Carpentry tools, groove-joint pliers, PVC saw, wiring tools, tiling tools, putty knife, screwdriver, adjustable wrench

☐ **Skills**
Connecting PVC pipe, basic carpentry, basic wiring, installing tiles

☐ **Prep**
Measure the space carefully, taking into account the framing, backerboard, and tile thickness.

☐ **Materials**
Whirlpool tub, waste-and-overflow unit, lumber and screws for framing, GFCI receptacle, cable, breaker, cement backerboard with screws, mortar mix, tile, mastic, grout, caulk, spacers, pipe thread tape, rag

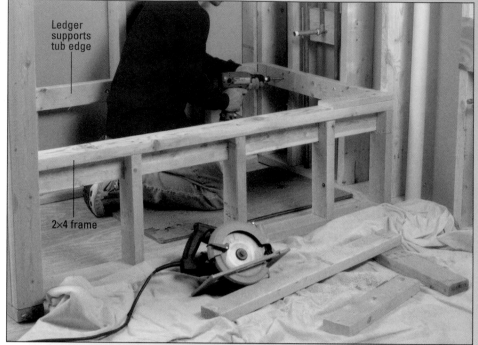

Ledger supports tub edge

2×4 frame

1 Build a frame following manufacturers directions. It's especially important to get the height right. You may snug the whirlpool up against one, two, or three walls. Where you snug the tub against the wall, attach a 2×4 ledger as you would for a standard tub *(page 155).* Where you will install tiles, plan the framing carefully, taking into account the thickness of the backerboard and tile (Steps 2 and 11). Most whirlpools require access to the plumbing at one end and the pump motor at the other end; check the manufacturer's directions.

Whirlpool Tub Installation

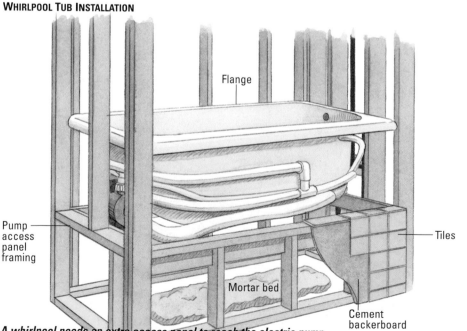

Flange

Pump access panel framing

Tiles

Mortar bed

Cement backerboard

A whirlpool needs an extra access panel to reach the electric pump. A 2×4 frame is covered with backerboard, then tiled. The whirlpool's flange rests on tile, but its weight must be supported by a mortar bed.

Ledger positioned to line up with tiled surround

Cement backerboard

Tile

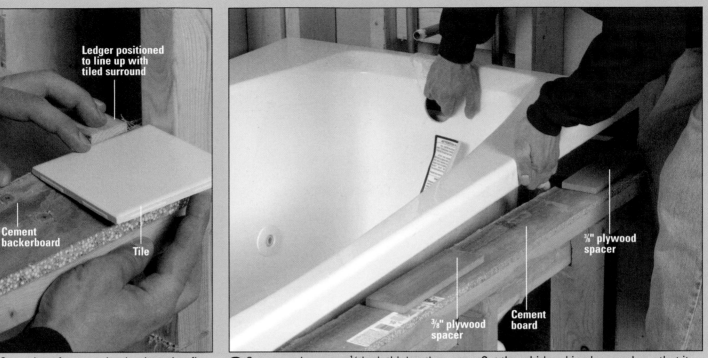

³⁄₈" plywood spacer

³⁄₈" plywood spacer

Cement board

2 Cut strips of cement backer board to fit where needed on top of the framing. Backerboard pieces should overhang the framing by ½ inch. You can also cut the side backerboard pieces but don't install them yet. Attach the backerboard using special backerboard screws.

3 Cut several spacers ⅛ inch thicker than the tiles you will install. (For ¼-inch-thick tiles, cut pieces of ³⁄₈-inch plywood.) Set the spacers on top of the backerboard wherever there will be tile.

Set the whirlpool in place and see that it fits. Be sure the bottom of the tub is at the correct depth so it will rest on the mortar bed (Steps 7 and 8).

Installing a GFCI receptacle

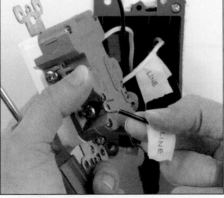

Most whirlpools plug into a GFCI receptacle, though some are hard-wired into an electrical box. For most models, you will need a 15-amp circuit that supplies only the whirlpool. Check the manufacturer's instructions. Consult with an electrician if you are not sure how to run cable and install a new circuit. Use cable that meets local codes; either NM cable, armored cable, or conduit with wires running through it. Run cable from the service panel to the whirlpool. Strip the cable and clamp it to an electrical box (left).

Wire a GFCI receptacle (center), wrap the connections, secure the receptacle in the box, and attach a cover plate.

Shut off power to the service panel. Strip the cable and connect the hot wire to a new electrical breaker (right). Connect the neutral and ground wires to the neutral and/or ground bus bar and snap the breaker into place. Restore power and test.

Installing a whirlpool tub (continued)

Framing square

Tub drain trap

4 Check to make sure the drain trap is positioned and at the correct height so that the whirlpool waste-and-overflow unit will slide into it (Step 9). Plan how you will make this connection, either from the basement or crawlspace below or through the access panel *(page 157)*.

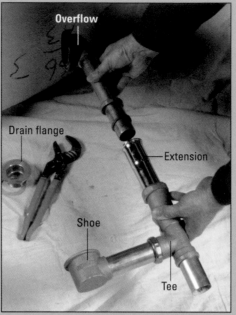

Overflow

Drain flange

Extension

Shoe

Tee

5 Assemble the waste-and-overflow unit. Some whirlpools come with a waste-and-overflow; if not you'll have to purchase a standard unit and add an extension (shown). Insert the shoe (cut to length if necessary) into the tee fitting.

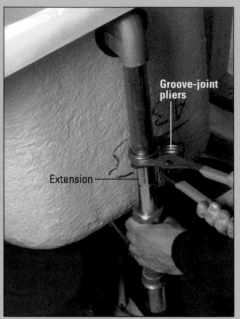

Groove-joint pliers

Extension

6 Set the tub on two overturned buckets. Install the overflow by slipping in the plunger assembly, tightening the screws on the cover plate, and screwing the drain flange into the shoe (see *pages 156–157*). Tighten the nuts on the drain extension.

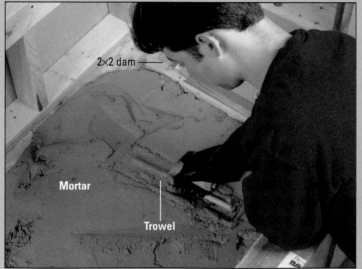

2×2 dam

Mortar

Trowel

7 Test-fit the whirlpool to see that the waste-and-overflow unit will slip into the drain trap. Remove the whirlpool. Screw 2×2s to the floor around the drain hole to keep mortar out of the hole. In a bucket or wheelbarrow, mix water with dry mortar mix. The mortar should be just wet enough to be poured. Smooth enough mortar onto the floor to support the bottom of the whirlpool.

Spacer

Mortar bed

8 Place spacers (Step 3) on the backerboard atop the side-panel frame. With a helper, gently set the tub in place. Guide the waste-and-overflow into the drain trap but do not tighten the connection. Push down on the tub until the lip rests on the spacers, but do not press hard. Allow the mortar to harden overnight.

9 Connect the waste-and-overflow to the drain and tighten the fittings *(pages 156–157)*. Support the pump motor with pieces of lumber and attach it in place with screws. Plug the cord into the GFCI receptacle. Follow the manufacturer's instructions for testing the whirlpool.

10 Install cement backerboard on all exposed sides. Drive backerboard screws every 6 inches or so. Wrap corners with fiberglass mesh tape.

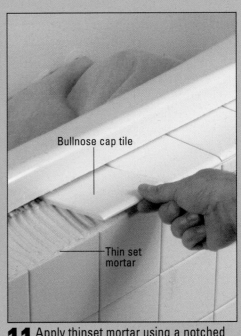

11 Apply thinset mortar using a notched trowel and set standard tiles on the side. When tiling the top edge, use bullnose caps for the outside corner for a finished look. After the thinset has dried, apply grout and clean the joints. Caulk the joint where the whirlpool rests on the tiles.

Adding the tub hardware

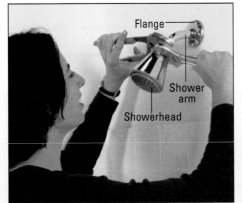

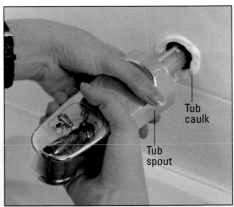

1 Once the wall is finished, remove the temporary nipple. Wrap pipe-thread tape around the ends of the shower arm and screw it into place. Slip on the flange. Twist on the shower head, then tighten with an adjustable wrench and groove-joint pliers. Protect the chrome with tape.

2 Following manufacturer's instructions, slide the escutcheon over the faucet and screw it into place. It should seal against the tiles with a rubber gasket. Attach the faucet handle.

3 Apply caulk around the spout hole. Choose a nipple of proper length for the spout and wrap pipe-thread tape around the threads of both ends. Twist the spout on by hand. Finish by wrapping the spout with a rag and tightening it against the wall with groove-joint pliers.

BUILDING A SHOWER ENCLOSURE

A new shower stall installed in a corner of a room will require you to build only one wall. If it's in the middle of a wall, two new walls are required. The walls may reach all the way to the ceiling, or they may stop partway up. In that case the top ledge must be covered with tile or another moisture-resistant surface. The opening can have a door, or you can simply install a curtain rod.

For a corner installation, a one-piece unit *(page 188)* is much simpler to install, though you have a limited choice of colors.

A 32-inch shower base will feel cramped; buy a base that is at least 34 inches. Some bases must be set in thinset mortar or in a bed of sand, while others can be simply placed on the floor.

For details on how to run drain and supply lines, see *pages 180-181*.

PRESTART CHECKLIST

☐ **TIME**
Two or three days to install a base, plumbing, tiled walls, and a shower door

☐ **TOOLS**
Carpentry tools, groove-joint pliers, drill, tools for plastic *(page 100)* and copper pipe *(page 98),* tiling tools, steel rod

☐ **SKILLS**
Working with plastic and copper pipe, framing a wall, installing tile

☐ **PREP**
Install a drainpipe with trap in the center of the base, as well as supply pipes, faucet, and shower riser

☐ **MATERIALS**
Shower base, roofing felt, PVC primer and cement, 2×4 studs, cement backerboard, backerboard screws, tiles, tile adhesive, grout, caulk, shower door

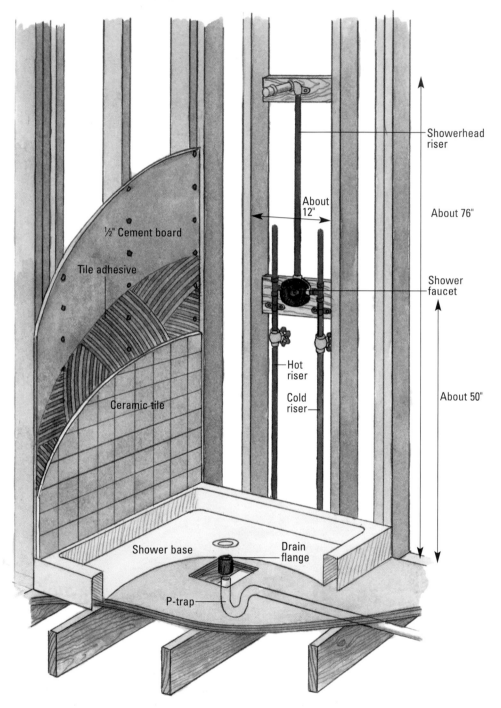

BUILDING A TILED SHOWER ENCLOSURE

½" Cement board

Tile adhesive

Ceramic tile

Showerhead riser

About 12"

About 76"

Shower faucet

Hot riser

Cold riser

About 50"

Shower base

Drain flange

P-trap

A shower drain should be installed at the center of the shower base. The flange should be level with the floor. Run the supply pipes after the framing is installed.

A. Installing the shower base

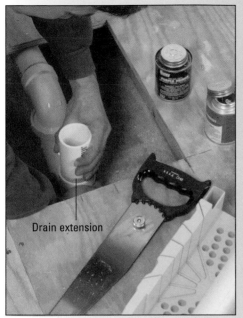

Drain extension

1 Set the shower base over the drain to make sure the drain is directly below the opening of the base. Remove the base, cut and cement an extension to the drainpipe. The extension should be flush with the floor.

Carpenter's level

Roofing felt

2 Place a layer or two of roofing felt to smooth any unevenness in the floor. (Some manufacturers may require a bed of mortar or sand.) Set the shower base over the drain to confirm that the drain is positioned where you want it. Check for level; shim with roofing felt as needed.

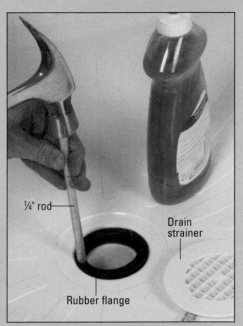

¼" rod

Drain strainer

Rubber flange

3 Using liquid soap as a lubricant, fit the rubber flange (provided with the shower base) over the drain extension and push it as far down as you can. Tap it all the way in place with a ¼-inch steel rod. Install the drain strainer.

REFRESHER COURSE
Installing a drain

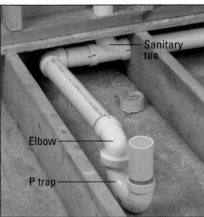

Sanitary tee

Elbow

P trap

See *pages 166–169* for instructions on running a new drain line. A shower drain should be connected directly to a trap. Drain lines must slope at a rate of ¼ inch per running foot and must be properly vented (see *pages 14–15*).

WHAT IF...
The base uses a PVC flange?

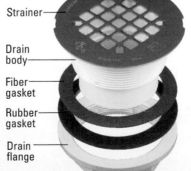

Strainer

Drain body

Fiber gasket

Rubber gasket

Drain flange

Cement the drain flange to the drainpipe; the flange should be flush with the floor. Set the gaskets on top of the flange. Place the shower base over the drain hole. Check that the gaskets are still in place. Screw the drain body through the hole in the base and into the flange. Attach the strainer.

STANLEY PRO TIP

Hire a pro when installing a mortar-laid shower base

A mortar-laid, tiled shower base can be customized to whatever style, size, and color you want. With it you can achieve a truly custom look. However, it is a major project in itself, requiring substantial prep work, including the services of a professional plumber.

Once the base of the shower is framed, a plumber should install the drain and join it to the CPE (heavy plastic) liner set inside the frame. A drain flange must be installed precisely so that water cannot seep under the liner. Then the area around the drain is filled with mortar, shaped so it slopes down toward the drain. When the mortar sets, tiles are installed on top.

B. Framing the shower

2×4 stud wall

Doubled 2×4 stud at outside corners

Protect base with a dropcloth

Cement backerboard

1 With the shower base in place, build 2×4 walls for the sides. Remember that the studs will be covered with ½-inch-thick cement board, plus the tiles (usually about ⅜ inch thick). No studs should be farther apart than 16 inches. On the plumbing wall, space the studs so you can position the shower faucet—a pair of studs spaced about a foot apart will accommodate most faucets. Install horizontal braces to support both the faucet and the shower head arm. Some bases may require a ledger *(page 155)*. Install the supply pipes and faucet, following instructions on *pages 180–181*.

2 Cut pieces of cement backerboard to fit. Cover all wood surfaces with the backerboard. Attach them to the studs with backerboard screws. Check that the wall surface is smooth and even because the tiles will follow any contours. Before tiling, fill the gap at the bottom with caulk.

One-piece shower units

Corner and rectangular shower stalls—made of acrylic fiberglass or polystyrene—are much easier to install than a custom-made enclosure. One-piece units are designed for new construction only because they are too large to fit through a door. Three-piece units are quickly assembled and are ideal for remodeling.

Two or three walls of these units must be installed up against solid walls. A corner unit can simply be installed in any corner that is reasonably square. A rectangular or square unit requires an opening of the correct width and height.

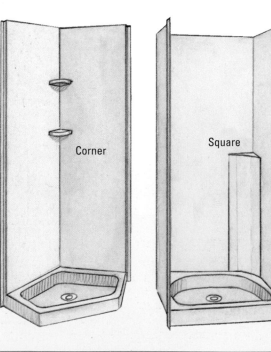

Corner

Square

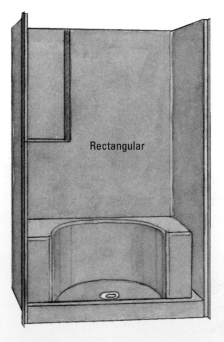

Rectangular

Ceramic tile

Grout float

3 Cover the backerboard with ceramic tile or with a prefab tub surround kit (see *pages 158–159*). Consult a book on tiling for guidelines on selecting, laying out, and cutting tile. In general, tiling should be planned to minimize small pieces. Wherever a tile edge will be exposed, install a bullnose

piece, which has one finished edge (see illustration below). Use a notched trowel to apply thinset mortar or organic tile adhesive and set the tiles. Use a tile-cutting hole saw for the faucet and showerhead stubouts.

Once all the tiles are applied, allow the adhesive to set overnight.

4 Mix a batch of latex-reinforced grout and use a grout float to first push the grout into the joints and then scrape away most of the excess. Wipe several times with a damp sponge, working to create consistent grout lines. Allow to dry, and buff with a dry towel. Caulk all the inside corners.

Caulk the edges of the stall

Bullnose

Backerboard

Caulk

Caulk

The bottom of a wall, where the tiles meet the shower base, must be installed correctly or water will seep behind the tiles and damage the studs. Install the backer board to the top of the base's flange and fill the gap below with caulk. Apply tiles and apply a bead of caulk.

Installing a shower door

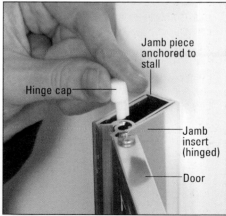

Jamb piece

Jamb piece anchored to stall

Hinge cap

Jamb insert (hinged)

Door

Measure the opening and select a door with a frame you can adjust to fit your unit. Follow manufacturer's instructions. In general, you'll begin by cutting the jamb piece to size and installing a bottom track and seal. Each jamb is made of two interlocking pieces. One attaches

to the stall with screws and anchors. When both jambs are installed, decide which way the door should swing and install the hinged insert with the clamps provided. Slide the door in place, cap, and add the door handle. Install the other jamb insert and adjust.

INSTALLING KITCHEN PLUMBING

Rough plumbing for a typical kitchen is much simpler than for a bathroom. Assuming there will be one sink and one dishwasher, only one drain line and one pair of supply pipes will be needed. All other connections—the drain and supply for the dishwasher, a supply line for an icemaker, and even a hot-water dispenser or a water filter—are made with flexible rubber or copper tubing that does not run through walls.

The finish plumbing, however, can get complicated. The underside of a typical kitchen sink may look like a bewildering maze of tubes, appliances, and trap lines.

This chapter eliminates the confusion by taking things one step at a time.

The master plan

Remodeling a kitchen involves many different operations. Usually, the most efficient order of work is the following:

■ Cover sensitive surfaces and remove old cabinets, flooring, and wall coverings.

■ Install the rough plumbing—the drain, vent, and supply lines.

■ Install electrical wiring and boxes and cut a hole for an exhaust fan, if included.

■ Apply new drywall and patch any damaged walls. Prime and paint.

■ Install the flooring, then cover it with a protective drop cloth.

■ Install the wall and base cabinets, as well as the countertops.

■ Do the finish electrical work—lights, receptacles, and switches.

■ Install the sink, faucet, garbage disposer, dishwasher, and any other plumbing appliances.

For more help on remodeling tasks other than plumbing, see books in the Stanley series such as *Basic Wiring, Advanced Wiring, Basic Tiling,* and *Interior Walls.*

Rough plumbing for a kitchen is simple, but the finish installation calls for patient, methodical work.

CHAPTER PREVIEW

Planning a kitchen
page 192

Running drain lines
page 194

Extending supply lines
page 196

Preparing the cabinets
page 198

Hooking up the sink
page 200

Any horizontal run of the revent must be at least 6 inches above the "flood level" of the sink—the rim of the sink. In this case, window framing is only a couple of inches above the countertop so a diagonal run of vent is needed. This prevents debris from settling in the vent should the sink back up.

If the drain line must travel more than 6 feet to reach the stack, you'll probably need to run the drain down through the floor and connect to the stack in the room below.

Sometimes it's easiest to dry-fit all or part of the drain and vent runs and then make the marks for cutting existing pipes and drilling holes. Use a level to check the vent and drain lines for correct slope—¼ inch per running foot. Fasten the dry run in place with duct tape. This allows you to accurately mark for tying into the stack. In addition, you can double-check slope and the final location of the drain stubout.

Installing a garbage disposer
page 204

Adding a hot water dispenser
page 206

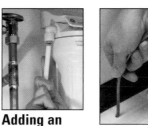

Adding an undersink filter
page 208

Hooking up an ice maker
page 209

Installing a dishwasher
page 210

PLANNING A KITCHEN

Many kitchen remodeling projects do not require new rough-in work. If the new sink is closer than 3 feet from an existing drain line, you can probably reach it by simply extending the trap. If supply lines need only to move over a few feet, you can probably attach a tee to one of the existing lines and route the new lines through cabinets, rather than inside walls. In this case, you may not need a plumbing permit; but check with your local building department to be sure.

The plan shown here calls for the standard trio of kitchen plumbing appliances—a double-bowl sink, a garbage disposer, and a dishwasher. Other appliances, such as an undersink filter (*page 143*) or a hot-water dispenser (*pages 206–207*), can be

added without much trouble either during the initial installation or sometime later. A kettle-filler faucet (*page 202*), however, requires pipes that run through walls.

The drain and vent line

The sink trap connects to the sanitary tee of a 2-inch drain line. The ideal height of the tee varies depending on the depth of the sink. (If the tee is lower than the ideal height, you can simply extend the trap downward. If the tee is too high, you may need to install a new tee at a lower point.)

The drain line must be properly vented; see *pages 14–15*. Often, the kitchen drain is connected to a separate stack, smaller in diameter than the main stack, which extends up all the way out the roof. It's

also possible to revent the drain line. Because kitchens are usually on the first floor, a revent line in a two-story house may need to travel up to the second floor or even to the attic.

Lots of grease gets poured down a kitchen sink. In many older homes, the kitchen drainpipe leads to an outside catch basin, which can be accessed periodically in order to scoop out the grease. If your system has no catch basin (or grease trap), at least be sure there is an easily accessible cleanout.

This plan calls for a cleanout located just below the sanitary tee.

The supply lines

The hot-water pipe supplies the faucet and the dishwasher; there should be a stop

KITCHEN PLUMBING OVERVIEW

When there is easy access from below, only the vent and stack need be installed in the wall—the drain runs through the basement or crawl space. See steps on pages 194–195 for how to install a drain line in the wall.

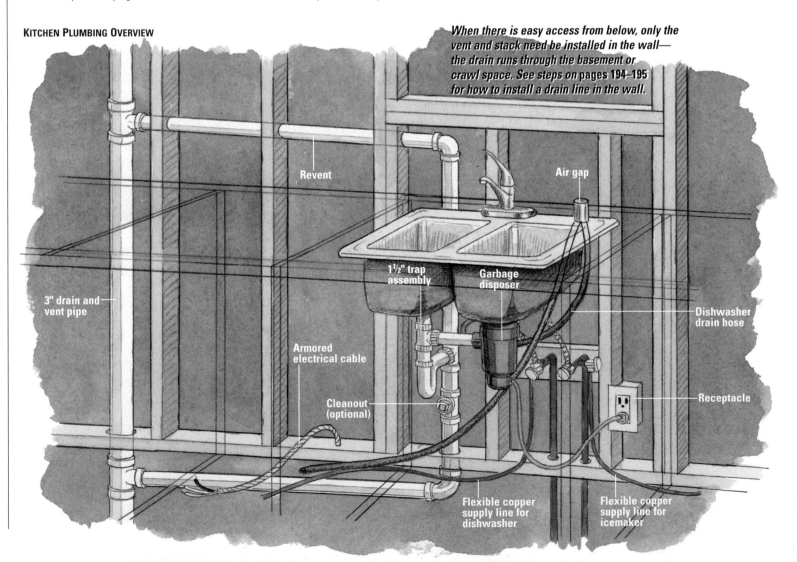

valve for each. The cold-water pipe supplies the faucet as well as a line that runs to the icemaker; there is a stop valve for each.

The sink, cabinets, and countertop

The window above a kitchen sink is typically 42 inches high, so any vent lines must be installed to either side of the window. A standard base cabinet topped with a countertop is 36 inches high. A special "sink base" cabinet has no drawers or shelves to make room for the sink and the plumbing.

A hole must be cut in the countertop to accommodate the sink *(page 199).* You can do this yourself if the countertop is plastic laminate. If the top is granite or solid-surface, hire a pro to cut the top.

Usually the dishwasher is positioned right next to the sink base to simplify running the drain and supply lines. (It is also the most convenient location for handling the dishes.) A 24-inch-wide opening in the cabinet houses a standard dishwasher.

Drawing a kitchen plan

On a piece of graph paper, draw a top view showing all the appliances, cabinets, electrical receptacles, and lights. Be precise, because every inch counts in a kitchen. A home center or kitchen supply source may have a computer program that will help you visualize possible layouts.

Kitchen designers often speak of a "work triangle," meaning that the sink, range, and refrigerator should all be within easy reach. This is easily accomplished in a kitchen that is U-shaped. If the kitchen is long and narrow, it's usually best to place one of the three elements on the wall opposite the other two. Make sure you can open the refrigerator without interfering with cooking or washing dishes.

Place the range at least 12 inches away from the sink. And leave 36 inches of counter space on either side of the sink for food preparation and draining dishes.

Most people prefer the sink to be placed in front of a window. The range should have a range hood above it, and the hood should vent to the outside.

If you plan to move or remove a wall, first check with a carpenter to make sure it's not load-bearing. If it is, you may be able to install a beam in its place.

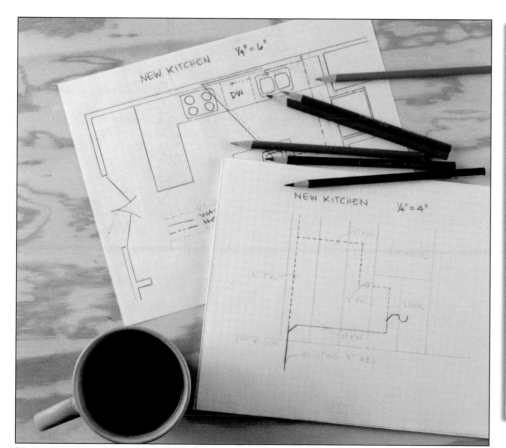

Make drawings *(pages 38–39)* to refine your plans and prepare for permit application. If you are tying into a DWV (drain-waste-vent) system with other fixtures, see the chart on *page 35* to confirm drain and supply pipe sizes. Start with a floorplan (shown), then settle specifics with a DWV elevation.

Standard specs

Check local codes for all pipe sizes and other dimensions. Here are some standard specs:

Drain and vent pipes
Sink: 2-inch drain; 1½- or 2-inch vent
Stack: 2 inches or larger
Sink drain: 18 inches above floor

Supply pipes
Faucet: ½-inch pipe
Faucet stubouts: Locate them where they can be easily reached once the sink is installed.

Other fittings
Include stop valves on the hot-water line for the dishwasher and sink.
Include stop valves on the cold-water supply for the sink and lines for other appliances such as an icemaker or hot- water dispenser.

RUNNING DRAIN LINES

If you need to run a new drainpipe, draw a simple plan, showing how it will be vented and where it will connect to the house's drain. Have your plan approved by a local plumbing inspector.

Because it needs to house only a 2-inch drain/vent pipe, a kitchen usually does not have an extra-thick "wet wall," as does a bathroom. Kitchen plumbing is sometimes run through an exterior wall; in that case, make sure the pipes are well insulated. In areas with cold winters, it is best to run supply pipes up from the basement through the floor rather than through the wall.

Remove all cabinets that are in the way; they are surprisingly easy to remove. Completely cover all cabinets and flooring that you will reuse to protect them from scratches.

If wiring is in the way, **shut off the power to the circuit** and test to make sure power is off. You may want to remove a cable before working on the drain.

See *pages 110–113* for how to run pipes through walls and connect to existing pipes.

PRESTART CHECKLIST

☐ **TIME**
About a day to run a new drain line with a revent

☐ **TOOLS**
PVC saw or circular saw, level, drill with hole saw, reciprocating saw, layout square

☐ **SKILLS**
Cutting and joining PVC pipe, running pipes through walls, connecting new pipe to old

☐ **PREP**
Clear the room of all obstructions; have your plans approved by an inspector

☐ **MATERIALS**
PVC pipe and fittings to suit local codes, fitting for joining to the drainpipe, PVC primer and cement, pipe straps

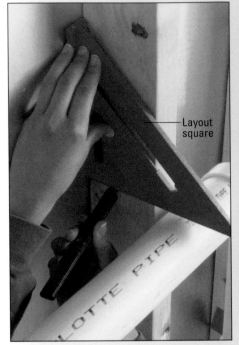

Layout square

1 Once you've put together a dry run of the drain and vent lines *(page 191)*, mark for cutting holes in the framing. Using a layout square, strike a line even with the top of the pipe. Then mark for the center of the pipe at the center of the stud.

2½" hole saw

2 For running 2-inch pipe, use a 2½-inch hole saw to drill through the studs (see *pages 166–171*). When possible, cut until the guide bit pierces the stud, then cut from the opposite side. Assemble the pipes in the wall, notching the studs where necessary.

INSTALLING A KITCHEN DRAIN-WASTER-VENT SYSTEM

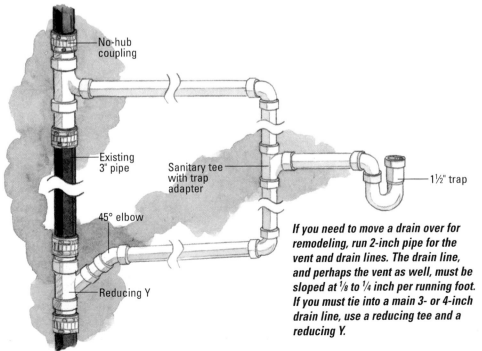

No-hub coupling

Existing 3" pipe

Sanitary tee with trap adapter

1½" trap

45° elbow

Reducing Y

If you need to move a drain over for remodeling, run 2-inch pipe for the vent and drain lines. The drain line, and perhaps the vent as well, must be sloped at ⅛ to ¼ inch per running foot. If you must tie into a main 3- or 4-inch drain line, use a reducing tee and a reducing Y.

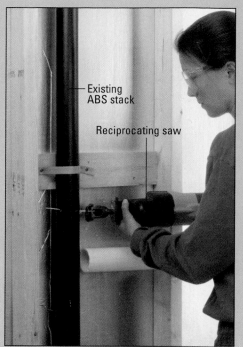

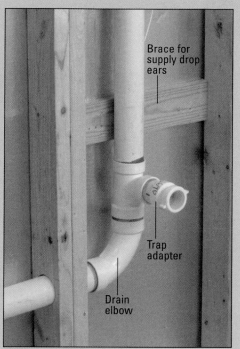

3 Having used the dry run to mark the existing stack, add braces and pipe straps to stabilize the drain. If the stack is cast iron, see *pages 108–109* for how to support it. Then cut away a section to make way for the new installation.

4 If the stack is ABS (shown in Step 3) or cast iron, use short lengths of PVC pipe and no-hub fittings to connect a sanitary tee for the vent and a Y and 45-degree street elbow for the drain. Then mark and cut a section of 2-inch PVC pipe to complete the stack.

5 Install a brace for the supply drop ears. Mark, prime, and cement *(pages 100–101)* the drain-vent system.

WHAT IF...
You install a sink in an island?

A sink installed in a kitchen island poses a special problem because there is no easy way to tie into a vent. The solution is a loop vent. This is a complicated setup, so consult with an inspector after you draw up your plans.

The drainpipe is run in the standard manner—a 1½-inch trap linking up 2-inch sink drain that runs down to a 3- or 4-inch drainpipe by means of a sanitary tee.

The vent pipe first loops up as high as possible, then runs down and over to a suitable vent pipe run up a wall. Because some water will likely enter the vent pipe, it must also be connected to the drainpipe using a sanitary tee fitting.

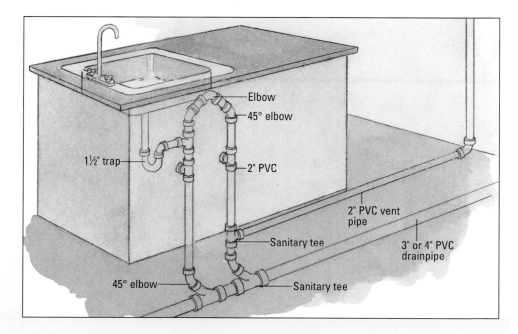

EXTENDING SUPPLY LINES

In a typical kitchen setup, hot and cold supply lines emerge from the wall just below the sink faucet, where they are connected to stop valves. Supply pipes should run inside walls rather than through cabinets to keep them safe from harm.

Because pipes under a sink are liable to get bumped, these pages show the most durable installation for emerging pipes, using drop-ear elbows and galvanized nipples to connect to stop valves.

Half-inch rigid copper pipe is large enough for most kitchen installations. (For information on how to cut and join copper supply pipe, see *pages 98–99*.)

These pages show separate stop valves for the hot and cold faucet lines, the dishwasher, and an icemaker. If you want to add a water filter, hot-water dispenser, or other appliance, you may need additional stop valves. Saddle tee valves, which simply tap into a pipe, are easy to install but are prone to clogging.

PRESTART CHECKLIST

☐ **TIME**
Several hours to run copper supply lines through a floor or wall

☐ **TOOLS**
Drill, level, combination square, propane torch, groove-joint pliers, C-clamps

☐ **SKILLS**
Cutting and joining copper pipe, running pipe through walls or floors

☐ **PREP**
Install the drain line and carefully plan the location of the supply lines; **shut off the water** before beginning work

☐ **MATERIALS**
Copper pipe and fittings, galvanized nipples, stop valves, flux, solder, nailing plates, shims

1 Where possible, run pipes through the centers of studs. Use a level or other long straightedge to mark for straight runs from stud to stud and use a combination square to mark for the center of studs. Drill ¾-inch holes to accommodate ½-inch pipe.

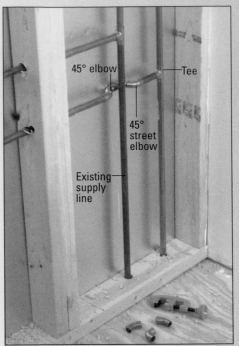

2 **Shut off water** and drain the lines you will tap into. Cut the existing pipes and install new tee fittings *(page 113)*. If you must run around a pipe or other obstruction, use 45-degree elbows and street elbows.

STANLEY PRO TIP

Choosing the right stop valve

Make sure each stop valve is the right size and type for both the pipe and the supply tube that it will attach to. A kitchen stop valve should have a ½-inch outlet.

If you will be joining to rigid copper pipe (rather than a galvanized nipple as shown above), buy a valve that sweats onto the pipe *(page 98)*, or one that joins with compression fittings (upper right).

If the pipe rises vertically through the floor, use a straight stop valve (lower left), rather than an angle stop.

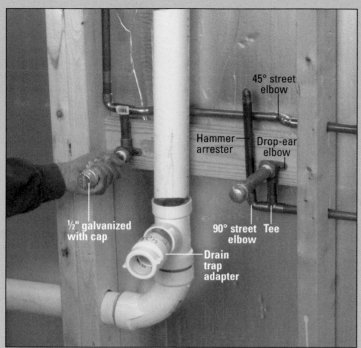

45° street elbow

Hammer arrester

Drop-ear elbow

½" galvanized with cap

90° street elbow   Tee

Drain trap adapter

3 Usually, the most convenient location for stubouts is on each side of the drain trap adapter, as shown. However, feel free to place them wherever they will be within easy reach but within 18 inches of the faucet inlets. At each stubout, install a hammer arrester and a drop-ear elbow. Do a dry run (shown), then sweat the fittings and reattach the drop-ears to the braces. Add nipples with caps; turn on the water and check for leaks.

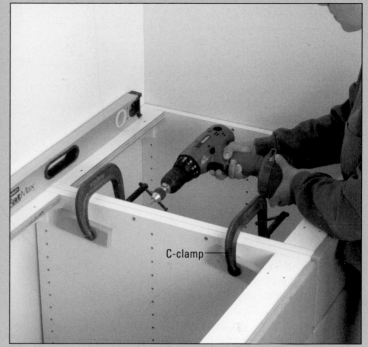

C-clamp

4 Install the wall covering, prime and paint the walls, and install the flooring. Install the kitchen base cabinets. Plumb and level them and attach them to each other (shown) and to the walls. If the sink base has a back, you'll need to drill holes for the stubouts.

WHAT IF...
Supply lines run beneath the floor?

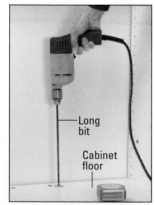

Long bit

Cabinet floor

To run pipes up through the floor from a basement below, install the cabinet first. Use a long drill bit to bore a locator hole down through the cabinet and into the space below.

ELECTRICAL CONNECTION FOR GARBAGE DISPOSER AND HOT-WATER DISPENSER

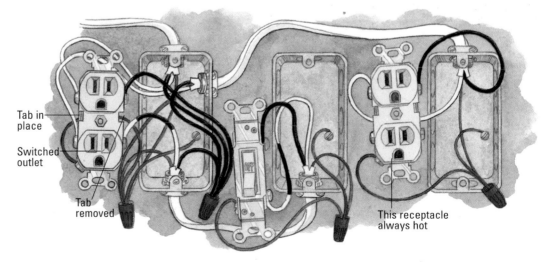

Tab in place

Switched outlet

Tab removed

This receptacle always hot

A garbage disposer should be plugged into a receptacle that is controlled by a switch. In the circuit illustrated above, a separate receptacle is always

hot, so you can plug in an appliance such as a hot-water dispenser. Shut off power before running wires and make sure that the new appliances will

not overload the circuit. Consult with a professional electrician if you are not completely sure of doing the job yourself.

PREPARING THE CABINETS

Once the drain and supply pipes have been installed and tested for leaks, run any electrical lines for receptacles and lights. Cover the walls with drywall, and prime and paint. Install the finish flooring, then protect it with cardboard or heavy paper and a drop cloth.

Purchase the sink, garbage disposer, dishwasher, and any other appliances. Unpack them and check the manufacturer's literature for the installation requirements. In particular, be sure about the dimensions of the opening for the dishwasher, as well as the size and location of the hole for its drain and supply lines.

A sink base cabinet has no drawers or shelves to leave room for all the appliances, tubes, and pipes that must fit inside it. Some sink bases are actual completed cabinets, while others consist of only the face and the floor.

PRESTART CHECKLIST

☐ **TIME**
A full day to install kitchen cabinets; plus several hours to run the electrical line for the dishwasher

☐ **TOOLS**
Hammer, drill, level, groove-joint pliers, adjustable wrench

☐ **SKILLS**
Measuring, drilling, and sawing accurately to install cabinets that are level and properly spaced

☐ **PREP**
Run and test all the rough plumbing

☐ **MATERIALS**
Cabinets, shims, screws, tees, nipples, pipe-thread tape, stop valves, 14/2 armored cable

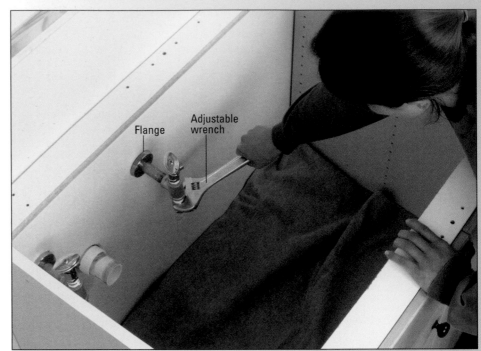

1 **Shut off the water,** and drain the line. For each supply, remove the cap from the nipple and slide on a flange to cover the hole at the wall. Wrap the nipple threads with pipe-thread tape, and install a tee. Wrap Teflon tape around the threads of two short nipples, and screw them into the tee fitting. Screw stop valves onto the nipples. Turn the valve handles off, and restore water pressure to test for leaks.

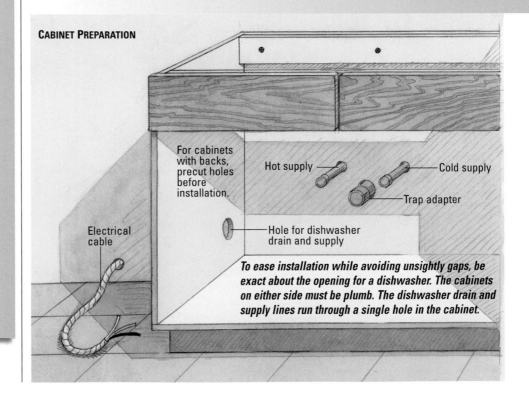

CABINET PREPARATION

For cabinets with backs, precut holes before installation.

Hot supply

Cold supply

Trap adapter

Electrical cable

Hole for dishwasher drain and supply

To ease installation while avoiding unsightly gaps, be exact about the opening for a dishwasher. The cabinets on either side must be plumb. The dishwasher drain and supply lines run through a single hole in the cabinet.

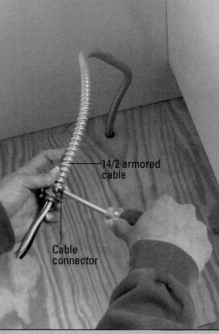

1½" hole saw

14/2 armored cable

Cable connector

24¼"

2 The dishwasher opening should be 24¼ inches wide for most models; check manufacturer's instructions. If installing a cabinet to the other side of the dishwasher (shown above), level from the sink base cabinet, plumb, and fasten it in place.

3 Run an electrical line for the dishwasher. Usually, a 14/2 armored cable connected to a 15-amp circuit is sufficient, but check codes and the manufacturer's literature. Be certain that the dishwasher will not overload the circuit. **Hire an electrician if you are not sure of your wiring abilities.**

4 The dishwasher instructions will tell you the best place to drill a hole for running the drain and supply lines. Usually a single 1½-inch hole is sufficient.

Cutting countertop for a sink

Saber saw

To cut a laminate countertop for a sink, place the new sink upside down on top of the countertop, centered over the base cabinet. Trace around the sink, then draw another line ¾ inch inside the first line. Cut along the second line using a saber saw equipped with a fine-cutting blade.

Choosing a sink

When it comes to sink materials, you generally get what you pay for. An inexpensive stainless-steel sink flexes when you push on it, scratches easily, and is difficult to keep clean. A higher-quality heavy-gauge (6- or 8-gauge) stainless-steel sink, such as one with a burnished finish, is a better choice. When choosing a stainless-steel sink, make sure the underside is well coated with sound-deadening insulation.

An enameled cast-iron sink comes in a variety of colors. It lasts much longer than an enameled steel sink. Acrylic sinks (like the one shown) have the look of enameled cast iron, and the higher-end models are nearly as durable. Both cast-iron and acrylic sinks have insulating properties so that water stays warm in them longer than it does in a stainless-steel sink.

Stainless steel

Heavy-gauge stainless steel

Cast iron

Acrylic

HOOKING UP THE SINK

Once you have cut the hole in the countertop *(page 199)*, set the sink into the hole to make sure it will fit.

It is possible to install the sink first and then attach the faucet, garbage disposer, and drain from below. However, you'll save yourself hassle and time if you connect most of the components to the sink before installing it. Spread a drop cloth on the countertop nearby and set the sink upside down on the cloth. The faucet holes should overhang the counter so you can install the faucet. Or better yet, set the sink on two sawhorses, padded with rags or towels.

Enameled-steel (shown) and stainless-steel sinks clamp to the countertop with special clips that are usually included with the sink. Test to make sure that the clips will work on your countertop before you install the plumbing. A cast-iron sink is heavy enough that it needs no clips.

PRESTART CHECKLIST

☐ **TIME**
About half a day to install a sink with disposer and dishwasher connections

☐ **TOOLS**
Drill, screwdriver, groove-joint pliers, adjustable wrench, strainer wrench or spud wrench

☐ **SKILLS**
Connecting a trap, installing a faucet and garbage disposer

☐ **PREP**
Install the rough plumbing, a switched receptacle, and the cabinets

☐ **MATERIALS**
Sink, faucet, garbage disposer, appliance extension cord, wire nuts, trap assembly, supply tubes, flexible copper line for dishwasher and icemaker supplies, drain hose (usually included with the dishwasher), air gap, plumber's putty, drop cloth

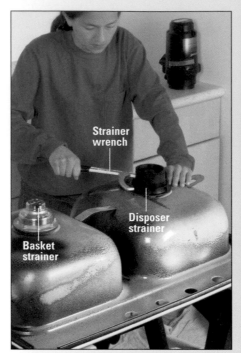

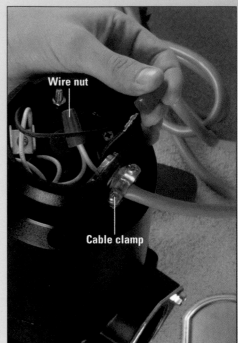

1 Install a standard basket strainer in one sink hole, and the garbage disposer strainer in the other hole. Make sure you know which strainer goes to which hole. Place a rope of putty under the lip of the strainer body and hold it in place as you slip on the washers and tighten the nut.

2 Following the manufacturer's instructions, dismantle the garbage disposer mounting hardware. Open the electrical coverplate and hook up an appliance extension cord using wire nuts. Replace the coverplate.

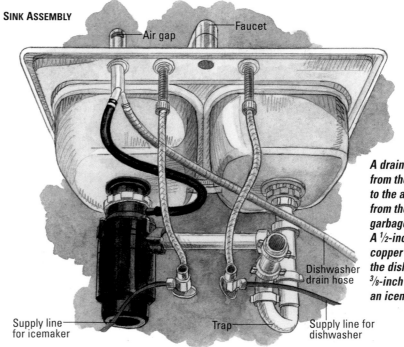

SINK ASSEMBLY

A drain hose runs from the dishwasher to the air gap and from there to the garbage disposer. A ½-inch flexible copper line supplies the dishwasher; a ⅜-inch line supplies an icemaker.

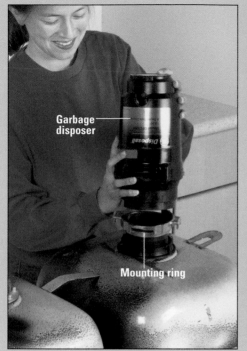

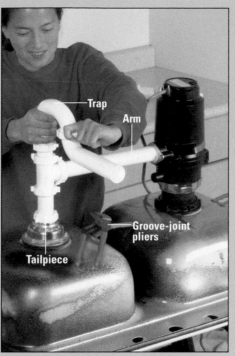

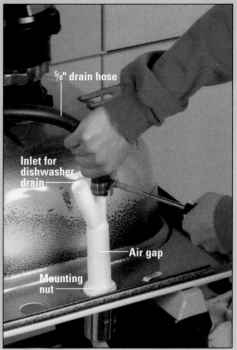

3 Slide the garbage disposer mount ring over the flange. Then install the cushion mount, making sure the groove on the inside fits over the lip of the sink flange. Position the disposer over the flange; push down and twist until the disposer is fully anchored.

4 Assemble the drain trap. Begin by installing the tailpiece and the arm that attaches to the disposer. Cut pieces to size as needed, then install the trap. Set the sink in the hole to see whether the trap lines up with the trap adapter in the wall; you may need to trim a piece or add an extension.

5 Attach the air gap with a mounting nut. Run a ⅝-inch hose from the air gap to the disposer. Secure the hose with hose clamps. If the drain hose is easily disconnected from the dishwasher, attach it to the air gap now. Otherwise attach it when you install the dishwasher *(pages 210–211)*.

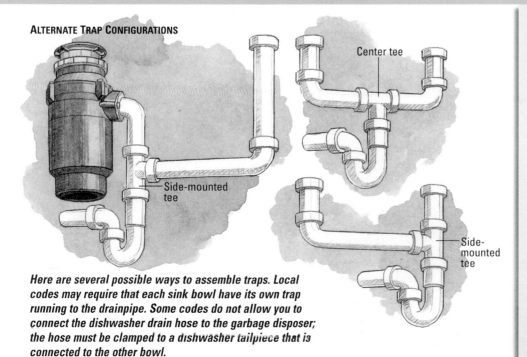

ALTERNATE TRAP CONFIGURATIONS

Here are several possible ways to assemble traps. Local codes may require that each sink bowl have its own trap running to the drainpipe. Some codes do not allow you to connect the dishwasher drain hose to the garbage disposer; the hose must be clamped to a dishwasher tailpiece that is connected to the other bowl.

STANLEY PRO TIP

Assembling a trap

When connecting the pieces of a chrome or PVC trap, don't forget the slip nut and washer for each joint. Where a tailpiece attaches to a strainer, a special type of washer may be used. You'll probably need to cut at least one pipe; use a hacksaw or a fine-toothed saw (for PVC only) and a miter box.

HOOKING UP THE SINK *(continued)*

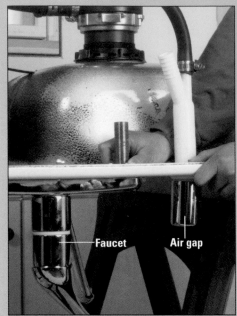

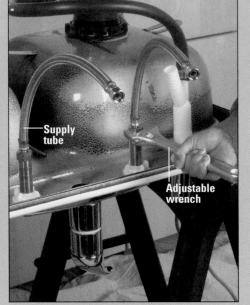

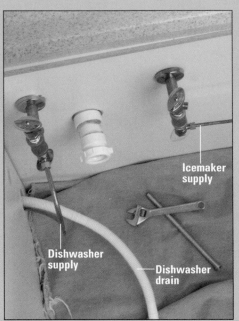

6 Install the faucet. If the faucet does not come with a plastic or rubber gasket, place a rope of putty under the faucet's flange to seal out water. Tighten the mounting hardware.

7 Screw flexible supply tubes onto the faucet inlets. Make sure their other ends are the right size to screw onto the stop valves. If the faucet has flexible copper inlets, use two adjustable wrenches to avoid kinking the inlets.

8 Before you set the sink into the hole, save yourself work later by hooking up as much plumbing as possible now. For instance, attach the supply lines for the dishwasher *(page 210)* and for the icemaker.

Installing a kettle-filler faucet

A faucet like this makes it easy to fill a large kettle while it is on the stove or countertop. This model supplies only cold water, but other types have cold and hot handles.

It is important to install the faucet firmly in the wall. Run a cold-water supply line up the wall. The last 2 feet or so should be extra-strong pipe, such as galvanized steel or brass. Install a threaded tee and a hammer arrester. Anchor a 2×6 or larger brace behind the pipe and the tee and attach the pipe and the tee using two-hole pipe straps.

Along with the faucet, buy a special inlet nipple, which has threads running all along its length in the same direction. A locking nut with washers allows you to screw the inlet nipple to the faucet at just the right depth so you can screw the faucet into the tee fitting at maximum tightness against the wall.

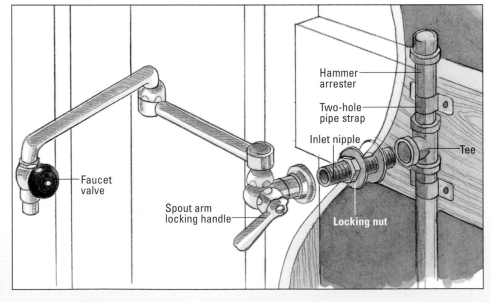

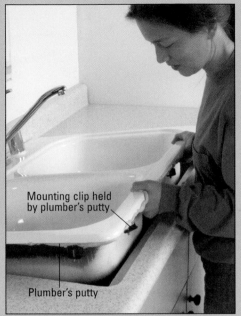

9 Place a rope of plumber's putty, thick enough to seal at all points, around the bottom lip of the sink. Position at least some of the mounting clips in the channels and hold them upright, using dabs of putty. Turn the sink right side up and carefully lower it into the hole.

10 From underneath, turn the clips so they grab the underside of the countertop. There should be a clip every 8 inches or so. Tighten each clip with a screwdriver or a drill equipped with a screwdriver bit.

11 Attach the trap to the trap adapter in the wall. Tighten all the connections with groove-joint pliers. To test, fill each bowl with water, then remove the stopper and watch for drips. Run the disposer with the water on and check for drips.

Installing a cast-iron sink

A cast-iron sink is very heavy, so have someone help you lift and position it. Apply a bead of silicone caulk around the hole. Carefully lower the sink into the opening. Avoid sliding it, which could compromise the caulk seal. Press down gently. Scrape away excess caulk with a plastic or wood scraper. Allow the caulk to set for several hours before attaching the plumbing.

Other sink installations

A flush-mounted or underhung sink makes for easier cleaning, but these styles require special countertop treatments.

Install a flush-mounted sink with its rim resting on plywood substrate. Install concrete backerboard around the sink and top it with tiles that partially rest on top of the sink flange.

Install and plumb an underhung sink after the substrate is installed. Then install tiles as shown, with cut pieces around the perimeter and bullnose trim pieces overlapping them.

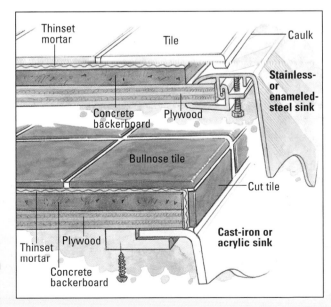

INSTALLING A GARBAGE DISPOSER

Replacing an existing disposer with one of the same size is simply a matter of disconnecting and reconnecting fittings. However, if there is no existing disposer, or if the new unit is a different size, you will need to reconfigure your sink trap.

A disposer must be plugged into an GFCI receptacle or directly wired to a junction box that is controlled by a switch. The switch is typically on the wall above the countertop. If the wiring does not exist under your sink, have an electrician do this work for you.

Local codes may regulate the use of disposers. In some areas they are banned because they add to the sewage load. Codes may require that a dishwasher drain hose be routed through an air gap before entering a disposer.

Installation, parts, and procedures vary considerably among disposer models. Follow the manufacturer's directions.

PRESTART CHECKLIST

☐ **TIME**
Between one and three hours, depending on changes to plumbing

☐ **TOOLS**
Screwdriver, groove-joint pliers, wire strippers

☐ **SKILLS**
Making simple electrical splices, installing a basket strainer

☐ **PREP**
Remove an existing disposer or part of the trap, and the strainer as well

☐ **MATERIALS**
Garbage disposer, wire nuts, appliance cord (thicker than normal extension cord) or armored cable ("whip"), trap parts

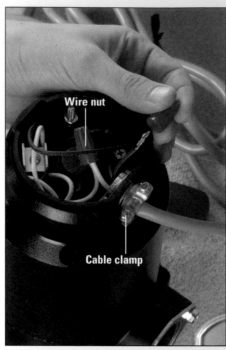

1 Remove the electrical cover plate from the bottom of the disposer. Install a cable clamp and run an appliance cord through it. Strip the wire ends and splice the wires—black to black, white to white, ground (green) to ground. Cap each splice with a wire nut. Replace the cover plate.

2 Remove the old strainer *(pages 50–51)* and clean the area around the hole. Press a rope of plumber's putty around the underside of the disposer sink flange. Press the flange into place. Have a helper hold the flange in position while you perform the next step from below.

GARBAGE DISPOSER INSTALLATION

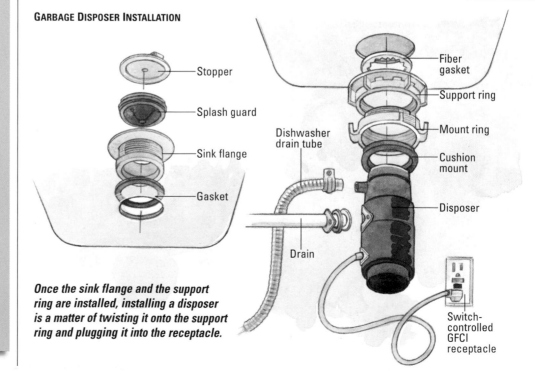

Once the sink flange and the support ring are installed, installing a disposer is a matter of twisting it onto the support ring and plugging it into the receptacle.

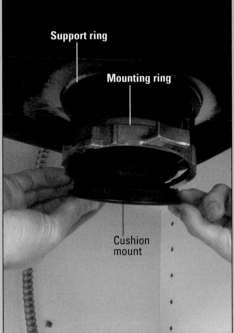

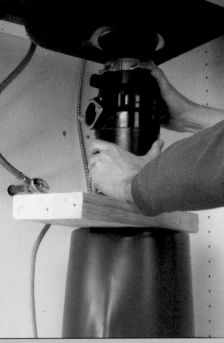

3 To install this type of mounting ring, slip on the fiber gasket and hand-tighten the support ring. Slide the mount ring over the flange and install the cushion mount, making sure the groove on the inside fits over the lip of the sink flange. Scrape out any excess putty on the inside of the sink.

4 If the disposer is not too heavy and you can get into a comfortable position, simply lift the disposer up onto the mounting ring and twist it so it catches and is firmly anchored. If you have trouble doing this, construct a simple platform to help support the disposer.

5 To connect to the drain line, either use the black elbow that comes with the disposer or discard the elbow and install a horizontal tailpiece, as shown. See *pages 46–47* for tips on assembling a trap.

Attaching a dishwasher

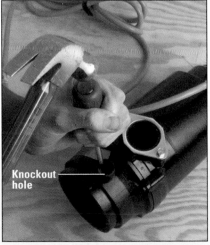

If you have a dishwasher, run its drain hose first to an air gap, then to the disposer's drain connection. Use a hose clamp to hold the hose firm.

USE THE BLACK ELBOW
Other disposer drain options

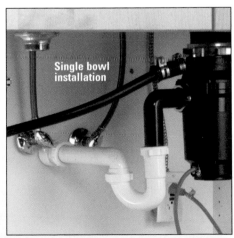

Some local codes require that the drain line turn downward as soon as it leaves the disposer. Most disposers come with a black elbow designed to make this turn.

If you have a single-bowl sink, install the black elbow that comes with the disposer and run the drain line directly into a trap.

ADDING A HOT-WATER DISPENSER

This handy appliance delivers water that's about 200° F to the countertop. It plugs into a standard electrical receptacle. Small copper tubes run from a cold water line to the dispenser's tank, then up to a spout by the sink.

Installation tips

To install the dispenser, you must have an electrical receptacle that is always energized (not switched on or off) near the sink. To supply a garbage disposer and a hot-water dispenser from a single receptacle, have an electrician install a "split" GFCI receptacle.

Position the tank and the copper lines out of the way under the sink. Usually, the rear wall is preferable to a side wall.

You can screw a saddle-tee valve into the pipe without shutting off the water to the pipe. However, the valve is liable to get clogged. For a more trouble-free installation, shut off the water and drill a hole first (as shown in Step 1).

PRESTART CHECKLIST

☐ **TIME**
If there is an existing electrical receptacle and an available knockout hole on the sink, about an hour

☐ **TOOLS**
Drill, adjustable wrench or small wrenches, groove-joint pliers, basin wrench, perhaps a hole saw

☐ **SKILLS**
Mounting a unit with screws, assembling appliance parts

☐ **PREP**
Clear out the cabinet below the sink; shut off water to a cold-water line

☐ **MATERIALS**
Hot-water dispenser, saddle-tee valve or stop valve

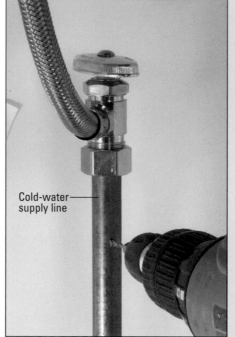

Cold-water supply line

1 **Shut off water** to a cold-water line; drain the line by opening a faucet at a lower level. Check the manufacturer's instructions for drilling a hole (typically about ⅛ inch in size) for the saddle-tee valve needle. Squirt a little multipurpose oil on the bit before drilling.

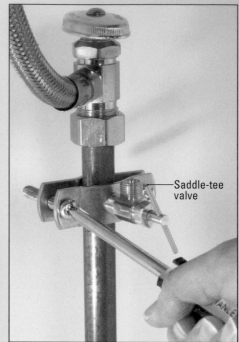

Saddle-tee valve

2 Position the two parts of a saddle-tee valve on the pipe, making sure the valve's point pokes into the hole. Tighten the screws. Turn the water back on and make sure the valve works and does not leak.

OVERVIEW OF HOT-WATER DISPENSER INSTALLATION

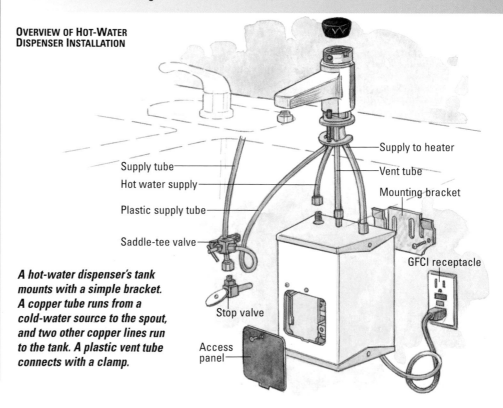

Supply to heater
Supply tube
Vent tube
Hot water supply
Mounting bracket
Plastic supply tube
Saddle-tee valve
GFCI receptacle
Stop valve
Access panel

A hot-water dispenser's tank mounts with a simple bracket. A copper tube runs from a cold-water source to the spout, and two other copper lines run to the tank. A plastic vent tube connects with a clamp.

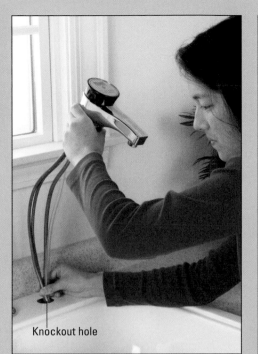

Knockout hole

3 Mount the spout first. Carefully slip the copper lines through the knockout hole. Have a helper hold the spout in position while you work from underneath. Slide on the washer and the mounting nut. Tighten the nut by hand. If that is not firm enough, use a basin wrench to tighten it further.

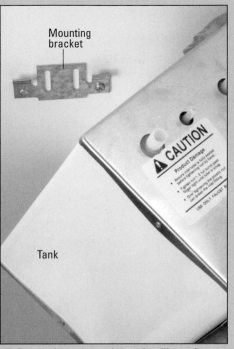

Mounting bracket

Tank

4 Determine where the tank will go; the copper lines must be able to reach it. Install the bracket with screws, then slip the tank onto the bracket.

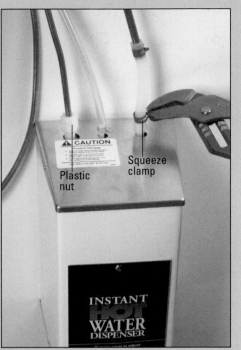

Plastic nut

Squeeze clamp

5 Connect the copper lines according to manufacturer's instructions. Bend the tubes carefully to avoid kinking; use a tubing bender to be safe (page 20). Copper tubes connect to the tank using a plastic nut and ferrule; plastic tubes are secured with squeeze clamps.

Other water connections

For a more secure supply connection, install a tee fitting in the cold-water line and add a new stop valve.

Another method is to replace a standard stop valve with one that has two outlets, one for the faucet and one for the hot-water dispenser.

STANLEY PRO TIP

Maintaining a dispenser

Water that comes from this unit is nearly boiling, so keep small children away from the spout.

The tank gets hot, too, so keep paper bags and other flammables away from it.

If you expect not to use the dispenser for a few days, unplug it to save energy.

If the unit gets clogged, shut off the saddle-tee or stop valve and disconnect the supply line. Hold the line over a bucket and slowly turn the water back on. If flow is slow, the problem is probably the saddle-tee valve. Shut off the water and replace the valve.

If water drips from the spout when the unit is not in use, turn down the temperature. If that doesn't solve the problem, replace the spout.

No knockout on sink?
Drill a hole in a stainless-steel sink using a metal-cutting hole saw. In an acrylic sink, use a standard hole saw.

ADDING AN UNDER-SINK FILTER

A simple cabinet-mounted water filter can reduce the amount of sediment in water, reduce water odor, and improve its taste.

Local water conditions vary, so check with a salesperson at a home center or hardware store to see which filter will work best for you. Most carbon-based units make water more palatable.

If your water is excessively hard, have a water softener company install and perhaps maintain a water softener.

The unit shown here purifies all the cold water that runs through a kitchen faucet. Also available is a unit that has its own faucet for a separate source of filtered drinking water.

For an easy-to-install alternative, consider a faucet-mounted water filter. Some purify all the water flowing through the spout, while others have a separate valve that allows you to choose either filtered or unfiltered water. Both screw onto the faucet in place of the aerator.

PRESTART CHECKLIST

☐ **TIME**
An hour or two

☐ **TOOLS**
Drill, screwdriver, tubing cutter, adjustable wrench, groove-joint pliers

☐ **SKILLS**
Attaching with screws, cutting pipe, and making simple connections

☐ **PREP**
Add a tee and stop valve to the cold water supply; clear out the cabinet

☐ **MATERIALS**
Water purifier, perhaps extra parts for connecting

Spout

Undersink mounting washer

1 Mount the spout to the knockout hole in the sink. Have a helper center the spout while you work below to tighten the mounting nut.

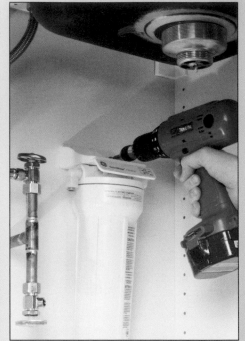

2 **Shut off the water** to the cold-water supply tube. Add a separate stop valve *(page 124–125)* or use one of the methods on *page 207.* Hold the filter in a convenient location and drive screws to attach it.

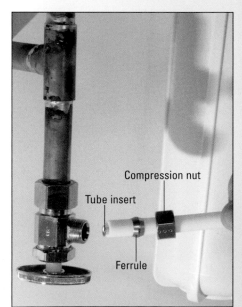

Compression nut

Tube insert

Ferrule

3 Trim to length the plastic supply tube for the filter. Poke the tube insert into the tube and slide on the compression nut and ferrule. Tighten the nut using a small adjustable wrench.

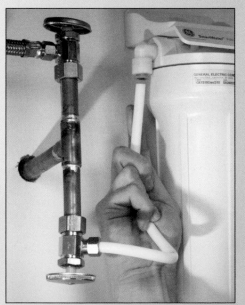

4 Connect the lines to the stop valve and spout, according to the manufacturer's instructions. Compression fittings make these connections easy. Water will now run through the filter before reaching the spout.

HOOKING UP AN ICE MAKER

Most new refrigerators have ice makers, but installation is typically an added expense. If you are retrofitting an ice maker to an older fridge, you will need to tap into a cold water line to supply the ice maker. In either case, doing it yourself is not difficult, as long as you work carefully with the copper tubing. If any kinks develop, don't try to "fix" them—cut them off or use a new piece of tubing.

For ice that tastes extra nice, install a water filter *(page 208)* and run the ice maker line through it.

As an alternative to the saddle-tee valve, install a new stop valve or a stop valve with two outlets *(page 207)*.

PRESTART CHECKLIST

☐ **TIME**
An hour or two for most installations

☐ **TOOLS**
Drill with long drill bit, adjustable wrench, screwdriver, tubing cutter, tubing bender

☐ **SKILLS**
Drilling holes, cutting and running copper tubing, making simple connections

☐ **PREP**
Locate a nearby cold-water pipe to tap

☐ **MATERIALS**
Copper tubing, saddle-tee valve

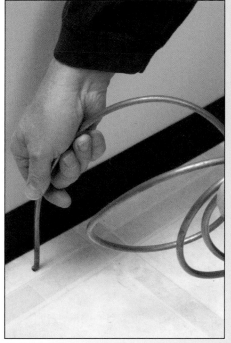

1 Behind the refrigerator, drill a hole through the floor to a basement or crawl space, or drill a horizontal hole to reach another room. Carefully unroll copper tubing and run it through the hole.

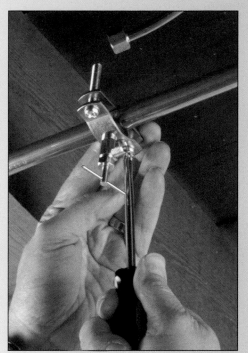

2 Install a saddle-tee valve on a cold water pipe *(page 206)* and hook the copper line to it by slipping on a ferrule and tightening a compression nut.

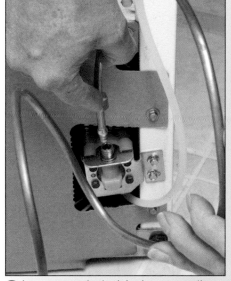

3 Leave enough slack in the copper line to allow you to slide out the refrigerator for cleaning. Connect the other end of the tubing to the ice maker connection on the refrigerator, using the same combination of a compression nut and a ferrule.

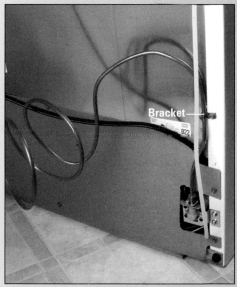

4 Moving the refrigerator for cleaning strains the compression fitting. Use one of the brackets provided with the refrigerator or the ice maker kit to firmly attach the copper tube to the fridge. Carefully bend the tubing into a coil as shown.

INSTALLING A DISHWASHER

Once you prepare the site correctly, installing a dishwasher is surprisingly easy. Make sure the opening is the correct size, and test-fit the dishwasher.

Run an electrical cable—preferably armored, though nonmetallic cable may be approved—into the space. Make sure it will not bump into the dishwasher's frame. In most cases, a 14/2 cable hooked to a 15-amp circuit will suffice. Make sure that hooking up to the dishwasher will not overload the circuit. Check *Stanley Advanced Wiring* for more information. Hire an electrician if you are unsure.

Most dishwashers come with a drain hose. The drain hose runs to an air gap mounted to a knockout hole in the sink *(page 201)*. From there, another length of hose runs to the garbage disposer. If there is no garbage disposer, it runs to a dishwasher tailpiece on the trap.

The water supply line is typically flexible copper, connected to its own shutoff valve. The cabinets on either side should be spaced according to manufacturer's instructions—usually 24¼ inches.

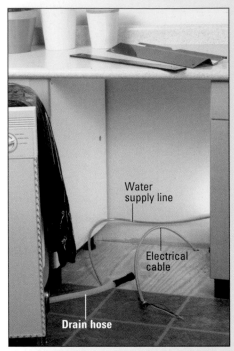

Water supply line

Electrical cable

Drain hose

Electrical cable

Water supply line

1 Using a tubing cutter, trim the supply tube to the needed length. Check to make sure the electrical cable is long enough to reach the junction box built into the dishwasher.

2 Push the dishwasher into the opening. As you do so, thread the drain line through the 1½-inch hole already cut in the cabinet. Make sure the lines do not become kinked or bent.

PRESTART CHECKLIST

☐ **TIME**
Once the electrical and plumbing lines are run and the cabinets installed, about an hour to install a dishwasher

☐ **TOOLS**
Tubing cutter, drill, screwdriver, adjustable wrench, groove-joint pliers

☐ **SKILLS**
Making simple plumbing and electrical connections

☐ **PREP**
Install the electrical and plumbing lines; install the cabinets and countertop

☐ **MATERIALS**
Dishwasher with drain hose, hose clamps, air gap, flexible copper supply line, electrical cable, wire nuts

DISHWASHER CONNECTIONS

Three connections are needed for a dishwasher: An electrical cable supplies 120 volts of power; a drain line runs to the trap or garbage disposer; and a supply line, hooked to a stop valve under the sink, brings water to the dishwasher.

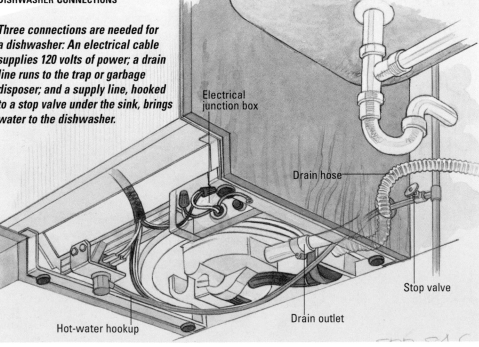

Electrical junction box

Drain hose

Stop valve

Hot-water hookup

Drain outlet

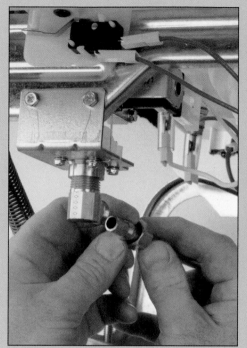

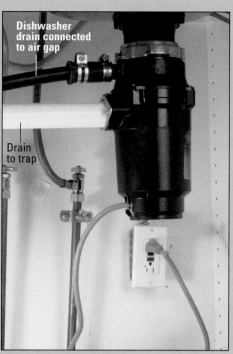

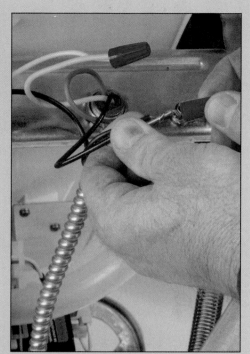

3 Slip a nut and ferrule onto the end of the supply line. Carefully bend the tubing and insert it into the supply inlet. Slide the ferrule down into the inlet and tighten the nut. Open the stop valve and check for leaks; you may need to tighten the nut further.

4 Run the drain line to the air gap, then to the garbage disposer or a tailpiece with a special dishwasher drain fitting. Slide a hose clamp onto the hose, slip the hose onto the fitting, slide the clamp over the fitting, and tighten the clamp.

5 Run the electrical cable through the cable clamp and tighten the clamp nuts to hold the cable firm. Strip and splice wires—black to black, white to white, and ground (green or copper) to ground. Cap each splice with a wire nut and install the electrical coverplate.

Anchoring and leveling the dishwasher

Slide the dishwasher in far enough so that only its decorative trim is visible. If the dishwasher won't go in far enough, pull it out and look for obstructions.

Stand back and check that the dishwasher looks straight in relation to the cabinets and the countertop. To raise or lower one or both sides, use groove-joint pliers to turn the feet at the bottom of the unit. Wiggle the dishwasher to test that it rests solidly on all four feet.

Once satisfied with the dishwasher's position, open the door and find the mounting tabs (usually on the top edge, sometimes on the sides). Drill pilot holes. To avoid drilling up through the countertop, wrap a piece of tape on the drill bit to mark the depth to stop at. Drive short screws into the holes to anchor the dishwasher to the countertop.

UTILITY ROOM & BASEMENT UPGRADES

Plumbing improvements in utility areas and basements can be relatively easy compared to other areas of the house. Often, there no walls that have to be removed to run new lines—and you won't have to mess up oft-used rooms while completing the project.

Water treatment

The high mineral content of local water can lead to staining, soap scum buildup, and a reduction in the ability of soap and detergent to get things clean. Such telltale signs indicate that your household water needs softening. Water softeners are pricey and are often rented by the month but if you install your own, it can pay for itself in two to three years.

Basement plumbing

Architects have equated a basement with digging a well and then trying to keep the water out. If your basement floods after heavy rainfall, you may want to install a sump pump. Digging a hole for the reservoir is the difficult part; you'll have to chop through a concrete floor then dig into hard-packed clay, gravel, and sand. But once the reservoir is in place, the plumbing is relatively easy.

If the main drain line is too high for a bathroom in the basement—or you don't want to break into the concrete floor to trench for drain lines—consider an upflush toilet unit. Once the drain and vent connections are made, these units are surprisingly easy to install and typically use standard toilets. Most units allow you to hook up sink and tub/shower drains as well. Once the bathroom is framed out and flooring and walls added, the unit will be completely hidden.

Adding a laundry area involves running hot and cold supply lines to the washer and tapping into a drain stack. A nearby utility sink is handy for heavy-duty washing up. The same techniques apply whether a laundry is upstairs or down.

Improvements to utility rooms and basements can be added with relative ease and speed.

CHAPTER PREVIEW

Installing a sump pump
page 214

Adding a water softener
page 216

Installing an upflush toilet
page 219

Setting up a laundry room
page 222

Are you tired of renting a water softener, paying someone else to maintain the system? The cost of buying a water softener and installing it yourself can be repaid in less than three years. As with most basement plumbing upgrades, the project requires little or no tearing into existing walls.

Upgrades such as this water softener installation can be ideal projects for homeowners; they rarely disrupt the use of other rooms and systems while they are under construction.

INSTALLING A SUMP PUMP

If your basement floods or becomes damp during wet periods, first try directing rainwater away from the house by changing your gutter downspouts. If that does not solve the problem, a sump pump may be the solution.

There are two basic kinds of sump pump installations. If you have no drainpipes under the basement designed specifically for handling rainwater, then dig a hole at a low point of the basement and install a perforated pit liner (you may have to perforate it yourself using a ⅜-inch spade bit). Water under the basement will slowly percolate into the liner.

If your house has rainwater drain pipes, it probably also has a pit already dug for a sump pump, with a drain pipe running into it. Purchase a non-perforated pit liner, and cut a hole for the drainpipe.

A wise add-on is a rechargeable battery backup unit, which will power the pump if a heavy storm causes a power outage. A pump-failure alarm is also a good idea.

PRESTART CHECKLIST

☐ **TIME**
About half a day to dig a pit and install a sump pump

☐ **TOOLS**
Sledgehammer or electric jackhammer, cold chisel, drill with masonry bit and spade bit, hole saw, PVC saw, small level, screwdriver, groove-joint pliers

☐ **SKILLS**
Basic carpentry skills, cutting and joining PVC drain pipe

☐ **PREP**
Locate a low spot in the basement near a wall so the pump won't take up usable space. If necessary, install a GFCI receptacle nearby.

☐ **MATERIALS**
Sump pump, pit liner, PVC drainpipe, primer, cement

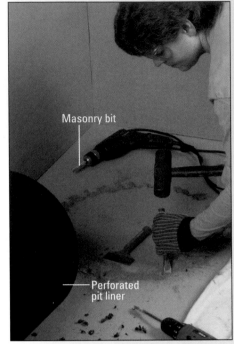

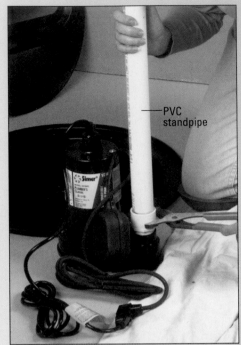

1 Use the pit liner to mark for cutting a hole in the basement floor. Using a masonry bit, drill a series of holes around the perimeter. (A concrete basement floor is usually 3 inches thick.) Chip out the concrete with a sledge and cold chisel or an electric jackhammer *(pages 21–22)*.

2 Dig the hole deep enough for the pit liner and set the pit liner in place. Make sure the liner is resting solidly on the ground so it can support the pump. Attach a PVC standpipe to the unit, using the adapter parts supplied by the manufacturer.

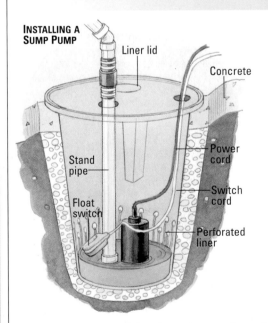

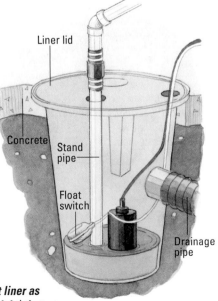

A retrofit sump pump (above) empties a perforated pit liner as water seeps in. Newer homes have drainage pipes (right) that feed into the pit liner. Both can use the same sump pump setup.

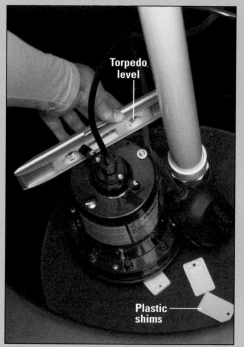

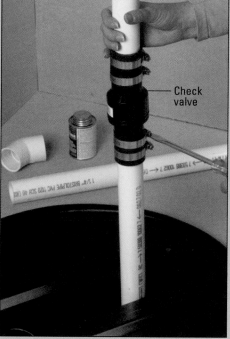

3 Set the pump on the bottom of the liner. It should be near the center so the float won't touch the side of the liner. Check to make sure the pump is level; shim underneath with plastic shims if necessary. Place the lid on the liner.

4 Just above the level of the floor, install a check valve, which ensures that water does not backflow into the pump. Run PVC pipe up and toward the exit point. Clamp the electrical wires to the side of the pipes. Plug the unit into a GFCI receptacle.

5 Cut a hole through the rim joist for the pipe to exit the house. Run PVC pipe out of the house and extend it so it carries water at least 6 feet away from the house. Water that is discharged near the house will seep back into the basement.

Pedestal sump pump

A pedestal-type sump pump has its motor above the water and is not waterproof. It is recommended for a basement that needs frequent draining; its float can be adjusted. This type is less expensive than a submersible but is also noisier.

Ejector pump for gray water

If your drain lines are above floor level and you want to install a utility sink, the simplest solution is a gray-water sump box. It must be connected to the house's drain and vent lines. To provide drainage for a toilet as well, install an upflushing unit (*pages 219–221*).

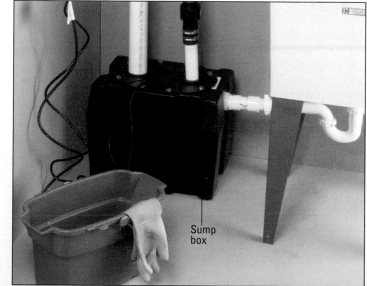

Sump box

INSTALLING A WATER SOFTENER

Hard water contains large amounts of minerals such as iron, calcium, and magnesium. Telltale signs include reddish stains, white mineral buildup in pipes and fittings, reduced cleaning ability of soap and detergent, and soap scum buildup. Hard water is not only a nuisance; it can also damage faucets and appliances.

A water softener captures minerals, then periodically flushes them away with a brine (saltwater) mixture. The more often it flushes, the more often you need to change the salt. The most efficient softener is one that flushes according to the amount of water used or the amount of minerals detected, rather than one that uses a timer.

The resulting water contains sodium, sometimes at levels undesirable for people high blood pressure and hypertension. If this is the case, consider a bypass line for drinking water, using bottled water, or installing a whole-house filter.

A water softening company will rent and maintain a water softener in your home. Check out the prices; it may be worth the extra price to have someone else change the salt and take care of maintenance.

PRESTART CHECKLIST

☐ **TIME**
A day to install a water softener

☐ **TOOLS**
Groove-joint pliers, screwdriver, tubing cutter, propane torch, flux brush, sandpaper, wire reaming brush

☐ **SKILLS**
Cutting and joining copper or steel pipe

☐ **PREP**
Plan to install the softener where water first enters the house, before it branches into hot and cold lines

☐ **MATERIALS**
Water softener, Teflon tape, solder, flux

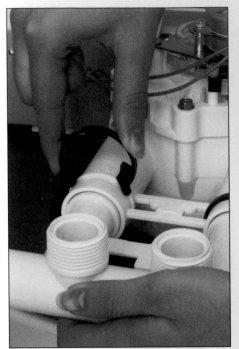

1 Install the bypass valve provided by the manufacturer. Lubricate the O-rings, push the valve into the ports, and slip on the clips.

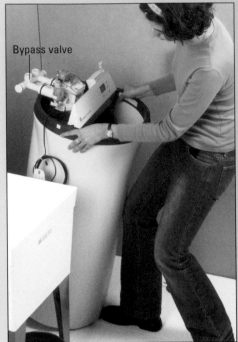

Bypass valve

2 Shut off gas or electricity to the water heater. Turn off the water supply at the main shutoff valve and open faucets on the lowest floor to drain the line. Provide a stable, level surface near the main water line for the softener to rest on, a place that is easily accessible. Position the unit.

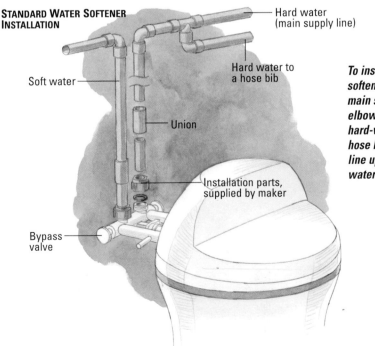

STANDARD WATER SOFTENER INSTALLATION

Hard water (main supply line)

Soft water

Hard water to a hose bib

Union

Installation parts, supplied by maker

Bypass valve

To install a water softener, break into the main supply line with elbows. To provide a hard-water supply to a hose bib, break into the line upstream from the water softener.

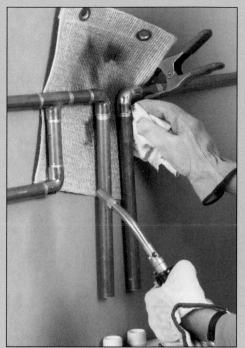

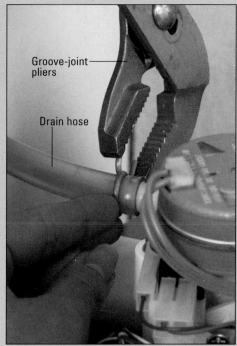

3 Break into the main supply line *(pages 98–99 or 106–107)* and install elbows. Make sure that hard water will enter the inlet, and soft water will exit via the outlet. If the main supply pipe is larger than ¾ inch, use reducer elbows. Local codes may require that you install three valves (below).

4 Install pipes leading down toward the bypass valve. Install the connecting parts supplied by the manufacturer and attach them by soldering a coupler on each line. Do all the soldering before installing any plastic parts.

5 Connect the drain hose to the softener unit using the clamp provided. The drain hose must end at a point at least 1½ inches above a drain, and it must be clamped firmly in place. Also connect the brine tank's overflow line.

THREE-VALVE INSTALLATION

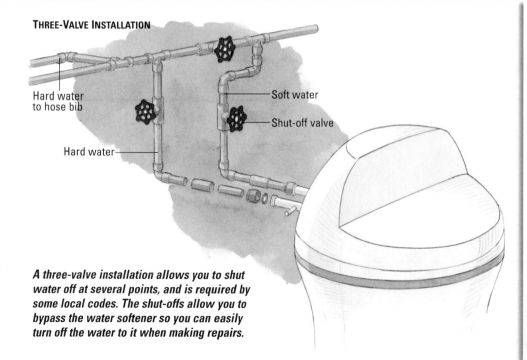

Hard water to hose bib

Soft water

Shut-off valve

Hard water

A three-valve installation allows you to shut water off at several points, and is required by some local codes. The shut-offs allow you to bypass the water softener so you can easily turn off the water to it when making repairs.

WHAT IF...
There is no drain nearby?

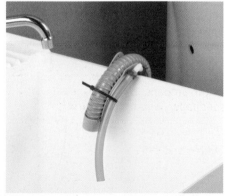

Where there is no nearby drain, run the drain tube to a utility sink. Firmly attach it, making sure the tube end is 1½ inches above the highest point to which water could rise. If the hose end were to become immersed, waste water could back up into the softener.

Installing a water softener (continued)

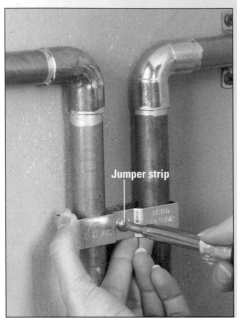

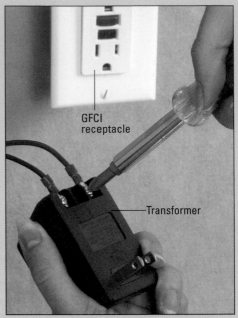

6 If your electrical system is grounded to the cold water pipe, the water softener will interrupt the path to ground. Install the jumper strip supplied with the unit (shown), or use grounding clamps and a #8 or thicker copper wire. If you're unsure how the house is grounded, call an electrician.

7 Carefully follow the manufacturer's instructions for expelling air from the water softener. Usually, this involves running water past the softener with the valve on "bypass," then pulling the valve out to the "service" position, which runs water through the softener and expels air.

8 Check for leaks in all the pipes. Attach the transformer to the wires for the unit. Plug the softener into a GFCI electrical receptacle. Open the softener's lid, and follow the manufacturer's directions for filling with water and salt.

Program the softener

Many water softeners have programmable controls that allow you to adjust the hardness of the water as well as the time when the recharging takes place.

To find the hardness level recommended in your area, consult with your building department, or call the manufacturer for a water testing kit. If you find that the water is too hard or too soft, adjust accordingly.

Set the softener to recharge when your family is unlikely to use water; while the unit is recharging, all the water in the house will be hard.

Maintaining a water softener

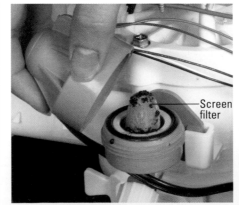

If the water shows signs of becoming hard, the softener's line might be clogged. With the valve set to "bypass," disassemble the nozzle and venturi housing. Remove the screen filter and clean away any debris by soaking the parts in clean water and brushing them with a toothbrush.

Sometimes the salt becomes crusty and forms a "bridge," either on top or at the bottom. Stir the brine with a broom handle or piece of wood; make sure the handle reaches the bottom. Break apart any congealed salt. A salt bridge may be caused by high humidity or by using the wrong kind of salt.

INSTALLING AN UPFLUSH TOILET

Installing a new toilet, shower, or tub in a basement can be a major undertaking. The concrete floor must be broken into and drainpipes installed, then new concrete must be poured.

An upflushing unit makes the job much easier. Instead of using gravity to drain, it has an electric pump that efficiently discharges waste up and away. A GFCI receptacle must be installed nearby.

Upflushing units usually are installed under or near the toilet. Most can serve a sink and a tub as well.

Some upflushing units, especially those installed in the '70s and '80s, were unreliable and needed frequent repairs. Newer units are more dependable. Ask a plumbing supplier about the track record of the model you are considering.

Plan plumbing for the entire bathroom. Run exposed pipes, or hide the pipes in walls. Make sure the unit's pump is powerful enough to send waste water the required distance to the house's drain.

PRESTART CHECKLIST

☐ **TIME**
A day to install an upflushing unit and a toilet

☐ **TOOLS**
Groove-joint pliers, screwdriver, level, drill, PVC saw, and deburring tool

☐ **SKILLS**
Planning and running drain and vent lines, basic carpentry skills

☐ **PREP**
Purchase a unit, draw a plan, consult with a plumbing inspector to make sure the plumbing will meet code

☐ **MATERIALS**
Upflushing unit, toilet, PVC pipe and fittings, primer, cement

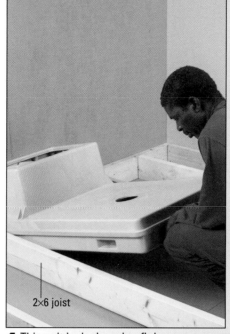

2×6 joist

Adjustable wrench

1 This unit is designed to fit between 2×6 joists. It must rest on a stable, fairly level surface. If necessary, build a simple 2×2 frame, mix and pour sand-mix hydraulic concrete, and set the unit in the concrete. Level in both directions. Allow the concrete to cure before proceeding.

2 Prepare the unit for the toilet: Install the iron support flange. Make sure that the toilet mounting bolts are in the correct positions and are long enough for mounting the toilet.

UPFLUSH TANK AND PUMP

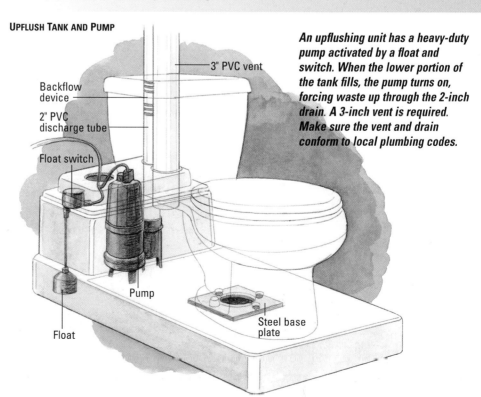

3" PVC vent

Backflow device

2" PVC discharge tube

Float switch

Pump

Float

Steel base plate

An upflushing unit has a heavy-duty pump activated by a float and switch. When the lower portion of the tank fills, the pump turns on, forcing waste up through the 2-inch drain. A 3-inch vent is required. Make sure the vent and drain conform to local plumbing codes.

Installing an upflush toilet *(continued)*

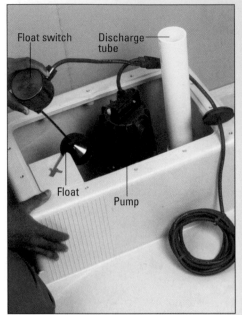

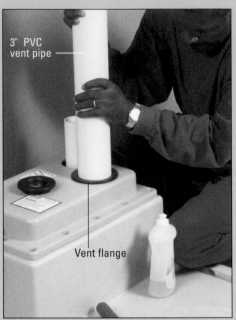

3 Assemble the float switch. Install the discharge pipe. Place the pump in the tank, and mount the float switch. Before sealing the unit, make sure the pump works. Attach a garden hose to a water supply and run it into the flange hole.

4 Connect the discharge to a drain pipe leading to a bucket or floor drain. Tape the temporary drainpipe joints—the pump is forceful. Plug the unit into a GFCI receptacle. Slowly fill the tank with water. The pump should come on and discharge water once water reaches the correct level.

5 Insert the rubber flange provided and insert 3-inch PVC vent pipe to the unit. (It's a tight fit; liquid soap helps.) Run the vent to the main stack. See *pages 166–171* for recommendations on proper venting. Be sure to configure the vent and drain in a code-approved manner.

What If…
A toilet must be placed well below the sewer line?

A macerating toilet is useful if a bathroom will be well below the sewer line (as much as 12 feet below), or if pipes must travel a long distance (up to 150 feet away) before connecting with the main sewer line. A macerating toilet has a rotating blade that grinds waste before pumping it away. Macerating units have smaller discharge and drain pipes. The flush cycle normally takes 15 to 18 seconds.

A macerating unit must be connected to a horizontal outlet toilet. Some manufacturers combine a toilet and pump. You can choose between stand-alone macerating toilets and units with connections for a tub/shower and a sink. (With either type, the tub/shower must be raised to facilitate drainage.)

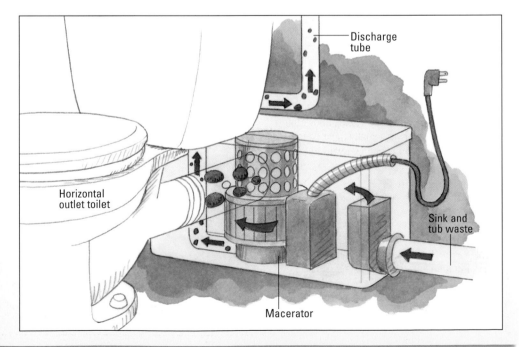

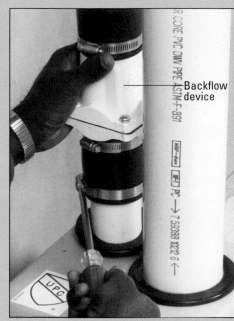

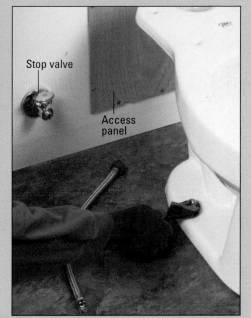

6 The discharge pipe connects to a backflow device to ensure that waste water will not flow back into the unit. (Be sure to install it correct and up—it is clearly marked.) Connect a 2-inch PVC drainpipe to the discharge unit, and run it toward the house's drain in a code-approved manner.

7 Connect the drain and vent pipes to the house's system. (See *pages 112–113* for ways to tie new pipes to old.) Plug the unit into a GFCI receptacle within reach from the access panel. Install the supply line. Install the subfloor and walls, being careful not to puncture the tank with any fasteners.

8 Finish the floor and walls and install the access panel. Install the toilet onto a wax ring where the bowl rests on the upflush unit *(pages 94–95)*. Connect the toilet to a cold-water supply line with a stop valve.

WHAT IF...
Other fixtures will be connected?

Additional plumbing fixtures—usually, a tub/shower and a sink—can be connected to an upflush unit. Drain pipes for these fixtures must flow downhill to the upflush unit.

This does not pose a problem for the sink, since its drain is usually 16 inches above the floor. The tub, however, usually must be raised so the drain line can flow downward to the upflush unit. One solution is to rest the tub on a shallow platform made of 2×4s and plywood. Vent pipes must be run in the standard manner *(pages 166–171)*.

Most manufacturers supply an extra flange for hooking up a tub/shower and sink drain to the tank. Follow the manufacturer's specs exactly for cutting the access hole for the drain.

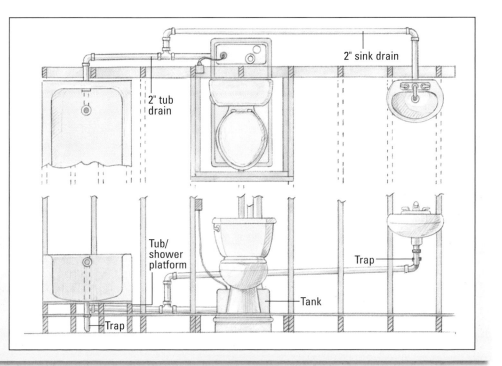

SETTING UP A LAUNDRY ROOM

A washing machine needs hot and cold water and a place for the water to drain. Hot and cold water must be brought to within a couple of feet of a washing machine. Install washing machine valves, which look like outdoor hose bibs but point straight down.

The washer drain hose hooks to a sink or a standpipe. The drain for either of these must slope downward at a rate of ¼ inch per running foot.

Many washing machines are self-leveling. Grab the machine by its control panel at the top rear, pull forward to slightly tilt the machine, and let it drop back solidly on all four feet. Adjust the front legs to make sure the machine is level in both directions.

PRESTART CHECKLIST

☐ **TIME**
About half a day

☐ **TOOLS**
Screwdriver, groove-joint pliers, propane torch, hacksaw, tubing cutter

☐ **SKILLS**
Working with copper and PVC pipe

☐ **PREP**
Locate the nearest supply and drain lines

☐ **MATERIALS**
Utility sink, washing machine with drain hose, solder, flux, PVC primer and glue, 1½-inch trap, pipes and fittings, masonry screws

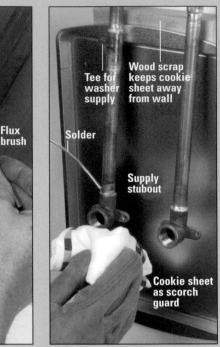

1 Shut off water to the supply pipes and drain the lines. To tap into a copper supply pipe, cut the pipe with a tubing cutter where you plan to install a tee fitting.

2 Apply flux and sweat the tee fitting in place (see *pages 116–117*). If there is not enough movement in the pipe, a piece of pipe and a slip coupling (shown above) may be necessary. Or try a compression fitting *(page 117)*.

3 Add lengths of pipe to reach the laundry tub, including tees to run pipes to the washer. At the end of each supply pipe, sweat on a brass supply stubout. Anchor the stubouts to the wall with masonry screws.

LAUNDRY ROOM OVERVIEW

Supply pipe

Washer drain hose

P trap

Supply pipes branch off to provide both the utility sink and the washing machine with hot and cold water. The machine's drain hose clips to the side of the utility sink, which has a P trap that connects to a house drain line.

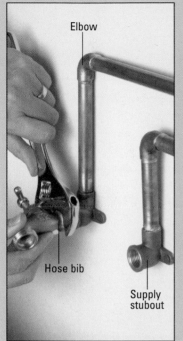

Elbow

Hose bib

Supply stubout

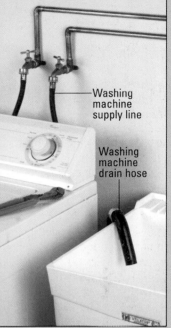

Adapter

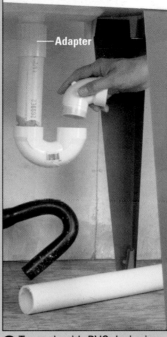

Washing machine supply line

Washing machine drain hose

4 Run copper lines to the washer. Add supply stubouts and anchor them to the wall with masonry screws. Apply pipe-thread tape and hand-twist each hose bib into its stubout; then tighten it with a wrench.

5 Install stop valves *(pages 124–125)* on the sink stubouts. A plastic utility sink is inexpensive and easy to assemble. Install a faucet onto the sink and connect supply tubes to the stop valves.

6 To work with PVC drainpipe, see *pages 100–101.* Tap into a drain line with a tee fitting, and run a drainpipe (sloped at ¼ inch per running foot) to the sink. Glue an adapter to the pipe end and attach the trap.

7 Set the washing machine in place and level it. Screw the machine's supply lines to the valves and tighten with pliers. Drape the drain hose over the side of the utility sink and clamp it firmly in place.

WHAT IF...
You extend steel pipe?

To tap into galvanized steel lines, cut and remove a section of pipe. Replace the section with a combination of lengths of threaded pipe, nipples, a tee fitting, and a union to suit your situation. Extend the supply line from the tee and attach a stop valve. (See *pages 106–107* for working with steel pipe.)

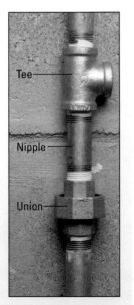

Tee

Nipple

Union

Making a direct drain connection

Where there is no room for a utility sink, install a standpipe for the drain. The pipe must be large enough to insert the washing machine's drain hose into it, and it must rise above the top of the machine's water level.

Washing machine supply box

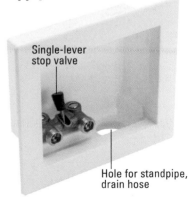

Single-lever stop valve

Hole for standpipe, drain hose

If your walls are not finished (the studs are exposed), or if you are able to run pipes through walls, consider installing a washing-machine supply box, which can be recessed into the wall for a neater look. It controls both hot and cold water with one valve and provides an outlet for a drain hose.

INSTALLING OUTDOOR PROJECTS

Running a water supply out of the house and to the yard may seem to be a daunting task only pros can handle. In some ways, however, it is actually easier than interior plumbing: pipes that are exposed or run in trenches are usually easier to install than pipes run through walls and floors. And most outdoor projects call for supply lines only—no drain and vent lines.

Because outdoor plumbing is not protected by interior walls, care must be taken to keep it from harm. Local codes set standards to make outdoor plumbing safe. Use only pipes and valves designed for outdoor use. Bury pipes deep enough so they will not be disturbed by normal gardening activity. Draw a map showing pipe locations so you can avoid hitting them if you do any later digging. Where pipes are exposed, clamp them firmly to stable structures.

Winterizing

If you have freezing winters, make sure you can drain all the lines in the fall. Run supply pipes at a consistent slope, so water cannot collect in low spots. Install valves, faucets, or sprinkler heads designed for draining. Or, plan to open up the system and blow compressed air through the pipes.

Some outdoor work—digging trenches by hand, for instance—is physically demanding. Unless you are used to such work, go at an easy pace and take plenty of breaks. Consider renting a machine or hiring laborers to make the job easier.

This chapter describes projects that are not difficult, especially if you have basic plumbing skills taught elsewhere in this book. All the installations make outdoor living more enjoyable and hassle-free. An outdoor kitchen equipped with running water means fewer trips to the kitchen. A window box drip irrigation system keeps flowers blooming on the hottest days and eliminates the chore of daily watering. And adding a new hose bib or two will mean less dragging of tangled hoses.

The same techniques used in these projects can be used for other outdoor installations, such as fountains, pools, or spas.

Basic plumbing skills, plus a few special materials, get most outdoor plumbing jobs done.

CHAPTER PREVIEW

Plumbing for an outdoor kitchen
page 226

Adding micro-sprinklers
page 228

Installing a hose bib
page 230

By combining several outdoor projects into one plan, you can choose the best locations for extending supply lines from the house and avoid having to add new connections later on. A simple scale drawing helps when checking local codes, buying materials, and checking for any underground hazards. Before you dig, ask your utility companies to mark the locations of gas, electric, communication, and water lines.

PLUMBING FOR AN OUTDOOR KITCHEN

Most decks and patios have a grill, so why not install other kitchen amenities? A small sink with a faucet helps with food preparation and reduces trips in and out of the house. And a gas barbecue unit that's built into a tiled countertop gives the cook plenty of convenient cooking and preparation space.

Construct the cabinets and countertops so they will survive years of weather. (You may want to cover the structure with a tarp when not in use.) Unless you live in a very dry climate, provide an awning or some other shelter from rain so the outdoor kitchen is at least partially protected.

If you have freezing winters, install plumbing that can be drained in the fall. Be sure you can shut off water inside the house. The drain line shown here runs to a simple dry well and needs no venting. It is acceptable for the "gray water" that a prep sink produces.

PRESTART CHECKLIST

☐ **TIME**
A day to run plumbing and a gas line for a sink and barbecue

☐ **TOOLS**
Groove-joint pliers, screwdriver, level, shovel, post-hole digger, hole saw, tools for joining copper and plastic pipe

☐ **SKILLS**
Installing PVC drain pipe, installing a sink, running supply lines

☐ **PREP**
Plan the location for your sink and barbecue; build the cabinet

☐ **MATERIALS**
Sink, gas-fired barbecue, supply pipes and fittings, drain pipes and fittings, trap, galvanized garbage can, gravel

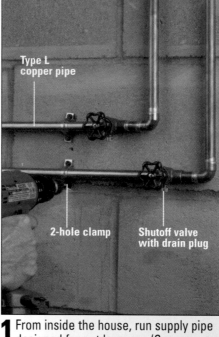

1 From inside the house, run supply pipe designed for outdoor use. (See *pages 98–99, 106–107* for running pipe.) Slope the pipes slightly to help them drain. Install shut-off valves with drain plugs at the lowest point. Attach the pipes firmly with two-hole clamps every 4 feet or less.

2 Run the supply pipe through the rim joist and to the outdoor kitchen routing up through the bottom of the sink/grill base cabinet. Sweat male threaded adapters to connect with the supply tubes for the sink.

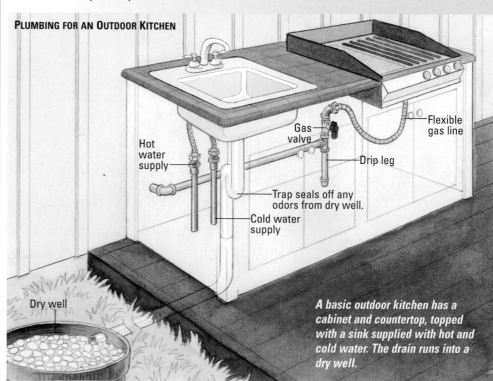

PLUMBING FOR AN OUTDOOR KITCHEN

A basic outdoor kitchen has a cabinet and countertop, topped with a sink supplied with hot and cold water. The drain runs into a dry well.

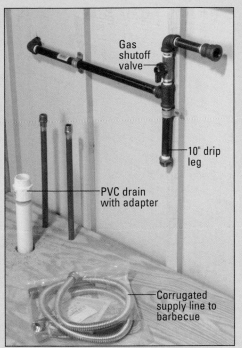

Gas shutoff valve

10" drip leg

PVC drain with adapter

Corrugated supply line to barbecue

Clam-shell digger

3 Install the PVC drain-pipe and adapter for the sink trap. To supply a barbecue with natural gas, run pipe that is code-approved for exposed outdoor gas lines in your region (see *pages 106–107* for how to install). Some barbecues may require a gas regulator. Install the sink and trap.

4 Dig a hole for a dry well at least 10 feet away from the patio or deck (check local codes). Dig a trench to it that slopes down and away from the house. Run the drain line—1½-inch PVC will probably be acceptable—in the trench. Check that it slopes at a rate of at least ¼ inch per foot.

5 Punch or drill a grid of holes, about ½ inch wide, in a garbage can. Set the can in the hole; its top should be 2 inches below grade. Mark where the pipe will enter and cut a hole for the pipe. Set the can back in the ground, install the pipe into the hole, and fill the can with coarse gravel.

WHAT IF...
The outdoor kitchen is a long way from the house?

As an alternative to bringing hot water all the way from the house, install a hot-water dispenser. This simple plug-in unit fits easily in the cabinet. With it, you need only run a cold-water line outdoors; a saddle tee and branch line runs to the dispenser. It is designed to supply nearly boiling-hot water, but you can turn the thermostat down to 140° F, which is within the range of normal hot tap water.

See *pages 206–207* for installation instructions. You will have to run 120-volt GFCI-protected electrical line to the unit; use only outdoor cable.

STANLEY PRO TIP

Using the drain

Wastewater in this system simply runs into the ground, so be careful what goes down the drain.
■ Keep a record of the dry well's location so you can easily find it if you ever need to dig it up.
■ Keep the strainer in the sink's drain hole so no solid material can pass down the drain.
■ Avoid pouring oil or grease down the drain; they can clog the system.
■ Use biodegradable dish soap to minimize damage to plants near the dry well.
■ Unless the soil is very dry, avoid running water for prolonged periods.
■ If you live in an area with freezing winters, dismantle the trap in the fall, and drain any remaining water.

Choosing the right materials

Codes for outdoor plumbing vary widely from area to area (and even from one town to a neighboring town), so check with your local building department before buying any pipes and fittings.

Among the options for supply pipes, PEX and CPVC are easy to run. If you install copper pipe, choose Type L or K, which are thicker and stronger than Type M.

PVC is the standard choice for drain pipe. You may want to run perforated drain pipe underground; this will allow some water to percolate out along the way to the dry well.

Gas pipe options include aluminum composite pipe (see *page 105)*, certain types of copper, green-coated steel, galvanized steel, and schedule 80 PVC (which is stronger than standard schedule 40).

ADDING MICRO-SPRINKLERS

Micro-sprinkler systems for containers and small planting areas are often referred to as "drip" irrigation. Many of these components spray or bubble water like larger systems designed for lawns and gardens. Correctly installed, these systems make it easy to deliver the right amount of water to plants.

Assembling the parts

A backflow prevention device keeps irrigation water out of your household water supply. A filter prevents tiny openings from getting clogged. Water is carried to the vicinity by ¾-inch supply hose, and ¼-inch distribution tubing delivers it to the containers. You may want to add a timer to turn the water on and off automatically.

Sprinkler companies make it easy to choose the right parts. You can choose from a variety of micro heads: bubble, mist, drip, or spray in quarter, half, or full circles.

If you intend to bury water lines or install a larger system, check local codes and talk with an inspector.

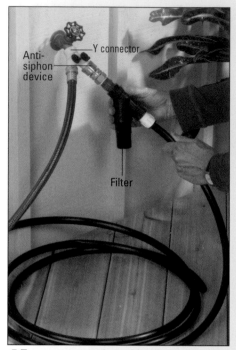

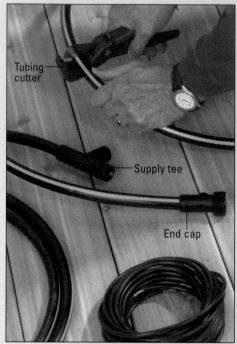

1 To connect to a hose bib, start with a dual shutoff Y-connector, so you can still connect a standard hose. Add an anti-siphon device to prevent backflow and a filter. Connect the ¾-inch supply hose with a compression fitting.

2 Run the hose to the area to be watered, and route it past the containers using push-in compression tees, elbows, and couplings. Cut the hose with a tubing cutter. Install an end cap at the end of the run.

PRESTART CHECKLIST

☐ **TIME**
Several hours to connect a simple watering system for five or six containers

☐ **TOOLS**
Groove-joint pliers, screwdriver, tubing cutter, hole punch, hammer

☐ **SKILLS**
Making simple plumbing connections

☐ **PREP**
Draw up your proposed system and show it to an irrigation retailer, or mail in a form to a sprinkler manufacturer

☐ **MATERIALS**
Micro-emitters and sprayers, ¾-inch supply hose, ¼-inch distribution tubing, connectors, caps, stakes, clips, clamps

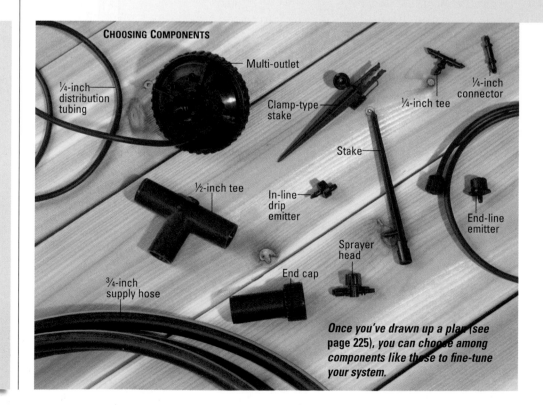

CHOOSING COMPONENTS

Once you've drawn up a plan (see page 225), you can choose among components like those to fine-tune your system.

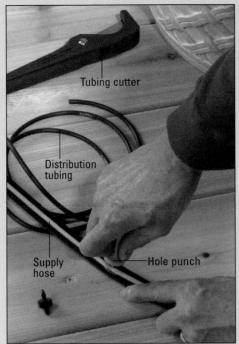

Tubing cutter

Distribution tubing

Supply hose

Hole punch

Emitter

Stake

Fastening cap

3 To connect ¼-inch distribution tubing to the supply hose, first poke the hose with a hole punch. Push a connector into the hole and slip the tubing onto the connector. If you make a mistake or change your mind, push a "goof plug" into the hole you no longer want to use.

4 Choose among a variety of heads, such as bubblers and sprayers. In most cases, the head slips onto the end of the tubing and the tubing connects to a stake which is driven into the soil. Some heads have adjustable sprays.

5 Position the emitters so the water sprays midway between the leaf canopy and the soil. Turn the water on, and reposition the heads for the best watering. Use plastic clips to hold the supply and distribution tubing in place.

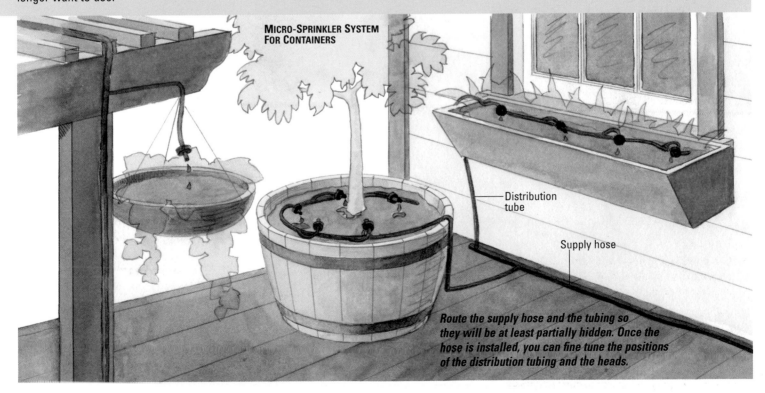

MICRO-SPRINKLER SYSTEM FOR CONTAINERS

Distribution tube

Supply hose

Route the supply hose and the tubing so they will be at least partially hidden. Once the hose is installed, you can fine tune the positions of the distribution tubing and the heads.

INSTALLING A HOSE BIB

A conveniently located hose bib (sometimes called a "sill cock") can save you from having to stretch a garden hose around the house. The most difficult part of installing a hose is breaking into a cold-water supply pipe and installing a tee fitting. The type shown has an extended stem so that the freeze-sensitive valve is indoors. Instructions on these pages include installing a shutoff valve so you can turn water off from the inside as well as the outside.

Choosing a hose bib

If you live in an area with freezing winters and the hose bib pipe will enter a heated room, buy a long-stemmed, frost-free sill cock (as shown at right), which shuts water off inside rather than outside. If you live in a warm climate, simply connect pipe to a standard hose bib.

If the hose bib will attach to a sprinkler system, install a hose bib with an anti-siphon device, which prevents water from backing up into the house and possibly contaminating your household water.

PRESTART CHECKLIST

☐ **TIME**
An hour or two to tap into a supply line and install a hose bib

☐ **TOOLS**
Tools for working with copper or galvanized pipe, carpenter's square, drill, drill bit, screwdriver, caulk gun

☐ **SKILLS**
Working with supply pipe

☐ **PREP**
Find a location that's convenient for attaching hoses and close to a cold-water pipe.

☐ **MATERIALS**
Hose bib, deck screws, silicone caulk, pipe and fittings, pipe-thread tape

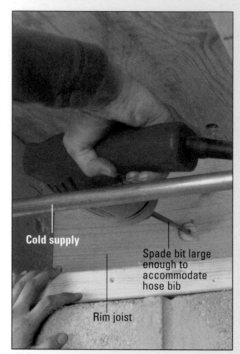

Cold supply

Spade bit large enough to accommodate hose bib

Rim joist

1 At a point slightly higher than the cold-water pipe you will tap into, drill a locator hole with a long, thin bit. Bore through the rim joist, sheathing, and siding. To avoid splintering the wood, drill part way from the indoors out, then finish by drilling from the outside in.

Gasket

Hose bib

2 From the outside, slip on the plastic gasket and push the hose bib through the hole. Apply silicone caulk around the hole and attach the hose bib by driving two deck screws that are coated to resist rusting.

FROST-FREE HOSE BIB INSTALLATION

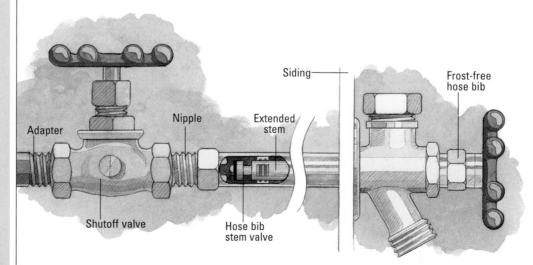

Adapter

Nipple

Siding

Extended stem

Frost-free hose bib

Shutoff valve

Hose bib stem valve

Plan for all the pieces you will need to install a hose bib. In this case, a short nipple connects the hose bib to the shutoff valve. The valve connects to the supply line with a sweated copper adapter.

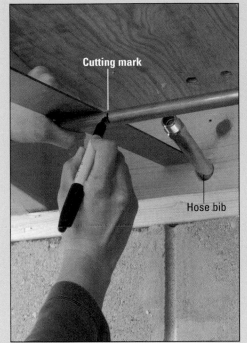

Cutting mark

Hose bib

3 Hold a carpenter's square or straight board alongside the hose bib location and mark the cold-water pipe for the location of the tee fitting. **Shut off the water.** Cut into the pipe and install the fitting.

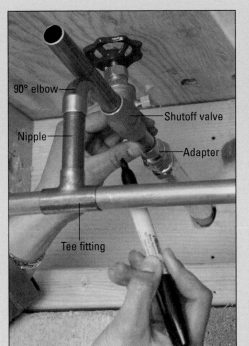

90° elbow

Nipple

Shutoff valve

Adapter

Tee fitting

4 Dry-fit a nipple and an elbow to the tee. Dry-fit an adapter, a nipple, and a shutoff. (A dielectric fitting is not needed if the bib is chrome-plated brass.) Make sure the hose bib slopes so it drains when turned off. Place the final nipple in the valve and mark it for cutting.

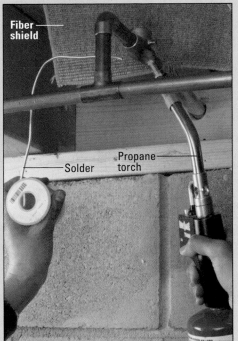

Fiber shield

Solder

Propane torch

5 Remove the inner parts of the shutoff valve. Protect the framing with a heat-proof fiber shield and sweat all the joints (see *pages 98–99).*

Galvanized-pipe connections

To break into a galvanized pipe, cut the supply pipe with a hack saw or reciprocating saw equipped with a metal-cutting blade (see *pages 106–107),* and remove pipe back to the nearest joint. Add sections of threaded pipe to reach the location of the hose bib.

Install a union and tee fitting and add a nipple and elbow to reach the level of the hose bib. (Build in a slight incline away from the hose bib.) Drill a finder hole and bore a 1⅛-inch hole (see Step 1, opposite). Add nipples and a union to reach a coupler attached to the hose bib.

If the supply line does not already have a stop valve in the near vicinity, add one between the union and the coupling.

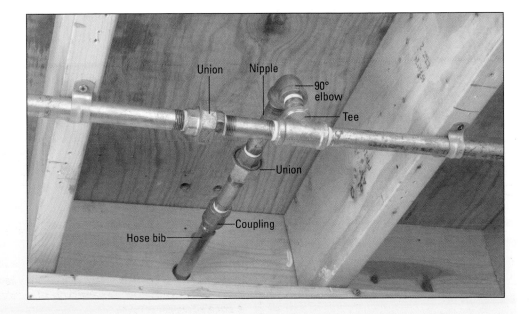

Union

Nipple

90° elbow

Tee

Union

Coupling

Hose bib

GLOSSARY

For terms not included here, or for more about those that are, refer to the index on *pages 235–240*.

ABS: One of the first plastic drain pipes used in homes. ABS (acrylonitrile-butadiene-styrene) is now forbidden in many municipalities in favor of PVC drainpipe.

Access panel: A removable panel in a wall or ceiling that permits repair or replacement of concealed items such as faucet bodies.

Adapter: A fitting that makes it possible to go from male endings to female endings or vice-versa. Transition adapters allow for joining different kinds of pipe together in the same run. Trap adapters help connect drainlines to a sink or lavatory trap.

Aerator: A device screwed to the spout outlet of most lavatories and sinks that mixes air with the water, which results in less water splash and smoother flow.

Air chamber: A short, enclosed tube on water lines that provides a cushion of air to control sudden surges in water pressure that sometimes result in noisy pipes.

Auger: A flexible metal cable fished into traps and drainlines to dislodge clogs.

Ballcock: The assembly inside a toilet tank that when activated releases water into the bowl to start the flushing action, then prepares the toilet for subsequent flushes. Also called a flush valve.

Basin wrench: Special plumbing tool with a long shaft to reach into small spaces to loosen or tighten hold-down nuts.

Basket strainer: A drain fitting on kitchen sinks that prevents debris from flowing into the drain and can be rotated so the sink can be filled.

Buffalo box: A type of whole-house shutoff where the valve is in a plastic or concrete box set in the ground.

Capillary action: The action that occurs when a liquid is drawn into a thin space between two solid surfaces, such as when molten solder is drawn into and around a copper pipe joint.

CPVC: Heat-resistant and as strong as PVC, CPVC (chlorinated poly-vinyl-chloride) is approved by many municipalities for indoor supply lines.

Catch basin: An underground grease catchment connected to a drain. Catch basins are commonly bypassed or abandoned.

Cleanout: A removable plug in a trap or a drainpipe that allows easier access to blockages inside.

Closet bend: The elbow-shaped fitting beneath a toilet that carries waste to the main drain.

Codes: See Uniform Plumbing Code.

Compression fitting: A brass or plastic fitting used to join pipe by tightening two nuts that force a ring-like ferrule into the fitting to assure a tight seal.

Coupling: A copper, galvanized steel, plastic, or brass fitting used to connect two lengths of pipe in a straight run.

Dielectric fitting: This fitting joins copper and steel pipe. By means of a specially-designed plastic washer, it insulates the pipes from an otherwise corrosive chemical reaction. See also transition fitting.

Diverter: A valve on a faucet that changes the flow of water from a faucet spout to a hand sprayer or, on a tub/shower faucet, from the tub spout to the shower head.

Drain-waste-vent (DWV) system: The network of pipes and fittings that carries liquid and solid wastes out of a building and to a public sewer, a septic tank, or a cesspool, and allows for the passage of sewer gases to the outside.

Drum trap: Found in older homes, this cylindrical trap is built into the floor and covered with a brass, chrome-plated, or expandable cap.

Elbow: A fitting used to change the direction of a water supply line. Also known as an ell. Bends do the same thing with drain-waste-vent lines.

Fall: A word used to express the slope drain lines are installed at to ensure proper waste drainage. Minimum fall per foot is $\frac{1}{4}$ inch.

Fitting: Any connector (except a valve) that lets you join pipes of similar or dissimilar size or material in straight runs or at an angle.

Fixture: Any of several devices that provide a supply of water or sanitary disposal of liquid or solid wastes. Tubs, showers, sinks, lavatories, and toilets are examples.

Fixture drain: The drainpipe and trap leading from a fixture to the main drain.

Flow restrictor: A device found in some shower heads to restrict the flow of water and thus reduce water use.

Flux: A stiff jelly brushed or smeared on the surfaces of copper and brass pipes and fittings before joining them to assist in the cleaning and bonding processes.

Hammer arrester: A shock absorbing device that provides a cushion of air to prevent water hammer.

Hose bib: A threaded faucet onto which a hose can be attached; also called a bibcock.

I.D.: The abbreviation for inside diameter. All plumbing pipes are sized according to their inside diameter. See also O.D.

Increaser: A fitting used to enlarge a vent stack as it passes through the roof.

Knockouts: Partially cut hole in a sink that may be punched open to allow addition of a fixture such as a sprayer

Loop vent: A vent installation for a kitchen island that loops as high as possible under the island and connects to a stack by means of a vent line that runs under the floor.

Main drain: That portion of the drainage system between the fixture drains and the sewer drain. See also fixture drain and sewer drain.

Nipple: A 12-inch or shorter pipe with threads on both ends that is used to join fittings.

No-hub fitting: A neoprene gasket with a stainless-steel band that tightens to join PVC drain pipe to ABS or cast-iron pipe.

Nominal size: The designated dimension of a pipe or fitting. It varies slightly from the actual size.

O.D.: The abbreviation for outside diameter. See also I.D.

O-ring: A round rubber washer used to create a watertight seal, chiefly around valve stems.

PE: Flexible PE (polyethylene) supply pipe is the newest type of plastic pipe. Many codes restrict its use.

PEX pipe: Cross-linked polyethylene plastic tubing. Where approved by local code, it may be used for radiant floor heating and hot and cold supply lines.

PVC: Polyvinyl-chloride (PVC) pipe is the most commonly accepted type of plastic drain pipe. PVC is sometimes also used for supply pipes, but most codes no longer allow it for hot water supply lines because heat causes it to shrink, weakening joints.

Packing: A plastic or metallic cord-like material used chiefly around faucet stems. When compressed it results in a watertight seal.

Pipe joint compound: A material applied to pipe threads to ensure a watertight or airtight seal. Also called pipe dope.

Pipe-thread tape: A synthetic pipe-thread wrapping that seals a joint.

Plumber's putty: A dough-like material used as a sealer. Often a bead of it is placed around the underside of toilets and deck-mount sinks and lavatories.

Plunger: A suction-action tool used to dislodge obstructions from drain lines. Also called a force cup.

PSI: The abbreviation for pounds per square inch. Water pressure is rated at so many PSIs.

Reducer: A fitting with different size openings at either end used to go from a larger to a smaller pipe.

Revent: A pipe that connects a fixture drain pipe to a main or secondary vent stack.

Riser: A pipe supplying water to a location or a supply tube running from a pipe to a sink or toilet.

Rough-in: The early stages of a plumbing project during which supply and drain-waste-vent lines are run to their destinations. All work done after the rough-in is finish work.

Run: Any length of pipe or pipes and fittings going in a straight line.

Saddle tee valve: A fitting used to tap into a water line without having to cut the line apart. Some local codes prohibit its use.

Sanitary fitting: Any of several connectors used to join drain-waste-vent lines. Their design helps direct waste downward.

Sanitary sewer: Underground drainage network that carries liquid and solid wastes to a treatment plant.

Seat grinder: Specialized tool used to smooth the seat of faucet valve.

GLOSSARY (continued)

Self-rimming sink: Common type of kitchen or bathroom sink that includes a formed lip that rests on the countertop, holding the sink in place.

Septic tank: A reservoir that collects and separates liquid and solid wastes, then digests the organic material and passes the liquid waste onto a drainage field.

Sewer drain: That part of the drainage system that carries liquid and solid wastes from a dwelling to a sanitary sewer, septic tank, or a cesspool.

Shock absorber: A device that provides a cushion of air to prevent water hammer.

Snake: A flexible metal cable fished into traps and drainlines to dislodge clogs; also called an auger.

Soil stack: A vertical drainpipe that carries waste toward the sewer drain. The main soil stack is the largest vertical drain line of a building into which liquid and solid wastes from branch drains flow. See also vent stack.

Soldering: A technique used to produce watertight joints between various types of metal pipes and fittings. Solder, when reduced to molten form by heat, fills the void between two metal surfaces and joins them together.

Stand pipe: A special pipe that connects a washing machine drain hose to the drain system.

Stop valve: A device installed in a water supply line, usually near a fixture, that lets you shut off the water supply to one fixture without interrupting service to the rest of the system. Stop valves are built into some tub/shower faucets.

Storm sewer: An underground drainage network designed to collect and carry away water coming into it from storm drains. See also sanitary sewer.

Stubout: A brass drop-ear elbow which has one threaded opening and two holes which can be screwed tightly against a wall. Some can be sweated; some have threaded ends.

Sweating: A technique used to produce watertight joints between copper pipe and fittings. A pipe and fitting are cleaned, coated with flux, and pushed together. When the fitting is heated to the proper temperature with a torch, solder is drawn into the joint by capillary action to make the seal.

Tailpiece: That part of a fixture drain that runs from the drain outlet to the trap.

Tee: A T-shaped fitting used to tap into a length of pipe at a 90-degree angle to begin a branch line.

Transition fitting: Any one of several fittings that joins pipe made of dissimilar materials, such as copper and plastic, plastic and cast iron, or galvanized steel and copper.

Trap: Part of a fixture drain required by code that creates a water seal to prevent sewer gases from penetrating a home's interior.

Uniform Plumbing Code: A nationally recognized set of guidelines prescribing safe plumbing practices. Local codes take precedence over it.

Union: A fitting used in runs of threaded pipe to facilitate disconnecting the line (without having to cut it).

Vent: The vertical or sloping horizontal portion of a drain line that permits sewer gases to rise out of the house. Every fixture in a house must be vented.

Vent stack: The upper portion of a vertical drain line through which gases pass to the outside. The main vent stack is the portion of the main vertical drain line above the highest fixture connected to it through which sewer gases from various fixtures escape upward and to the outside.

Water hammer: A loud noise caused by a sudden stop in the flow of water, which causes pipes to repeatedly hit up against a nearby framing member.

Water supply system: The network of pipes and fittings that transports water under pressure to fixtures and other water-using equipment and appliances.

Wet wall: A strategically placed cavity (usually a 2×6 wall) in which the main drain/vent stack and a cluster of supply and drain-waste-vent lines are housed.

Y: A Y-shaped drainage fitting that serves as the starting point for a branch drain supplying one of more fixtures.

INDEX

METRIC CONVERSIONS

U.S. Units to Metric Equivalents			Metric Units to U.S. Equivalents		
To convert from	Multiply by	To get	To convert from	Multiply by	To get
Inches	25.4	Millimeters	Millimeters	0.0394	Inches
Inches	2.54	Centimeters	Centimeters	0.3937	Inches
Feet	30.48	Centimeters	Centimeters	0.0328	Feet
Feet	0.3048	Meters	Meters	3.2808	Feet
Yards	0.9144	Meters	Meters	1.0936	Yards
Square inches	6.4516	Square centimeters	Square centimeters	0.1550	Square inches
Square feet	0.0929	Square meters	Square meters	10.764	Square feet
Square yards	0.8361	Square meters	Square meters	1.1960	Square yards
Acres	0.4047	Hectares	Hectares	2.4711	Acres
Cubic inches	16.387	Cubic centimeters	Cubic centimeters	0.0610	Cubic inches
Cubic feet	0.0283	Cubic meters	Cubic meters	35.315	Cubic feet
Cubic feet	28.316	Liters	Liters	0.0353	Cubic feet
Cubic yards	0.7646	Cubic meters	Cubic meters	1.308	Cubic yards
Cubic yards	764.55	Liters	Liters	0.0013	Cubic yards

To convert from degrees Fahrenheit (F) to degrees Celsius (C), first subtract 32, then multiply by ⅝.

To convert from degrees Celsius to degrees Fahrenheit, multiply by ⅘, then add 32.